MILTON STUDIES

II

MILTON STUDIES

STUDIES

II   ❧ *Edited by*

James D. Simmonds

UNIVERSITY OF PITTSBURGH PRESS

MILTON STUDIES

is published annually by the University of Pittsburgh Press as a forum for Milton scholarship and criticism. Articles submitted for publication may be biographical; they may interpret some aspect of Milton's writings; or they may define literary, intellectual, or historical contexts—by studying the work of his contemporaries, the traditions which affected his thought and art, contemporary political and religious movements, his influence on other writers, or the history of critical response to his work.

Manuscripts should be from 3000 to 8000 words in length and should conform to the *MLA Style Sheet*. They will be returned only if sufficient postage is enclosed (overseas contributors enclose international reply coupons). Manuscripts and editorial correspondence should be addressed to James D. Simmonds, Department of English, University of Pittsburgh, Pa. 15213.

Milton Studies does not review books.

Within the United States, *Milton Studies* may be ordered from the University of Pittsburgh Press, Pittsburgh, Pa. 15213.

Overseas orders should be addressed to Henry M. Snyder & Co., Inc., 440 Park Avenue South, New York, New York, 10016, U.S.A.

ISBN 0-8229-3174-5 (Volume I)

ISBN 0-8229-3194-x (Volume II)

Library of Congress Catalog Card Number 69-12335

Copyright © 1970, University of Pittsburgh Press

All Rights Reserved

Manufactured in the United States of America

CONTENTS

MILTON STUDIES

II

PARADISE LOST
AND THE THEME OF EXODUS

John T. Shawcross

The myth of exodus is distinguished from the myth of return by repetitive stages of ritual, moving linearly through time, rather than by cyclic recurrence. Exodus mythologizes the means by which man will eventually reach heaven: through successive stages of trial and purgation. The Exodus of the Israelites from the bondage of Egypt into a wilderness is a metaphor for faith in the outcome of trial and purgation; it is a type of the leading of Jesus into the desert. *Paradise Lost*, while frequently citing biblical accounts connected with the Exodus, presents the original mythic occurrence of exodus as Adam and Eve leave their formerly secure world to embark upon the wilderness of life. The successive exoduses of man are shown in Books XI and XII. The exodus myth exists further in the fabric of the poem in the roles played by Moses, Raphael, and Michael. The aim of successive exoduses is to transform the hardened heart into "th'upright heart and pure," to achieve the Paradise within. The *hortus conclusus* out of which Adam and Eve emerge to face the world before them indicates the source of the myth: the delivery of the child from its mother's womb.

THE RISE of mythic criticism has been sharp in recent years. Concentration on the cycle of birth, growth, death, and rebirth has led to an emphasis on the Christ figure in literature, and *Paradise Lost* has justifiably received attention as a poem in which myth operates and in which the *figura* of the Son has a strikingly significant role. But woven into the fabric of biblical thought is also the myth of exodus, made concrete as symbol by the delivery of the Israelites from Egypt under the leadership of Moses. It has been only seldom discussed as

3

a recurrent motif in the Bible and not at all specifically as a mytho-
poeic theme in literature. I would argue that it lies, consciously or unconsciously, behind much human thought and thus in the substratum
of structure for many works of literature. An obvious example is Kenneth Patchen's "What is the Beautiful?"; I cite only some lines at the
beginning and the end:

> The narrowing line.
> Walking on the burning ground.
> The ledges of stone.
> Owlfish wading near the horizon.
> Unrest in the outer districts.
>
> Pause.
>
> And begin again.
> Needles through the eye.
> Bodies cracked open like nuts.
>
> . . . .
>
> Pause.
>
> And begin again.
> Tents in the sultry weather.
> Rifles hate holds.
> Who is right?
> Was Christ?
> Is it wrong to love all men?
>
> Pause.
>
> And begin again.
>
> . . . .
>
> I believe that only the beautiful
> Shall survive on the earth.
> I believe that the perfect shape of everything
> Has been prepared.
>
> . . . .
>
> Man beckons to man on this terrible road.
> Hundreds of years will pass before the light
> Shines over the world of all men . . .
> And I am blinded by its splendor.
>
> Pause.
>
> And begin again.

Patchen here employs historical eras of life, but not as cycle; they are rather stages moving toward a blinding splendor. With each stage a dialectic has effected the (at least temporary) removal of all ill of the past and the passage into an advanced future. Herein lie the differences between these two myths: the myth of return repeats the ritual cyclically; the myth of exodus consists of repetitive stages of ritual moving linearly.[1]

Over the years ideas of myth have confounded these two basic myths by assigning an ending to the cycle at the end of time. The long seasons roll on, only to repeat themselves until the Second Coming occurs. But such a break in pattern when the Second Coming occurs is inconsistent with the cyclic content of the myth of return; cycle, rather than being the basic myth of the Bible, is a metaphor drawn from natural observation. The problem of the confounding of the two myths can be seen in Revelation when we learn that the serpent's bondage beneath the ground is not eternal (Chapter xx), for we had been led to see this as the end of mortal time and the beginning of eternity. The myth of return incorporates no progression as it recurs eternally, and thus no point of completion of the endless rounds can be conceived. The Second Coming will not occur simply because time has elapsed. An equation has been made by founders of Christian thought between Christ's death and the death of vegetation or the daily descent of darkness and between Christ's resurrection and the rebirth of vegetation or the daily return of light. (The influence of fertility rites in the formation of Christianity is well documented.) This has led to assignment of the time of resurrection on the basis of planetary motion (and conflation with the Passover) near the vernal equinox, with the symbolism of that equinox and the sign of the Ram (Aries) typifying a new beginning with its attendant hope. The end of the cycle, therefore, has become, in the interpretation of the New Testament, an eternal resurrection at the end of time; and Milton sees this as Death's becoming the Gate of Life (*Paradise Lost* XII, 571), or as an "endles morn of light" ("At a Solemn Music," l. 28). But these metaphors are not part of the myth of exodus, although the concepts of eternity are, nor are they logical adjuncts to the myth of return.

Exodus as myth epitomizes (or typifies) the ritual that must constantly be undertaken to achieve the dream of reunion with the godhead. As Northrop Frye asserts, "myth accounts for, and makes communicable, the ritual and the dream."[2] The significant differences in the myths lie in the achievements which exodus accomplishes. The ritual involved in exodus is a constant forward motion through successive stages of action and time, each a beginning again, an involvement in false security and error, and a removal from that involvement to a period of trial or purgation as things begin again. It is not cyclic. The mythic quest is thus mankind's constant striving forward to its dream through the ritual of exodus; the cyclic myth allows a questing theme only in the early hope that comes with rebirth. In *Paradise Lost* the perverse quest of Satan, which takes on some of the attributes of the less heroic argument (see IX, 13 ff.), is the obverse of Man's quest, for his dream is uncreation—that is, a return of all created things to their chaotic state (cf. his offer to "reduce" the universe "To her original darkness" in II, 981 ff., and the parallel language here and in the last lines of the poem on the expulsion).[3] The ritual by which he will hope to achieve his dream (for he does have hope although he tries to deceive himself) is the constant corruption of mankind through the hardening of the heart.

A problem that one encounters in dealing with biblical myth is that one must interpret the Bible, seeing it not as revealed word but as archetypal literature. This is, of course, what exegetes have been doing for centuries while maintaining its "truth"; yet in the modern world of criticism there is still a tendency to read most biblical stories or events as unique. I would suggest instead that exodus, as well as Christ *figurae*, exists in the Old Testament because of its archetypal source in man's explanation of life in time, and as such, from a Christianized point of view, it is a type, whose antitype is the New Testament account of the Son's temptation in the wilderness.

The occurrence and recurrence of exodus before and after the symbolic event of Moses' leading the chosen people into a wilderness,[4] from thence to move ultimately to a land of milk and honey, are types of the leading of Jesus into the desert where he will be confronted by Satan. Hebrews iii, 7–19 justifies the typological argument I advance: "Wherefore as the Holy Ghost saith, Today if ye will hear his voice, harden not your hearts, as in the provocation, in the day of temptation in the wilderness: when your fathers tempted me, proved me, and saw my works forty years. . . . For some, when they had heard, did provoke: howbeit not all that came out of Egypt by Moses. But with whom was he grieved forty years? was it not with them that had sinned, whose carcasses fell in the wilderness? And to whom sware he that they should not enter into his rest, but to them that believed not? So we see that they could not enter in because of unbelief." The myths of birth-rebirth and of exodus exist together: the one serving as metaphor for repetition in time, the other as symbolic means to achieve return with the path by which return will be achieved clearly laid out. Whereas the cyclic myth takes on a chronological panorama of time (deriving largely from seasonal observation) and the monomyth crystallizes recurrence through resurrection, the exodus myth points to stages within time, renouncing the past and heralding the future. It is not cyclic but linear in time-perspective, developed and advanced by stages which progress toward the millennium and its eschatological completion with the Judgment of the Son. Here the messianic function of Christ crystallizes renewal through delivery from bondage, the final delivery antithetically binding "the dragon, that old serpent, which is the Devil, and Satan" in "the bottomless pit" with "a great chain" (Revelation xx, 1–2). The end of time will see the coincidence of resurrection and such renewal, and with this Milton believed would come the "reducing" (or leading back) of the saints "Under thir Head imbodied all in one" (VI, 779).[5]

The theme of exodus, thus seen, is patently significant to *Samson Agonistes,* the story of the Great Deliverer of the chosen people from Philistian yoke. Samson, like Moses, does not enjoy the new stage of history made possible through trial and purgation, but he does take his place in the rolls of the saints. And it is patently significant to *Paradise Regain'd,* with Jesus' metaphoric renunciation of his past as mere man through his growing realization of his Godhead, the source of tension in the poem. He is now ready to face the future in renewal and realization of his divine nature. The angelic host sing:

> Hail Son of the most High, heir of both worlds,
> Queller of Satan, on thy glorious work
> Now enter, and begin to save mankind.   (*PR* IV, 633–35)

It is by emulation of the Son, who has internalized Paradise, that man can be assured that Satan "never more henceforth will dare set foot / In Paradise to tempt" (*PR* IV, 610–11). The theme of exodus emphasizes trial and resistance if a type of Christ is involved, or trial, fall, and repentance if a mere man, until time have a stop with the fall of the mystic Babylon.[6] In the fall and destruction of Babylon will be found "the blood of prophets, and of saints, and all that were slain upon the earth" (Revelation xviii, 24)—that is, those who have resisted the evil which Babylon represents. The belief in ultimate arrival at the land of milk and honey through such trial is symbolized by the angel's words to St. John, who had asked for the angel's open book of life: "Take it, and eat it up; and it shall make thy belly bitter, but it shall be in thy mouth as sweet as honey" (Revelation x, 9). The taste of honey prepares one, like Jonathan, to speak the Word of God, since thereby his eyes have been enlightened. It creates a paradise within and gives a preview of the ultimate paradise, for it moves through bitterness and through the renunciation of such false advisers as Saul, human but not spiritual father. (The foregoing remarks are obviously significant for a study of *Samson Agonistes*.) With the end of time will come the end of exodus, for the trials and progressions forward will no more be needed and the unconscious remembrance of the race will have been blotted out. This view casts a further meaning on the prophecy that "God shall wipe away all tears from their eyes; and there shall be no more death, neither sorrow, nor crying, neither shall there be any more pain; for the former things are passed away" (Revelation xxi, 4). That the theme of exodus informs *Paradise Lost* will, I hope, become clear as we explore the motif, particularly through the antitype of the temptation in the wilderness. Through this theme we will find greater meaning than heretofore for the "Paradise within . . . happier farr" (XII, 587).

Exodus is a leading out or a deliverance. As Eric Voegelin has noted,[7] the exodus is Israel's metaphor for its unique conception of faith. It represents a break not only with the Egyptian gods, but with the order they represent; it becomes a symbol of the replacement of false gods by true gods. Thus it symbolically delivers one from the past which has become the secured existence of any established order, whether political or ideational. The past has created faith in an image (perhaps in an idol); the exodus dashes that image and replaces it with an image of faith. Exodus must occur frequently for the sons of Adam, for they repeatedly devise the various oracles and pagan gods enumerated in the *Nativity Ode*, be they Mammon or

Dagon, material wealth or pleasure. The birth of the Son as Man routed those false gods and prepared for the symbolic means of exodus for man from their control. Those who had preceded Christ in history had the memory of exodus as symbol. Those who have come after the age of Christ have not only that memory but the example of the Son to create the fairer Paradise within—that is, faith.

Yet exodus also underlies the Platonic myth of the cave, symbolizing man's self, his life, and his history.[8] The highest good, God, is not the goal attained by exodus: it is rather the means to renewal. And as one moves slowly upward from the cave through the dialectic, he is fortified to proceed to the next stage. One must grow accustomed to the new light before proceeding onward; it is only after many successive exoduses that man will reach the highest good. Analogue with the allegory of the cave is found in Exodus xxxiii, 20, when God says: "Thou canst not see my face: for there shall be no man see me, and live." God's blinding splendor would destroy in the same way that Zeus' appearance to Semele as himself (lightning) destroyed her. One must move by stages to be able to look on God, the blinding splendor that answers Patchen's title question. The myth of exodus therefore acts as a symbol of the renewal of faith at certain stages of history through the renunciation of false beliefs, through the testing of man against the lures of Satan, and through leading him to a new Promised Land, each a successive type of God's Heaven. These successive stages advance from the specific (for Eden was the earthly Heaven) to the more general, or from the local to the universal—the Paradise within. According to Voegelin, "The promised land can be reached only by moving through history, but it cannot be conquered within history. The Kingdom of God lives in men who live in the world, but it is not of this world."[9] Studies of the Edenic quest—the attempts to fetch back the Age of Gold—are tangent to my argument, but they have not recognized the myth of exodus as here described.[10]

As the Israelites are delivered through the Red Sea, they enter a wilderness (or desert) which they must wander to reach the Promised Land. Of course, not all the Israelites accept Moses' leading forth (Exodus xiv, 11–12) any more than modern man accepts renunciation of the world outside the shadows of the cave. The period of wandering in the desert becomes a time of privation, to the extent of forty years (a generation): "And the children of Israel did eat manna forty years, until they came to a land inhabited; they did eat manna, until they came unto the borders of the land of Canaan" (Exodus xvi, 35). This symbol of privation repeats itself in the forty days and nights spent by Moses upon Mount Sinai (Exodus xxiv, 18), those earlier of Noah's flood (Genesis vii, 17), and those later fasted by Jesus in the wilderness (Matthew iv, 2). The hoped-for rebirth of the nation of the chosen people of God through exodus becomes a symbol of the rebirth of the individual soul rededicating itself to God. The desert in which the people wander lies directly in the path to the Promised Land. The concept of "wander" itself implies errant steps, and indeed the Israelites "sin a great sin" (Exodus xxxii, 30), as Adam had (XI, 427), and will repeatedly do so. Exodus—that is, deliverance from bondage—is therefore no guarantee for the future: it calls for continued exercise of the faith evoked by God's great hand in working deliverance. The meaningfulness of God's act of deliverance (whether through miracle or dialectic) is clearly seen when we remember the significance for Milton of Psalm 114, which commemorates the Passover: "Shake earth, and at the presence be agast / Of him that ever was, and ay shall last." "The memory of Israel preserved the otherwise unimportant story," Voegelin writes, "because the irruption of the spirit transfigured the pragmatic event into a drama of the soul and the acts of the drama into symbols of divine liberation. . . . Through the illumination by the spirit the house of institutional bondage became a house of spiritual death."[11]

Paradise Lost records the memory of exodus through specific references to it and to Moses,[12] through the theme which organizes and develops certain concepts of the poem, and through its "great Argument." Among the allusions to the book of Exodus are these:

> the Red-Sea Coast, whose waves orethrew
> *Busiris* and his *Memphian* Chivalry,
> While with perfidious hatred they pursu'd
> The Sojourners of *Goshen,* who beheld
> From the safe shore thir floating Carkases
> And broken Chariot Wheels.   (I, 306–11; xiv, 23–30)

> As when the potent Rod
> Of *Amrams* Son in *Egypts* evill day
> Wav'd round the coast, up call'd a pitchy cloud

> Of *Locusts*, warping on the Eastern Wind,
> That ore the Realm of impious *Pharaoh* hung
> Like Night, and darken'd all the Land of *Nile*.
>
> (I, 338–43; x, 12–15)
>
> Nor did Israel scape
> Th'infection when thir borrow'd Gold compos'd
> The Calf in *Oreb*.   (I, 482–84; xii, 35; xxxii, 4)

These references early in the poem equate Satan and the fallen angels
with Pharaoh and the Egyptians, then with the locusts (recalling
Apollyon and the locusts of the bottomless pit in Revelation ix,
1–11), and with the false gods of Egypt and the idol fashioned by
Aaron after the Exodus.[13] The history of the Exodus is retold in
Paradise Lost in XII, 151–269. Although Satan and his cohorts are not
mentioned in this passage the attentive reader has been prepared
from the beginning to recognize that this stage in history is analogic—
indeed, almost allegoric. The chosen people, having fallen into
bondage of a "sequent King" (XII, 165), a "lawless Tyrant, who
denies / To know thir God, or message to regard" (XII, 173–74), can
be seen not only as descendants of Adam and Eve but as representations of the first parents who had fallen into bondage of Satan through
his envy. The bondage of the chosen people is a type of bondage of
man by Satan; it repeats the pattern that the first fall set forth. And
Milton alludes to this patterning which life undergoes by utilizing
the equation of Satan and Pharaoh. God sends signs and judgments
to Pharaoh (XII, 175 ff.), just as Satan is shown a sign in the sky
after he is found at the ear of Eve (IV, 995 ff.) and at what becomes
the beginning of mortal time when Satan is defeated in the War in
Heaven (VI, 775–76, 789–90), and he has the judgment of serpentine
nature placed on him (X, 164 ff., and X, 504 ff.) after the fall.
(Milton calls Pharaoh "The River-dragon" [XII, 191], and, since the
infernal locusts were identified with scorpions in Revelation, the
transmutation of the fallen angels in Book X is into locust-like swarms
including "Scorpion and Asp" [X, 522–24].) The history of the
Exodus recorded in Book XII is one statement of the constant fall that
the descendants of Adam and Eve undergo. Each fall becomes a
successive stage upward to the final judgment, for each fall discrimi-
nates for mankind another factor of the dialectic. At the end of time
Man should be able to face God's bright splendor directly, not through

shade or agencies, not through clouds (also suggesting repentance) or fire (also suggesting suffering). The pattern underlying the fall integrates all history and argues for a linear progession of time, the past renounced and the future heralded.

Moses, a type of Christ in his role as prophet, appears frequently in *Paradise Lost*. Book XII, 235–44, explicitly indicates Moses' function as a *figura*:

> But the voice of God
> To mortal ear is dreadful; they beseech
> That *Moses* might report to them his will,
> And terror cease; he grants what they besaught
> Instructed that to God is no access
> Without Mediator, whose high Office now
> *Moses* in figure beares, to introduce
> One greater, of whose day he shall foretell,
> And all the Prophets in thir Age the times
> Of great *Messiah* shall sing.

A prophet is one who proclaims revelation. In Book I Milton addresses the Heavenly Muse that inspired Moses on the secret top of Oreb and Sinai (Exodus iii, 1; xix, 18; xxiv, 12–19; xxxiv, 2–3) to aid him in asserting Eternal Providence. The role of Moses itself is divided between Raphael and Michael, God's messengers to Man, and is the artifact for one of the roles for the creator of the poem— the poet as narrator—a topic too complex for consideration here. Raphael in Hebrew means "medicine of God"; he is likened by Milton to Hermes, whose medical powers are symbolized in the caduceus he carries—two intertwined serpents around a winged staff, representing knowledge and wisdom. Milton emphasizes the fact that Hermes is a *figura* of Christ at this point in the narrative (V, 285–87) by calling him "*Maia's* son," that is, one born of mortal woman and the godhead. Moses' kinship with Hermes is seen in references to his rod in I, 338; XII, 198; and XII, 211–12. It had become a serpent when dashed to the ground (iv, 3) and with this rod Moses was empowered by the Lord to do signs (*signa*).[14] Such signs, of course, depict knowledge and the wisdom which should flow therefrom. When the signs were given "in the sight of the people . . . the people believed" (iv, 30–31). Raphael warns Adam to be obedient and have faith through example (*signa*), and to put the potential lure of Eve's beauty behind him. He offers knowledge and wisdom. The kinship of

Raphael to Moses points to his prophetic role: God's ways are revealed and there is shortlived belief. But like the chosen people Adam and Eve will fall into bondage.

In Adam and Eve's Paradise, so markedly different from the wildernesses faced by Moses and Jesus or even from Dante's "dark forest of life," which Milton expressed in *Comus* as a "wild surrounding wast" (1. 403), we are to see the original model of the antecedents to exodus. With exodus from Paradise will come desiccation, as the imagery of the final lines shows. Incapable of performing the prophetic role themselves, Adam and Eve fail in their test of faith through succumbing to *concupiscentia carnis,* that is, the bodily temptation of need usually seen through hunger. The doctrinal answer to this lure is that "man does not live by bread alone, but by every word that proceedeth out of the mouth of God" (Matthew iv, 4). The role of the prophet is to present the Word of God to the people. The metaphor depends on the Word of God as food for the soul, just as actual food will strengthen the body and make it healthy. (The significance of the eating metaphor during Raphael's visit and revelation in Books V and VI is thus understood: the argument over the metaphor has been blind to symbolic language.) The fall occurs when Eve disregards God's Word by the partaking of actual food at noon, as if in need. (Eve's temptation, of course, also reflects, though imperfectly, the remaining two lures: *concupiscentia ocularum* and *superbia vitae,* the world and the devil.) Adam's temptation is likewise bodily and through supposed necessity. He succumbs to the lure of the flesh, "fondly overcome with Femal charm" (IX, 999). With their fall comes the loss of Paradise, that which had been, in Voegelin's words, "the secured existence of an established order."[15]

It is thus through Adam and Eve's inability to resist the formulation of false gods, through their negation of faith, and through their passive acceptance of a secured existence that the need for exodus was sown. Once fallen, they must be led forth to reformulate a concept of true Godhead through repentance and then through further trial. Theirs will be uneasy thoughts and uneasy steps, though some will see only the mirage of security. Milton has worked into his narrative the cause of exodus and, as we will see, continuing exoduses and the great Christian antitype when Jesus is led into the wilderness.

Moses' role as Michael is equally instructive of the weaving of exodus into the fabric of the poem. Just as the trumpet had sounded when Moses gave the law of God to the people after the Exodus, so a trumpet precedes God's commission to Michael to lead Adam and Eve out of Paradise (xix, 16–19, xx, 18; XI, 72 ff.) and to denounce their banishment and the future. Moses has been "sent from God to claim / His people from enthralment, and . . . return / With glory and spoil back to their promis'd Land" (XII, 170–72). So Michael, a Christianized form of Hermes as conductor of the dead to the Elysian fields, will start mankind out on its journey back to God with the expulsion. His ultimate Hermetic role is seen at the end of the War in Heaven, a role played by the Son—the antitype—at the end of time, when he leads the faithful angels back to God—reduces them— so that they become embodied within the Godhead whence all substance has derived in the creation *ex Deo*. Michael like Moses is a revealer of God's law but neither is the exemplar that will lead the fallen into Canaan. For this we must wait for Christ. Milton wrote:

> So Law appears imperfet, and but giv'n
> With purpose to resign them in full time
> Up to a better Cov'nant, disciplin'd
> From shadowie Types to Truth, from Flesh to Spirit,
> From imposition of strict Laws, to free
> Acceptance of large Grace, from servil fear
> To filial, works of Law to works of Faith.
> And therefore shall not *Moses*, though of God
> Highly belov'd, being but the Minister
> Of Law, his people into *Canaan* lead;
> But *Joshua* whom the Gentiles *Jesus* call,
> His Name and Office bearing, who shall quell
> The adversarie Serpent, and bring back
> Through the worlds wilderness long wanderd man
> Safe to eternal Paradise of rest.   (XII, 300–14)

The circumstance requiring the Exodus of the Israelites out of Egypt is analogous to the expulsion of Adam and Eve out of Paradise: each had fallen into bondage to a false god through lack of faith and wisdom. The house of institutional bondage, whether Egypt or Eden, had become a house of spiritual death, literally in Eden through the sin which "Brought Death into the World, and all our woe." The excesses following the fall in Book IX symbolize that spiritual death. Fisch notes that ". . . the Jewish commentators had glossed the word *play* (*saheq*) as a reference to sexual orgies following the violation of the divine command. This again serves to relate the corruption of Adam and Eve to the archetypal frame of the Exodus."[16] His references are to Book IX, 1027–28 ("But come, so well refresh't, now let us play, / As meet is, after such delicious Fare") and to Exodus xxii, 6, after the exodus ("And they rose up early on the morrow, and offered burnt offerings, and brought peace offerings; and the people sat down to eat and to drink, and rose up to play"). Echoes of the Red Sea with its stretches of wilderness (Exodus xiii, 18), the dried land of passage through which they move eastward to their final home with a cloud by day and a pillar of fire by night to lead them, can be seen in Milton's description of the expulsion:

> The Cherubim descended; on the ground
> Gliding meteorous, as Ev'ning Mist
> Ris'n from a River o're the marish glides,
> And gathers ground fast at the Labourers heel
> Homeward returning. High in Front advanc't,
> The brandisht Sword of God before them blaz'd
> Fierce as a Comet; which with torrid heat,
> And vapour as the *Libyan* Air adust,
> Began to parch that temperate Clime; whereat
> In either hand the hastning Angel caught
> Our lingring Parents, and to th'Eastern Gate
> Led them direct, and down the Cliff as fast
> To the subjected Plain.   (XII, 628–40)

With this we should compare Milton's description of Moses' leading the chosen people forth under the guidance of God:

> Such wondrous power God to his Saint will lend,
> Though present in his Angel, who shall goe
> Before them in a Cloud, and Pillar of Fire,
> By day a Cloud, by night a Pillar of Fire,
> To guide them in thir journey, and remove
> Behind them, while th'obdurat King pursues:
> All night he will pursue, but his approach
> Darkness defends between till morning Watch;
> Then through the Firey Pillar and the Cloud
> God looking forth will trouble all his Host
> And craze thir Chariot wheels: when by command
> *Moses* once more his potent Rod extends

> Over the Sea; the Sea his Rod obeys;
> On thir imbattell'd ranks the Waves return,
> And overwhelm thir Warr: the Race elect
> Safe towards *Canaan* from the shoar advance
> Through the wild Desert, not the readiest way,
> Least entring on the *Canaanite* allarmd
> Warr terrifie them inexpert, and fear
> Return them back to *Egypt,* choosing rather
> Inglorious life with servitude.
>
>   (XII, 200–20; Exodus xiv, 19–29)

We have moved from references to Exodus and Moses in *Paradise Lost* to the theme itself. It is by the temptation in the wilderness that Jesus will undergo that the Son will overcome Satan simply by obeying God. "All this is carefully worked out in *Paradise Lost,*" as Harris Fletcher has noted, and, he continues, the poem "opens with the idea fully formed, see Book I:1–5. Then in Books 3:94–95, 107, 203–205; 5:501, 512–514, 522, 536–537, 541, 611–612; 6:687, 902, 912; 7:159; 8:325; and 12:386–435, the situation involving man's obedience is repeatedly woven into the main theme, or becomes the main theme of the poem."[17] The last citation is pertinent:

>   nor so is overcome
> *Satan,* whose fall from Heav'n, a deadlier bruise,
> Disabl'd not to give thee thy deaths wound:
> Which hee, who comes thy Saviour, shall recure,
> Not by destroying *Satan,* but his works
> In thee and in thy Seed: nor can this be,
> But by fulfilling that which thou didst want,
> Obedience to the Law of God, impos'd
> On penaltie of death, . . .
> The Law of God exact he shall fulfill
> Both by obedience and by love, though love
> Alone fulfill the Law.

On the one hand the garden itself has been the place of temptation, though not a wilderness because the fall has not yet occurred, and Man has fallen to that temptation. On the other hand the wilderness that Adam and Eve face as they leave Paradise becomes the theater for continued temptation—with resistance by some and fall by others. The rejection of the security which their world afforded before has given rise to uncertainty and possible fears in the future. Only reliance upon God's Word—that is, upon God's Providence—will allay such perturbations of the mind and soul. The exodus or expulsion in the poem has been preceded by avowals of faith by both Adam and Eve. They greet the new world before them with hope and faith. The final lines are replete metaphorically:

> Som natural tears they drop'd, but wip'd them soon;
> The World was all before them, where to choose
> Thir place of rest, and Providence thir guide:
> They hand in hand with wandring steps and slow,
> Through *Eden* took thir solitarie way.   (XII, 646–49)

The last line, deriving as it does from Psalm cvii, 4, reenforces the deliverance by God and alludes to the Exodus again, for this is one of the psalms dealing with the freedom from Egyptian bondage: "O give thanks unto the Lord, for he is good: for his mercy endureth for ever. Let the redeemed of the Lord say so, whom he hath redeemed from the hand of the enemy. . . . They wandered in the wilderness in a solitary way." Adam and Eve's wandering in the wilderness is equated with the chosen people's wandering in their wilderness, quite unmistakably. The place of rest that Adam and Eve and their progeny shall take is metaphoric, not simply a reference to daily rest. Whether they rest in Heaven or in Hell is for them to choose by obedience and faith, or not. Their steps will be wandering (errant, unsteady) and they will be slow, but eventually, many exoduses onward, Man will be able to arrive at the land of milk and honey, and enter in to bliss. This exodus, solitary as it is, becomes a rededication of the individual to God through renewal and rebirth. The sum of wisdom, Michael has told Adam, is to know that

> to obey is best,
> And love with fear the onely God, to walk
> As in his presence, ever to observe
> His providence, and on him sole depend
> . . . suffering for Truths sake
> Is fortitude to highest victorie.   (XII, 561–70)

Perhaps we are reminded that "Blessed is the man that walketh not in the counsel of the ungodly, nor standeth in the way of sinners, . . . But his delight is in the law of the Lord" (Psalms i, 1–2). The dropping of the natural tears and the wiping of them soon away recalls the prophecy of Revelation already quoted. Recognition of the allusion restresses that the former things are passed away, and that a new life lies before mankind. The significance of exodus as a beginning again in a stage in time is unavoidable.[18]

The vision that Adam has of the world to come in Books XI and XII consists of a number of stages in time separated by various exoduses, with a major break in continuity as we reach the story of Noah and the flood. Michael's words to Adam shortly thereafter define exodus as suggested in this paper:

> Thus thou hast seen one World begin and end;
> And Man as from a second stock proceed.
> Much thou hast yet to see, . . .
> This second sours of Men, while yet but few;
> And while the dread of judgement past remains
> Fresh in thir minds, fearing the Deitie,
> With some regard to what is just and right
> Shall lead thir lives, . . . till one shall rise [Nimrod]
> Of proud ambitious heart, who not content
> With fair equalitie, fraternal state,
> Will arrogate Dominion undeserv'd
> Over his brethren, and quite dispossess
> Concord and law of Nature from the Earth,
> Hunting (and Men not Beasts shall be his game)
> With Warr and hostile snare such as refuse
> Subjection to his Empire tyrannous.   (XII, 6–32)

Milton's language indicates that Nimrod is a type of Satan, who again enthralls the chosen people. We may be sure that others in the future will rise Satan-like to pervert, although Michael, after reciting the Mosaic Exodus, comes swiftly to David the King and then to Jesus. Adam's reaction to all he sees through these two books articulates with the polarities of good and evil as the stages of history are played out. There are steps forward—sometimes even large ones for Adam and thus for the attentive reader—but the journey will not end until the Son

> shall come
> When this worlds dissolution shall be ripe,
> With glory and power to judge both quick and dead,
> To judge th'unfaithful dead, but to reward
> His faithful, and receave them into bliss,
> Whether in Heav'n or Earth, for then the Earth
> Shall all be Paradise, far happier place
> Then this of *Eden*, and far happier daies.   (XII, 458–65)

This Paradise, the Paradise within which those who emulate the Son
will achieve, can emerge only through successive trials and transformation of the hard heart into "th'upright heart and pure" (I, 18).[19]

After the Judgment on Adam and Eve in Book X and their repentance, they stand "in lowliest plight . . . Praying, for from the
Mercie-seat above / Prevenient Grace descending had remov'd /
The stonie from thir hearts" (XI, 1–4). God's miraculous powers were
frequently seen in a kind of alchemical transformation of making
"glassy flouds [flow] from rugged rocks . . . and . . . soft rills from
fiery flint-stones gush," as Milton paraphrased Psalm 114.[20] The well-
known emblem printed on the title page of Henry Vaughan's *Silex
Scintillans* depicts the same miracle of removing the stony from a
heart. The hardened heart and the means to transform it are mentioned often by Milton. Just after the defeat of Satan in the War in
Heaven, for example, we read:

> In heav'nly Spirits could such perverseness dwell?
> But to convince the proud what Signs avail,
> Or Wonders move th'obdurate to relent?
> They hard'n'd more by what might most reclame,
> Grieving to see his Glorie.   (VI, 788–92)

The hardening of Pharaoh's heart (read Satan's) is repeated often
in the verses of Exodus xiv, and these supply Milton's lines when
describing the Exodus:

> and oft [God]
> Humbles his stubborn heart, but still as Ice
> More hard'n'd after thaw.   (XII, 192–94)

It is the pure in heart that are blessed, Jesus says in the Sermon on
the Mount, for they shall see God; that is, they will be able to face
His bright splendor once all hardness of heart has been transformed.

To effect this, God will send a Comforter (the Holy Spirit of
John xv, 26)

> who shall dwell
> His Spirit within them, and the Law of Faith
> Working through love, upon thir hearts shall write,
> To guide them in all truth, and also arm
> With spiritual Armour, able to resist
> *Satans* assaults, and quench his fierie darts.   (XII, 488–92)

This passage occurs almost at the end of the poem, but the thought had initiated the poem as well—another factor bringing the poem into a circle and a continuum. The poet had asked instruction from the Spirit, "that dost prefer / Before all Temples th'upright heart and pure" (I, 17–18). By the end of the poem we see the beginning of the search for the means to that purification which the latterday poet professes. The means to such purification of heart, which the poet admonishes his readers to seek, lies in 1 John iii, 2–3: "we know that, when he [the Messiah] shall appear, we shall be like him; for we shall see him as he is pure." The role of the Son throughout *Paradise Lost* is the center of God's Eternal Providence, which Milton wishes to assert and which will thereby justify God's ways toward men to men. The Son encompasses the Eternal Providence of God, as I have suggested elsewhere;[21] and the theme of the poem is Love. The temptation in the wilderness will exemplify the means for a man to make exodus effectual, and the resurrection will assure all men of faith. Thus have we moved to the "great Argument" of the poem in its relationship to the theme of exodus.

The message of exodus is that the stony must be purged from fallen man's heart and he must believe that his redeemer liveth. My reading of the poem thus gives special urgency to the Father's words in VII, 154–61:

> in a moment [I] will create
> Another World, out of one man a Race
> Of men innumerable, there to dwell,
> Not here, till by degrees of merit rais'd
> They open to themselves at length the way
> Up hither, under long obedience tri'd,
> And Earth be chang'd to Heav'n, and Heav'n to Earth,
> One Kingdom, Joy and Union without end.

The "degrees" are the stages which successive exoduses will reach continuously through time, until the Second Coming. The process of purification of heart which is symbolized in the myth of exodus is expressed by the Father in III, 188–202 (my italics):

> for I will *clear thir senses* dark,
> What may suffice, and *soft'n stonie hearts*
> To pray, repent, and bring obedience due
> · · · · · · · ·

And I will place *within* them as a *guide*
My Umpire Conscience, whom if they will hear,
Light after light well us'd they shall attain,
And *to the end persisting, safe arrive.*
This my *long sufferance* and my day of grace
They who neglect and scorn, shall never taste;
But *hard* be *hard'n'd, blind* be *blinded* more,
That they may *stumble on,* and deeper fall;
And none but such from mercy I exclude.

The purgative way, through successive trials and exoduses of the race of men, will lead to illumination by truth, and finally at the end of time to reunion with God. The trials which mankind will undergo (see specifically those in Books XI and XII) will be trials by potential drowning (Noah's flood) and trials by potential burning (the conflagration of 2 Peter iii, 10). These successive stages partake of alchemy, an object of which was to produce pure and indestructible gold from baser metal. The alchemical matter of the poem has not been fully explored, but perhaps here we can note a point or two. Alchemical transformation resulted from "killing" the base metal and then from experimentation involving water and fire and the philosopher's stone. "Killing" alchemically represented sexual union, the partners of which were Sol and Luna, symbols of fire and water. Too much dominance of either of the two Great Sexes would destroy the experiment. The desirable union of Adam and Eve would agree with these principles, and so we see them go forth solitary, hand in hand: they are as one and must continue as one, lest either destroy the other. The way in which Milton transposes the imagery of water and fire is astounding,[22] but just the final lines of the poem will underscore its importance to the theme of exodus: the mist, the river, the marish, the tears; the blazing sword, the torrid heat, the Libyan air adust, the parching of the temperate clime. The pure heart, like indestructible gold, will result from its "killing"—from humility—and its reformation through the amalgam of suffering and repentance. Through such trial will come the Paradise within as and when the pure heart is forged. The philosopher's stone—the catalyst, as it were—in these trials is faith, seen as obedience and love, both in God and in one's marriage partner.

The sexual connotation of the alchemical lore is related to exodus through birth symbolism. The repeated vision of the New Heavens and Earth that will emerge out of the phoenix-like final conflagration, or the myth of creation (often alchemically expressed in the poem), is sufficiently well known not to be cited. But we can note, first, the presage of the birth of the Promised Seed (that which brings forth repentance and hope in the poem), and it is the Promised Seed that will lead man out from bondage to Satan; and, second, the graphic delivery of Adam and Eve from the *hortus conclusus,* or enclosed garden, which is Paradise. Here the "great Argument" and the theme of exodus coincide. The *hortus conclusus* of Song of Songs iv, 12 has usually been interpreted as a womb symbol and as the garden of Paradise. Like the child who has come to depend upon a secured existence within its mother's womb with its ambiotic waters of life, Adam and Eve issue forth to a desiccated world adust (with its obvious pun on mortality). They proceed "to th'Eastern Gate" (again, a womb symbol), moving fast down the cliff to the subjected plain. Like the child who must grow into manhood, Adam and Eve and their progeny must face the wilderness of life with each successive generation.

The exodus of Moses is expressed in similar birth metaphor, once we recognize it—the sea, of course, being a female archetype:

> [God] them lets pass
> As on drie land between two christal walls,
> Aw'd by the rod of *Moses* so to stand
> Divided.   (XII, 196–98)

This graphic symbolism is startling, but the pervasiveness of the myth of creation in the poem should obviate disbelief. The myth of exodus, we see, has derived from Man's attempt to explain his life in time: it owes much in the recesses of human thought to the observation of human gestation. The myth of exodus is plainly an archetype of birth; its stages through history are the movement of generations through history, each hopefully an advance over the preceding generation. And the forty days or years of biblical privation and trial are the days of generation. A modern example of this use of exodus can be seen in Joyce's *A Portrait of the Artist as a Young Man,* a novel which is a womb in which the gestation of its hero is expressed in imagery following the course of pregnancy. The novel ends with the exodus of Stephen Dedalus from his maternal life—from mother and country —to a world to be forged into the artifacts of immortality.

Milton as creator of the poem and as prophet reveals God's Word in order to lead man to purification of heart. The book of life is bitter, and the poem has its tragic effect. But it can also be as sweet as honey. Milton is able to act as creator through the inspiration of his Celestial Patroness, who brings God's Word nightly to his ear (again, a womb symbol). The poem we are reading is the fruit of the union of poet and Spirit; it is delivered forth to the wilderness of Man's world as Adam and Eve descend to the subjected plain from the cliff above. Its envoi might be: Go forth; "be fruitful, multiplie, and fill the Earth, Subdue it" (VII, 531–32).

As myth of linear time and the continuum of life, the theme of exodus is remarkable in *Paradise Lost*, for it opposes the cyclic myth of birth–rebirth while it lies hidden, obscure, through strategic manipulations of time. The displacement of time in the poem at first yields a confused time-perspective for the reader, with its beginning occurring chronologically after the narrative of Books V and VI, with the report of creation which has occurred somewhere around the end of Book II and the beginning of Book III given in Books VII and VIII, and with the foreview of life after the poem has ended given in Books XI and XII. Once recognizing the uses of time just outlined, however, the reader feels enjoined to conclude a pattern of cyclic time, for it seems to repeat itself in various ways. But Milton, I suggest, does this consciously to mislead those who wish to believe that "the future would be like the past" and that "no single event could have universal significance."[23] The fact is, the poem moves steadily forward from the first line to the last with only a few countable days elapsing. All events are momentous, and all are unique. Time, Milton is urging, moves forward constantly to that final day of Judgment so prominently discussed in Books III, VI, X, and XII.[24] The citation in Book X comes after we have seen the effects of Judgment, when the heavenly audience sings Halleluia:

> Just are thy ways,
> Righteous are thy Decrees on all thy Works. (X, 643–44)

Milton is quoting Revelation xv, 3: "And they sing the song of Moses the servant of God, and the song of the Lamb, saying, Great and marvellous are thy works, Lord, God Almighty; just and true are thy ways, thou King of Saints." The making of Saints, which is the intention of exodus, will result from God's just ways. The myth of exodus—certainly not that of return—asserts eternal providence and justifies God's ways toward men.

University of Wisconsin

NOTES

1. I use the term "myth" as suggested by G. van der Leeuw in *Religion in Essence and Manifestation: A Study of Phenomenology* (New York, 1963), II, 413–14: "It is the reiterated presentation of some event replete with power. . . . The mythic occurrence, then, is typical and eternal; it subsists apart from all that is temporal. If nevertheless we attempt to fix it in time, we must place it at either the beginning or the end of all happening, either in the primeval era or at the conclusion of time, that is before or after time. . . . Thus the event becomes 'eternal': it happens now and always and operates as a type."

2. *Anatomy of Criticism* (Princeton, 1957), p. 106.

3.   by constraint
Wandring this darksome Desart, as my way
Lies through your spacious Empire up to light,
Alone, and without guide, half lost, I seek
What readiest path leads where your gloomie bounds
Confine with Heav'n.   (II, 972–77)

The World was all before them, where to choose
Thir place of rest, and Providence thir guide:
They hand in hand with wandring steps and slow,
Through *Eden* took thir solitarie way.   (XII, 646–49)

All quotations are from my edition of *The Complete English Poetry of John Milton* (New York, 1963).

4. Harold Fisch has recently noted that the story of Adam, Eve and the serpent "is felt to have reference to the most 'epical' of all biblical stories, the Exodus from Egypt. It is notable that Rashi prefaces his comment on Genesis I:1 with the remark, no doubt strange to Christian readers of *Paradise Lost,* that the justification for beginning the Scriptures with the Creation and the doings of Adam and Eve is that this is the necessary preliminary to the Exodus and the Conquest of Canaan"; see "Hebraic Style and Motifs in *Paradise Lost,*" *Language and Style in Milton* (New York, 1967), ed. Ronald David Emma and John T. Shawcross, p. 38. Implied is a relationship between the expulsion and the Exodus. Mother Mary Christopher Pecheux has pointed out that "the reiterated references to Abraham throughout Michael's prophecy [in Books XI and XII] function as a device to show the symbolic unity of the wanderings of the Chosen People and of the human race. The Exodus from Egypt itself, the greatest of all these journeys, is associated with both the past and the future: first with Abraham . . . (XII, 258–260) and then with the Savior . . . (XII, 313–314)"; see "Abraham, Adam, and the Theme of Exile in *Paradise Lost,*" *PMLA,* LXXX (1965), 371.

5. Again cf. Satan's address to Chaos in II, 981 ff.

6. Cf. Milton's argument in *Areopagitica* (London, 1644): "that which purifies us is triall, and triall is by what is contrary" (p. 12).

7. Eric Voegelin, *Order and History*, Vol. I of *Israel and Revelation* (Baton Rouge, La., 1956), p. 113.

8. I am greatly indebted to Professor Christine Downing of Douglass College for many theological concepts underlying my thesis. Mrs. Downing's exacting view of the exodus myth can be found in "How Can We Hope and Not Dream? Exodus as Metaphor: A Study of the Biblical Imagination," *Journal of Religion*, XLVIII (1968), 35–53.

9. *Order and History*, p. 114.

10. Closest to my view for *Paradise Lost* is the discussion of Mother Mary Christopher Pecheux: ". . . the exile motif is harmonized with the concept of the journey of the epic hero. The virtues of Abraham are precisely those which Abraham as Christian hero is called upon to practice, while both Abraham's setting forth to the land of Canaan and Adam's exile from Paradise are types of the Christian wayfarer, moving slowly but always with confidence towards the heavenly Jerusalem which awaits him in the dim future" (op. cit., pp. 365, 371).

11. *Order and History*, p. 113.

12. James H. Sims, *The Bible in Milton's Epics* (Gainesville, Fla., 1962), pp. 259–73 passim, lists sixty allusions to Exodus in *Paradise Lost*.

13. James Whaler ("The Miltonic Simile," *PMLA*, XLVI [1931], 1047) has demonstrated the patristic identification of Pharaoh and Satan. John Steadman ("The Devil and Pharaoh's Chivalry," *MLN*, LXXV [1960], 197–201), going beyond Whaler, shows that the destruction of the Egyptian army was equated with the punishment of the rebel angels, that the Red Sea was a type of the fiery lake of Hell, and that the immersion of Pharaoh's army symbolized baptism (and this we can read as a stage in time when a new beginning will again occur) and also the Day of Judgment (implying a relationship that I have here urged). Sims equates Satan and his cohorts in Book VI with Pharaoh and his host (p. 224), and Fisch ("Hebraic Style and Motifs in *Paradise Lost*," p. 39), besides noting like identifications, calls the "Chrystal wall of Heav'n, which op'ning wide, / Rowl'd inward, and a spacious Gap disclos'd / Into the wastful Deep" (VI, 860–62) at the expulsion of the rebel angels from Heaven the same as the two crystal walls of the Red Sea in Michael's vision (XII, 197).

14. "The serpent, too, becomes likened with the serpent which Moses miraculously produced before Pharaoh (Exodus 7:9), with Pharaoh himself, and with the fiery serpents which beset the Israelites in the wilderness (Numbers 21:6–7)," Fisch, p. 39.

15. *Order and History*, p. 113.

16. "Hebraic Style and Motifs in *Paradise Lost*," p. 50.

17. Harris F. Fletcher, ed., *John Milton's Complete Poetical Works* (Urbana, Ill., 1948), IV, 10.

18. Although we cannot explore the mirror activities of Satan in this paper, we perhaps can mention one explicit parody of the theme of exodus. When Satan returns to Hell in Book X to tell of his bad success (and also of the Judgment upon the fallen angels), he boasts:

> Thrones, Dominations, Princedoms, Vertues, Powers,
> For in possession such, not onely of right,

> I call ye and declare ye now, returned
> Successful beyond hope, to lead ye forth
> Triumphant out of this infernal Pit
> Abominable, accurst, the house of woe,
> And Dungeon of our Tyrant: Now possess,
> As Lords, a spacious World, t' our native Heav'n
> Little inferiour, by my adventure hard
> With peril great atchiev'd.   (X, 460–69)

As he ends expansively, "What remains, ye Gods, / But up and enter now into full bliss" (X, 502–03), the devils transform with a hiss of strident sounds into all manner of reptilian beasts.

In like fashion Milton built his poem on antithetic concepts like good:evil, light:dark, the dove-like creature generated:the vain empires hatched. The "paradise within" (XII, 587) is the obverse of Satan's "hell within" (IV, 20). The way in which the hell within is intensified is the reverse of Adam and Eve's story: Satan leaves Hell behind on purpose only to internalize hell through successive acts of disobedience and fraud.

19. Some while ago Ruth Mohl argued that the theme of *Paradise Lost* is the making of the great man; see *Studies in Spenser, Milton, and the Theory of Monarchy* (reprinted, New York, 1962). She wrote: ". . . so far as Milton was concerned, the term *the greater Man* was by no means limited to Christ. To him all mankind were 'sons of God,' capable of becoming better, nobler beings" (p. 83); "To him, apparently, the way to produce finer human beings is not to belittle them but rather to insist on their divine origin, their great capacities for intellectual and spiritual development, and, above all, their ability, in the light of knowledge and right reason, to know and love and obey and humbly walk with God. Such men are 'greater men,' well on their way toward 'perfection.' But there are other greater men as well: those who, having fallen, repent and regain right reason and are restored to their oneness with God. . . . Adam at the close of *Paradise Lost*, is such a 'greater man,' for he, too, has 'regained Paradise' and thus restored the possibility of happiness for all mankind" (p. 85).

20. George Herbert's "The Altar" is built on the equation of stone and heart, and should be read against the background of the hardened heart.

21. "The Son in His Ascendance: A Reading of *Paradise Lost*," *MLQ*, XXVII (1966), 388–401.

22. Note, for example, the oxymoronic and infernal parody of the "burning lake," Milton's version of the fire and ice of Hell, and of the river Phlegethon which winds its way through the Wood of the Suicides.

23. The words are Laurie Zwicky's ("Kairos in *Paradise Regained:* The Divine Plan," *ELH*, XXXI [1964], 271) for the meaning of cyclic time.

24. See my article, "The Balanced Structure of *Paradise Lost*," *SP*, LXII (1965), 696–718, for structural arrangements within the poem. References to the final day in Books VI and XII emphasize the cause and effect of Judgment; those in Books III and X, the hope for man which the pyramid structure implies.

SERPENT ERROR:
PARADISE LOST X, 216–18

Leslie Brisman

Milton's simile in *Paradise Lost* X, 218 carries the reader through a chain of associations at first sight uncomfortable but ultimately redemptive. The similes frequently recapitulate the pattern of the fall, and references to snakes in particular distinguish literal from spiritual meanings. Here Milton echoes the Bible and Ovid in a way that makes the reader's acceptance of allusion an acceptance of grace and the pattern of God's ways. The crucial word is "or." With it the reader turns from one explanation to another, a miniature of the Christian turn from a death of the old self to a rebirth in both personal and historical terms. In granting the redemptive connotation of the words, "or as the Snake with youthful Coat repaid," the reader participates in the act of grace that is the repaying of the snake, or, more immediately, the clothing of the first parents. Such an act of participation is characteristic and essential to the experience of reading *Paradise Lost*.

R EADERS OF *Paradise Lost* have long taken pleasure in the moral burden of ambiguous words which require an act of participation to keep the meaning from falling into erroneous ways. And recent criticism has been as searching in the methodology of that participation as it has been in uncovering instances that call for it.[1] In what follows I wish both to indicate what must be brought to one more passage and to generalize about the relationship of the act of reading to poetic intent.

After the fall, Milton describes Christ serving as well as judging mankind:

As Father of his Family he clad
Thir nakedness with Skins of Beasts, or slain,
Or as the Snake with youthful Coat repaid.[2]   (X, 216–18)

How surprising it is to bring in the snake here may be indicated by comparing a serpentine image from the story of creation. Raphael describes streams which

or under ground, or circuit wide,
With Serpent error wand'ring, found thir way. (VII, 301–02)

Though three suspect words are used there in an innocent context, and side by side, the reader is not disturbed but delighted in his ability to distinguish fallen from unfallen meanings. The distance between the two is the temporal distance overlooked between poet and reader, who confront each other with the familiarity that is knowledge: Milton and we know the difference, know how to choose the innocent connotations while being aware of the rejected possibilities. The "fallen" connotations are justified not only by our awareness of the difference between fallen and unfallen nature, but in the phrase that follows, "found thir way," a verbal miniature of chaos resolved into order, good brought out of evil. One may argue generally that such is the way the pun works in *Paradise Lost*, establishing a sense of community between poet and reader, who are bound together in the knowledge they share of another realm of meaning. Satan's puns may be seen as a parody of that sense of community, an attempt (which we, as fallen creatures, share) to establish a secondary meaning in defiance of the heavenly host.[3] It is no accident that ambiguous language is most dense around the incident of the cannon, the most physical image of disruption; its noise and openness violate the tacit agreements that keep secondary meanings emblematic of a higher reality rather than an uprise against it.

But by Book X the differentiation of Satanic from innocent meanings of "snake" is clearly more difficult. Indeed, the passage above follows the condemnation of the serpent animal itself, and the poet is remarkably open about his difficulty with the distinction between physical and metaphysical meanings:

To Judgment he proceeded on th' accus'd
Serpent though brute, unable to transfer
The Guilt on him who made him instrument
Of mischief, and polluted from the end

Of his Creation; justly then accurst,
As vitiated in Nature: more to know
Concern'd not Man (since he no further knew)
Nor alter'd his offense.   (X, 164–71)

Clearly some distinction, "though in mysterious terms," must be
made between the serpent animal and Satan, though one would do
well to question the reason Milton dwells on rather than passes over
the difficulty. Frye says, "both Satan and Christ divide the world into
the material and the spiritual, but for Satan the material
is real and the spiritual is imaginary, or, as he says, 'allegoric.' "[4] The
distinction must be kept in mind in approaching the simile in line
218, where interpreting literally puts the reader in the devil's party.
On the other hand, if we do not suppress the diabolic overtones of
"snake" the association is equally uncomfortable. It is a passage
about mercy, yet the poet seems to insist on our not forgetting the
fact of the fall. It will not do to dismiss the naming of the snake as
the most obvious way of getting around the existence of skins without death; death was brought into the world with the eating of the
apple, and animals could have been described as leaving carcasses
around. Indeed, just a little further on Milton presents that possibility
in simile, when Death is attracted to earth as ravenous fowl are
"lur'd / With scent of living carcasses designed / For death, the
following day" (X, 276–78).

But one need not stop to work out the chronology, or to wonder
whether "the following day" could refer by analogy to the day on
which Christ killed animals to clothe Adam or metaphorically (in
just the distinction Adam contemplates) to future mortality. For
Milton did not need to raise the issue in X, 218 at all, any more than
he did the Ophion allusion or the transformation of the devils into
snakes later. All these references to snakes are beyond what the story
itself necessitates.

The serpent keeps coming up as just the figure for distinguishing
literal from spiritual meanings. Satan says:

True is, mee also he hath judg'd, or rather
Mee not, but the brute Serpent in whose shape
Man I deceived.   (X, 494–96)

Later, Adam's lesson on the difference between visual, material reality
and prophetic truth is based on the interpretation of "serpent":

> Needs must the Serpent now his capital bruise
> Expect with mortal pain: say where and when
> Thir fight, what stroke shall bruise the Victor's heel.
>   To whom thus *Michael*. Dream not of thir fight,
> As of a Duel, or the local wounds
> Of head or heel.   (XII, 383–88)

What is extraordinary is how Milton associates the lesson about the spiritual meaning of a word with the lesson about the spiritual meaning of history. Fully to understand the relationship of "snake" to "Satan" is to understand the redemption that will be brought out of the fall. Stanley Greenfield points to the salvational suggestion behind the ultimate simile of the poem, XII, 628–32:

The suggestion of redemption receives powerful support here, I believe, from the implicit comparison, in the simile, of the Cherubim to a snake: the words "gliding" and "glide" within two lines (one beginning and one ending), as well as the overtones of evil . . . insinuate such a picture. The "snake" at the laborer's heel, then, brings to mind the promise of redemption, the bruising of the snake's head by the Seed's heel.[5]

It is with the awareness of this possibility that the reader questions why the snake should be brought into the simile in Book X when Milton would have appeared to share Christ's mercy by not bringing that up. The poem's first annotator was struck by the difficulty:

the sense of their Sin (wrought by the Temptation of that subtle Animal,) which introduced the necessity of those dreadful Disguises, must have given them the utmost horror and detestation for that Creature, so as not to cover their Nakedness with any thing borrow'd from the occasion of their Crime.[6]

Against the opinion "that the *Protoplasts* first cloathed themselves with Serpents Skins," Hume points to Milton's greater delicacy: "Our Author better supposes, there may be some Creatures that cast their skins as well as Snakes." The point of such commentary is to direct attention away from the question why Milton brings up snakes at all in admiration of the detail that he does not say the first parents used snake skins necessarily. Hume seems to miss the point, for the passage is not about Adam's choice of covering, nor even Christ's choice of gift to man, but what is verbally, in simile, given to the reader. Newton does not conceal his annoyance, and calls it a notion which we may presume he borrow'd from some commentator rather than advanc'd of himself. It seems too odd and extravagant to be a fancy of his own, but he might introduce it out of vanity to show his reading. Pliny indeed mentions some lesser creatures shedding their skins in the manner of snakes, but that is hardly authority sufficient for such a notion as this.[7]

It is not Milton's vanity but Newton's in pointing to Pliny "to show his reading." In Milton's passage it is not the poet's vanity but the reader's: expecting words of comfort, he is taken aback by one more reminder of the fall and the lesson the poet ties to it. Mention of the snake is followed by the line "And thought not much to clothe his Enemies," which Bentley found so out of place as to be marked as the insertion of a moralizing editor.[8] The moral is Milton's, of course. He has been speaking of Christ's judgment, and now echoes Isaiah: "He put on the garments of vengeance for clothing and was clad with zeal as a cloke. According to their deeds, accordingly he will repay" (lix, 17–18). As that justice is tempered with mercy "unto them that turn from transgression," so the sentenced Adam is pitied and clothed by Christ. Analogously we, the "enemies" of Christ (in the sentence of Isaiah and in Romans v, 10), are clothed "with the garments of salvation . . . with the robe of righteousness" (Isaiah lxi, 10). The reader is made to share in the awesomeness of granting that grace in repaying his enemy, the snake, with the redemptive connotation of the line, "as the Snake with youthful Coat repaid." It is as if to say, if such meaning is offensive to the reader, how much more offensive is man's sin in the sight of God. Reading *Paradise Lost* thus involves a surrender, which Hume, Newton, and Bentley were not prepared to make, of the feeling that the reader "deserves" some comfort for having come this far, "deserves" to share unambiguously in the grace bestowed on Adam. Rather, in recognizing the guilty meaning of "snake" and the redemptive meaning of "youthful Coat," the reader participates first in the fall and then in the act of grace. It is as though Christ will deign to associate the reader with Adam in bestowing grace as the reader deigns to associate the serpent animal with mankind in the redemptive repayment; the way we are invited to participate is part of that grace itself. Alone, the snake allusion may seem too small to support such cosmic architecture; but such moments, in their rhythmic recurrence, redeem individuality from insignificance

as the particular image shares in miniature the larger pattern of fall
and redemption.

In choosing to grant such meaning the reader participates in
the choice the text itself offers: "or slain, / Or as the Snake with
youthful Coat repaid." The alternatives are in little what they are
for Christ. Man must die, "die hee or justice must." The slain beast,
like slain man, is the verdict of justice, the given condition brought
to a moment of choice. The "or" which hinges two interpretations of
the origin of beast skins reflects the archetypal "or," the alternative
offered to history by Christ. Not "hee," man, must die, but justice
itself and its verdict when the Son substitutes his death, repaying
the original debt that "brought Death into the World" with the
"youthful Coat" that is eternal life. The tone of the option is thus free
from the indifference with which James H. Sims would dismiss it:

Here the mood of free choice is established by the alternatives Milton
refers to as present in the Biblical text alluded to: "Unto Adam also, and
his wife, did the LORD God make coates of skinnes and cloathed them"
(Gen. 3:21). The reader may take his choice and believe either that God
killed the animals to provide coats for the man and woman or that the
skins were really shed to be naturally replaced by the new skins of the
animals.[9]

Rather, as the reader turns from the first to the second interpretation,
he participates in the great turn from death to eternal youthfulness,
from pre-Christian to Christian history, sharing in the choice that re-
deems Adam and all mankind, the choice Christ offers that is grace.

The poem thus associates at the moment of choice three heroes
—Adam, Christ, and the reader. Allusion binds them together, and
in this passage another thread strengthens the fabric of that identification. It is Hercules, who like Christ is a subduer of snakes and
the son of the Deity.[10] The battle with protean Neptune (defeated
in the form of a snake) recounted in *Metamorphoses* IX has parallels
with the war against Satan, and Milton specifically echoes Ovid's
description of Herculean power at the time of death in II, 541–46.
The irony, as so often in *Paradise Lost*, depends on reading back-
wards as well as forwards and interpreting allusions in light of each
other. It was the arch-serpent himself who first offered the tempta-

tion of associating the death that is eating the fruit with the Herculean transformation, saying to Eve:

> So ye shall die perhaps, by putting off
> Human, to put on Gods, death to be wished.   (IX, 713–14)

The kind of death Adam and Eve first discover is described with a reference that again weaves in Hercules. Gone is

> native righteousness,
> And honor from about them, naked left
> To guilty shame: he cover'd, but his Robe
> Uncover'd more. So rose the *Danite* strong
> *Herculean Samson* from the Harlot-lap
> Of *Philistean Dalilah*, and wak'd
> Shorn of his strength, they destitute and barren
> Of all thir virtue.   (IX, 1056–63)

In contrast to the robe of righteousness Christ metaphorically bestows in Book X, mention of a robe here does not even have the reality, let alone the substantive, redemptive connotations of that allusion. Is Milton anticipating the covering with fig leaves, is it a robe of shame, or is it like the veil of innocence, no longer extant even metaphorically? The reference leaves Adam, like Samson, like Hercules, more naked still. But though deceived by woman and condemned, Adam, like Samson, like Hercules, is granted grace, and the bestowing of skins of beasts that is a sign of Christ's mercy echoes the Ovidian description of the redemption of the classical hero:

> utque novus serpens posita cum pelle senecta
> luxuriare solet, squamaque nitere recenti,
> sic ubi mortales Tirynthius exuit artus,
> parte sui meliore viget, maiorque videri
> coepit et augusta fieri gravitate verendus.[11]

The coat of Nessus is mercifully repaid with the coat of immortality and eternal youth, as man, "or slain," will be repaid with the "youthful Coat" of salvation. Accepting the serpent's old coat, symbol of death and corruption, man is led in time to a redemption beyond time. To accept the implied association of the reclothed snake with reclothed man is to accept the world of Miltonic metaphor, the reintegration of wandering, "erring" implication into a higher order. Christ's mercy in clothing the naked is Milton's power to repay the reader who finds Biblical and classical echoes and acknowledges both the burden and the redemptiveness of the bestowed significance.

Yale University

NOTES

1. The most thorough study devoted to reader reaction is that of Stanley Fish, *Surprised by Sin: The Reader in "Paradise Lost"* (London, 1967).

2. Quotations are from the text of Merritt Y. Hughes, *John Milton: Complete Poems and Major Prose* (New York, 1957).

3. The tradition of snickering at Miltonic puns, summarized by Ernest Edward Kellett, "Puns in Milton," *London Quarterly Review*, CLIX (1934), 469–76, is best ignored. But see, for example, Robert Walker French, "Verbal Irony in *Paradise Lost*" (doctoral dissertation, Brown University, 1964). "The reason why Milton associates punning with a sinful nature" is discussed by Northrop Frye, *The Return of Eden: Five Essays on Milton's Epics* (Toronto, 1965), esp. pp. 80, 115, 118–43.

4. *Return of Eden*, pp. 128–29. Frye, who finds that "the cursing of the serpent is an unavoidable part of Milton's source," explains the passage thus: "Milton does not know why the serpent was cursed, and it is characteristic of a curious flat-footed honesty in Milton's mind that he should spread so obvious a bewilderment over a dozen lines of blank verse" (p. 56).

5. "Milton's *Paradise Lost*, XII, 629–632," *Explicator*, XIX (1961), 57.

6. Patrick Hume, *Annotations on Milton's "Paradise Lost"* (London, 1695), p. 270.

7. Thomas Newton, *"Paradise Lost"* . . . *With notes of various Authors* (London, 1750), III, 235–36.

8. "This Line is certainly of the Editor's Manufacture. It's quite superfluous; it divides what's naturally connected; and it changes the Sentiment, from a *Family* under a gracious Master and *Father*, to the Condition of *Enemies*." Richard Bentley, *Milton's "Paradise Lost"* (London, 1732), p. 315n.

9. James H. Sims, *The Bible in Milton's Epics* (Gainesville, Fla., 1962), p. 120.

10. Milton compares Christ to Hercules in "The Passion," 13–14, and in *PR* IV, 563–68. Other points at which Milton touches subject matter pertaining to Hercules may be located from Charles Grosvenor Osgood, *The Classical Mythology of Milton's English Poems* (New York, 1900). Perhaps the most significant single statement about Milton's use of Ovid and the classics generally is Davis P. Harding, *The Club of Hercules: Studies in the Classical Background of "Paradise Lost"* (Urbana, Ill., 1961). See also Harding's earlier work, *Milton and the Renaissance Ovid*, Illinois Studies in Language and Literature (Urbana, Ill., 1946), XXX, no. 4. A comprehensive collection of Ovidian material in Milton is Mary Campbell Brill, "Milton and Ovid" (doctoral dissertation, Cornell University, 1935). Miss Brill notes the serpent parallel on p. 210.

11. Ovid, *Metamorphoses,* ed. Frank Justus Miller (Cambridge, Mass., 1916), IX, 266–70, pp. 20–22. Golding's translation (IX, 320–26) reads:

> And as the Serpent slye
> In casting of his withered slogh, renewes his yeeres thereby,
> And wexeth lustyer than before, and looketh crisp and bryght
> With scoured scales: so Hercules as soone as that his spryght
> Had left his mortall limbes, gan in his better part to Thryve,
> And for to seeme a greater thing than when he was alyve,
> And with a stately majestie ryght reverend to appeere.

(*Ovid's Metamorphoses: The Arthur Golding Translation,* ed. John Frederick Nims [New York, 1965], pp. 231–32).

SYMBOLIC LANDSCAPE IN *PARADISE LOST*

John R. Knott, Jr.

Milton reshaped the tradition of the earthly paradise in significant ways. His Eden is never static or pictorial, and its landscape is novel in its fluidity, spatial depth, and sense of order. By emphasizing the repose of Adam and Eve and their harmony with the landscape Milton made his paradise resemble a Christianized Arcadia; it has affinities with the Arcadian landscapes of such painters as Giorgione and Poussin as well as with literary Arcadias. The elegiac mood that distinguishes Eden from simpler kinds of pastoral extends to other descriptive passages in the poem. In its landscape as in other features heaven is the true image of perfection. This perfection is reflected in Eden and parodied in the grotesque distortions of the landscape of hell. The devastation that results from the Fall shows that Eden, unlike the fictional Arcadia, cannot absorb the presence of death. When Adam descends to the "subjected plain," he must replace the *otium* of his life in Eden with an inner peace, self-attained and independent of the external world.

I N 1753 Joseph Warton, obviously not a man to echo received opinion, said exactly what he thought of Milton's Eden:

Sapphire fountains that rolling over orient pearl run nectar, roses without thorns, trees that bear fruit of vegetable gold and that weep odorous gums and balms are easily feigned, but having no relative beauty as pictures of nature, nor any absolute excellence as derived from truth, they can only please those who when they read exercise no faculty but fancy and admire because they do not think.[1]

The objections of such modern critics of Milton's stylized natural description as T. S. Eliot and F. R. Leavis are not very different from Warton's in tone and bias.[2] The preference for realistic and detailed "pictures of nature" that Warton helped to establish and we take for granted makes it understandably difficult for a modern reader to appreciate the conventional modes of representing the earthly paradise, and for that matter any natural scene, that Milton inherited. But the important question to ask in responding to *Paradise Lost* is what kind of "truth" we should be seeking. Should paradise be sharply particularized, so that it appears as a recognizable, precisely defined place? Or should it represent a kind of imaginative truth by imaging a state of innocence and bliss beyond normal human experience? C. S. Lewis, a persuasive defender of Milton's conception of Eden, has argued that it had to be conventional, "immemorial" rather than original, to make us know that "the garden is found."[3] A narrow literalism would have defeated Milton's purpose of exposing the reader to a condition of life that is more nearly mythic than historic. He knew that we must shake off our bondage to the familiar, and temporarily forget our normal sense of time, if we are to respond fully to a prelapsarian world.

Writers found different ways of appealing to "fancy" in describing the earthly paradise, even though they might all agree that spring was eternal there and the fruit golden. Milton's Eden is not to be compared with those medieval versions of paradise that have richly jewelled gates, or palaces, or fountains. Actually Milton's "Saphire Fount," "Orient Pearl," and "sands of Gold" need not be taken as literally as Warton supposes.[4] One can find similar diction in *Comus,* in Sabrina's "silver lake" and "coral-pav'n bed," and her chariot "Of Turquoise blue and Em'rald Green," intended to suggest the stream itself. Milton's problem in representing paradise was to show nature perfected without making it unbelievable. We are asked to take some things on faith: thornless roses, an unvarying climate, fruit of "golden rind." Yet these features are part of an idealized scene that can stand for a heightened version of the nature we know.

It should be recognized that while this walled, mountaintop garden is traditional, Milton reshaped the tradition of the earthly paradise. No one would confuse Milton's earthly paradise with Dante's, a *locus amoenus* in the medieval manner, with all the elements of the ideal landscape: trees and fragrant flowers, fresh water, birds singing, a gentle breeze.[5] Dante's paradise is charming because it is so delightfully naturalistic; it could be a typical spring scene if there were not clearly something marvelous in the atmosphere of the place and in the encounter of Dante and Matilda. Milton's garden offers not a "pleasance," as Dante's does, but a landscape more like the environs of Spenser's Bower of Bliss as they are viewed by Guyon, with groves, streams, hills, and valleys.[6] Like Spenser's false paradise, Eden is shown through the eyes of an antagonistic visitor who is nevertheless susceptible to the allure of the place and includes conventional earthly paradise motifs as well as all the pleasures of nature that the author can represent. Of course these natural delights are flawed for Spenser by the artifice behind them. In many ways Milton's Eden is closer to Spenser's true paradise, the Garden of Adonis, where both harvest and spring are "continuall," decking with fresh colors the "wanton pryme," and where "all plenty and all pleasure flowes."[7]

Yet Milton's handling of the familiar materials is distinctly original. For example, he does not resort to the rhetorical device that Patch has called the "negative formula," by which such discomforts as disease and old age are specifically excluded from the earthly paradise.[8] This technique, which can be found in Homer's account of Olympus in *The Odyssey* and countless subsequent descriptions of Elysium, the Golden Age, the Fortunate Isles, and the earthly paradise, can be illustrated by the earthly paradise of the fifth century African, Dracontius:

> In sun's hot rays it burneth not, by blasts
> Is never shaken, nor doth whirlwind rage
> With fierce-conspiring gales; no ice can quell,
> No hailstorm strike, nor under hoary frost
> Grow white the fields.[9]

Instead of defining his Eden by exclusions Milton overwhelms us with its sensuous appeal, avoiding details from the fallen world that would cloud our perception of the place itself. We do not hear of "pinching cold and scorching heate" (X, 691), storms, or Boreas and Thrascias and the rest of the company of the winds until after the Fall, when they have become a reality. This minor deviation from tradition is characteristic of Milton's effort to avoid unnecessary rhetorical trappings in his description of Eden. However conventional his subject, he could at least present old motifs in new ways, working them into a freshly conceived vision of the place.

Milton's paradise is never static, or simply pictorial, as so many others are, because everything in his description works to lead the reader into the "Garden of bliss" and make him participate in delight. He conveys this delight partly through the conversations of Adam and Eve and the series of tableaux in which he shows them, partly by presenting the features of the Garden in convincing ways rather than declaring their existence in the manner of someone proving the authenticity of his version of the myth by trotting out the familiar properties. We know that the trees of the Garden bear golden fruit and are perpetually in flower because we see them as they actually appear to Satan ("Blossoms and Fruits at once of golden hue / Appeerd" [IV, 148]). The detail derived from patristic tradition, "And without Thorn the Rose" (IV, 256), is offered as an aside; it adds the final touch to a line that subtly lifts the description into the realm of the miraculous:

> or the flourie lap
> Of som irriguous Valley spred her store,
> *Flours of all hue, and without Thorn the Rose.* (IV, 254–57)

Most references to eternal spring in accounts of the earthly paradise or the golden age are only slightly more elaborate than the Ovidian assertion, "Ver erat aeternum."[10] But Milton has "Universal *Pan* / Knit with the *Graces* and the *Hours*" (IV, 266–67) lead on "Eternal Spring" in a graceful dance that complements the harmony of trembling leaves and the song of the birds and is an expression of the vibrant life of the Garden as well as an emblem of order. Nature is perpetually fresh and growing in Eden, as if always in the first hour of existence; each morning the plants "spring" with new life from the unbelievably fertile soil. Even the flowers seem alive and not static or decorative. In most ideal landscapes flowers are said to enamel, or paint, meadows and fields; comparisons with tapestry are frequent. But Milton makes his flowers a manifestation of the abundance of paradise and thus another proof of God's bounty:

> Flours worthy of Paradise which not nice Art
> In Beds and curious Knots, but Nature boon
> Pour'd forth profuse on Hill and Dale and Plain. (IV, 241–43)

At one point Adam and Eve are shown reclining on a "soft downie Bank *damaskt* with flours" (IV, 334), but the description of Adam sitting "On a green shadie Bank *profuse* of Flours" (VIII, 286) is more characteristic of Milton's manner in *Paradise Lost*.

The fragrance of the Garden more than any other traditional feature communicates a sense of intense and inescapable sensuous delight. Milton goes far beyond the customary brief reference to rich odors. Fragrance, from the omnipresent flowers and the heavier, more exotic scent of "Groves whose rich Trees wept odorous Gumms and Balme" (IV, 248), is for him synonymous with delight. When Raphael enters the "spicie Forrest" on his way to Adam, it is as if he has entered a region, or state, of bliss:

> Thir glittring Tents he passd, and now is come
> Into the blissful field, through Groves of Myrrhe,
> And flouring Odours, Cassia, Nard, and Balme;
> A Wilderness of sweets; for Nature here
> Wantond as in her prime, and plaid at will
> Her Virgin Fancies, pouring forth more sweet,
> Wilde above rule or Art; enormous bliss.   (V, 291–97)

This is an active nature, gratifying the sense of smell with an irresistable profusion of odors. The air itself, "pure now purer" to Satan as he approaches the Garden, "to the heart inspires / Vernal delight and joy" (IV, 154–55). Delight, like nature, is always vernal in the Garden; although Adam and Eve surely know some variation in their pleasures, Milton gives the impression that pleasure in some form is continuously in the process of being realized. Thomas Greene has argued that the spices of the Garden contribute to a "lulling heaviness" in its atmosphere and offer an "invitation to indolence,"[11] but this should be true only for someone not acclimatized to such a special atmosphere: Satan, or the fallen reader with his dulled senses. We have trouble accepting a higher order of sensuous pleasure than we know from experience, just as we may find it hard to be comfortable with a nature that is not domesticated but wantons "as in her prime." Excess can be alarming when we are taught to prefer moderation. Spenser's Bower of Bliss is suspect because Art "too lavishly" adorns the meadow with flowers, but nature in Eden cannot be too lavish. Its energies should be wondered at, not questioned.

The dynamic character of Milton's Eden is apparent in the landscape as a whole. The scene presented in two long descriptive passages early in Book IV is more convincing than the panorama Spenser offers in the Bower of Bliss episode for several reasons. The most obvious is the sustained movement of Milton's blank verse. In one skillfully modulated sentence that extends for forty lines (IV, 223–63) Milton directs the reader's vision over the landscape, moving from simple, geographical fact ("Southward through *Eden* went a River large") to the marvelous (brooks "Rolling on Orient Pearl and Sands of Gold," fruit with "Golden Rind") without violating the illusion of reality. The scene has spatial depth, as Spenser's does not, largely because it is presented as a prospect.[12] Milton brings Satan, and thus the reader, into the scene by stationing him on the Tree of Life, whereas Spenser simply sets Guyon aside before embarking on his *descriptio*. Moreover, Milton indicates the relationship of features to one another by continually shifting his perspective, providing what Eisenstein has called "cinematographic instructions" in commenting on other passages from *Paradise Lost*.[13] Milton directs our attention to the course of the streams of the Garden and moves from sunny field to shady bower, from groves of spice trees to others of fruit trees. Interspersed are lawns and downs with grazing flocks, "palmie" hillocks, and valleys spreading their store of flowers. Elsewhere ("Another side") are "umbrageous Grots and Caves." By contrast, Spenser's landscapes seem two-dimensional, simple lists of features with little indication of spatial relationships:

> There the most daintie paradise on ground
> It selfe doth offer to his sober eye,
> In which all pleasures plenteously abownd,
> And none does others happinesse enuye:
> The painted flowres, the trees upshooting hye,
> The dales for shade, the hilles for breathing space,
> The trembling groues, the Christall running by;
> And that which all faire workes doth most aggrace,
> The art, which all that wrought, appeared in no place.[14]

Ariosto and Tasso are no better at suggesting space in a landscape scene, nor is Sidney, for all the subtle harmony of his descriptions:

There were hilles which garnished their proud heights with stately trees: humble valleis, whose base estate semed comforted with refreshing of silver rivers: medows, enameld with al sorts of ey-pleasing floures: thickets, which being lined with most pleasant shade, were witnessed so to by the chereful deposition of many wel-tuned birds: each pasture stored with sheep feeding with sober security, while the prety lambs with bleting oratory craved the dams comfort: here a shepheards boy piping, as though he should never be old: there a young shepherdesse knitting, and withal singing, and it seemed that her voice comforted her hands to work, and her hands kept time to her voices musick.[15]

To find a firmly outlined scene one must look to the seventeenth century, to Denham's stylized but reasonably accurate description of the topography of the Thames valley in *Cooper's Hill* (1642), which Dr. Johnson credited with establishing the genre of local poetry.[16]

Milton adapted the technique of the prospect to the description of an imaginary scene, an ideal landscape as opposed to an idealized one drawn from an actual model. While he placed the Garden geographically, and marked its center and circumference, his landscape has a fluidity that Denham's or Pope's comparable one in "Windsor Forest" do not. Milton suggests the actuality of the Garden without allowing its contours to harden. Groves and bowers are not located precisely, nor are "Hill and Dale and Plaine." And the use of "or" as a connective makes the parts of the landscape seem interchangeable, as if to suggest that all views are equally pleasant:

> Betwixt them Lawns, or level Downs, and Flocks
> Grazing the tender herb, were interpos'd,
> Or palmie hillock, or the flourie lap
> Of som irriguous Valley spred her store.   (IV, 252–55)

Once we are within the Garden the limiting wall disappears. Here are "*All* Trees of noblest kind for sight, smell, taste," "Flours of *all* hue"; as we are told at the very beginning of the description, Satan is "To *all* delight of human sense expos'd" (my italics). Spenser insists that "all" pleasures abound in the Bower of Bliss, but Milton is more emphatic. He would have us imagine "more" than "Natures whole wealth," because the delights of the "blissful Paradise / Of God" are beyond measure. Thus its landscape must have a sense of openness, of "Variety without end," that the topography of the Thames valley, or any identifiable place in the familiar world, cannot.

Eden is also an ordered world in which, as Northrop Frye has suggested, we cannot lose our way.[17] Adam and Eve may wander anywhere in the landscape of the Garden without becoming disoriented; in this environment they would have continued "secure," both safe and without cares, if it were not for the intrusion of Satan and for Eve's desire for knowledge beyond that gained from her life in the Garden. The order of the landscape is a matter of proportion and balance.[18] Upon first awaking Adam discovers around him a scene of "Hill, Dale, shadie Woods, and sunnie Plaines" (VIII, 262). Satan sees in the landscape of the earth a "sweet interchange / Of Hill and Vallie, Rivers, Woods and Plaines" (IX, 115–16). Because Milton provided a justification for this landscape in heaven ("For Earth hath this variety from Heav'n / Of pleasure situate in Hill and Dale" [VI, 640–41]), topography becomes a manifestation of the order of the universe as well as a source of pleasure. It is the visible design of God.[19] Both Spenser and Sidney pair complementary landscape features, "High reared mounts" and "Low looking dales," but without emphasizing contrast as an ordering principle. Instead Spenser offers simple variety:

> So all agreed through sweete diversity,
> This gardin to adorne with all variety.[20]

A line from Joseph Beaumont's insistently allegorical description of Eden could be taken as a commentary on Milton's landscape: "Sweet *Order* with *Variety* did play."[21] The evolution of this sense of an ordered nature can be seen in Pope's careful balance of opposites in "Windsor Forest":

> Here Hills and Vales, the Woodland and the Plain,
> Here Earth and Water seem to strive again,
> Not Chaos-like together crush'd and bruis'd,
> But as the World, harmoniously confus'd:
> Where Order in Variety we see,
> And where, tho' all things differ, all agree.[22]

Milton has vegetation contribute to the order of his natural world in subtle ways. In the final movement of the magnificent account of creation, "stately" trees rise "as in dance," bringing to perfection the landscape planned by God:

> With high woods the hills were crownd,
> With tufts the vallies and each fountain side,
> With borders long the Rivers.   (VII, 326–28)

Within the Garden trees are not scattered at random but form groves, alleys, and bowers (with shrubs and flowers). Such features can be found in contemporary gardens; Bacon, for one, included alleys and arbors in his prescription for an ideal garden.[23] To make gardeners of Adam and Eve, who labor to keep their paths and bowers "from Wilderness" (IX, 244–45), Milton had to introduce human standards of orderliness. But in clearing their paths Adam and Eve do not control or shape nature, which remains "Wilde above rule or Art" (V, 297). Wherever Milton got the idea for his alleys of trees, he presents them as part of the order in the mind of God, one more example of the way in which God has combined order with delight in the Garden. How far one could go in the opposite direction can be seen from the excesses of Du Bartas, whose Eden has not only alleys and arbors but "love-knots" of roses tended by angels and even topiary work; there is a maze ornamented with the shapes of satyrs, centaurs, whales, and "thousand other counterfaited corses."[24] Milton's "sovran Planter" (IV, 691) worked in less capricious ways.

Helen Gardner has called Eden a "landscape garden" of the sort that reached perfection in the garden parks of the eighteenth century. I would prefer to think of Milton's paradise as a garden on a divine rather than a human scale, more extensive and wilder than even a garden conceived as "nature in miniature" could be.[25] It has affinities not only with previous representations of the earthly paradise but with the literary landscape of Arcadia, invented by Virgil[26] and rediscovered and elaborated by Boccaccio, Sannazzaro, and Bembo.[27] Milton's Eden shares with this idealized pastoral world common natural delights, flocks if not shepherds, and a harmony of human figures with their natural setting. Arcadia, or its various equivalents in the pastoral poetry of the Renaissance, is among other things a place where life is easy; its inhabitants, like Adam and Eve, are often shown against a natural background in attitudes of repose. Adam and Eve, of course, enjoy their repose only after labor sufficient to make "ease / more easie" (IV, 329–30).

A scene such as the one in which Adam and Eve are shown reclining on a flowery bank ("Under a tuft of shade") eating their supper fruits is an example of what Curtius has called the "motif of bucolic repose."[28] Curtius traces this motif to Virgil's first eclogue, which begins with Tityrus reclining under a beech tree playing his pipe, reflecting on the *otium* of the shepherd's life: "O Meliboee, deus nobis haec otia fecit." The farmers described in the *Georgics* possess a similar *otium*, a leisure that implies freedom from care:

> at secura quies et nescia fallere vita,
> dives opum variarum, at latis otia fundis
> speluncae vivique lacus et frigida Tempe
> mugitusque boum mollesque sub arbore somni
> non absunt.[29]

The comparable sense of *secura quies* in the pastoral poetry of the Renaissance derives from the way figures are related to their landscape. If one needs an emblem to represent the Arcadian world, it should be a reclining or seated figure, suggesting by his relaxation and his harmony with nature a profound calm of mind.[30] Milton's tableau is perhaps the richest statement of this motif in English poetry. Yet the frisking of all the animals about Adam and Eve in itself sufficiently indicates that their "ease" goes beyond the *otium* of pastoral poetry. As Adam is reminded in his discourse with Raphael on astronomy, their contentment depends upon obedience. He is taught to live

> The easiest way, nor with perplexing thoughts
> To interrupt the sweet of Life, from which
> God hath bid dwell farr off all anxious cares,
> And not molest us, unless we our selves
> Seek them with wandring thoughts, and notions vaine.

> (VIII, 183–87)

There is little emphasis on the repose of Adam and Eve in the tradition of the earthly paradise before Milton; the closest thing to it is the enervating repose shown in the false paradises of Ariosto, Tasso, and Spenser. But there is one notable presentation of a pastoral Eden in hexaemeral drama, Giambattista Andreini's *L'Adamo* (1613). Andreini skillfully relates Adam and Eve to a lush natural setting and, like Milton, compares Eve with flowers and pictures her among them. His most sophisticated use of natural description is in the scene in which he shows Adam greeting Eve on her return, unaware that she has sinned. Adam enthusiastically points out to Eve an enticing stream that flows through a meadow and then falls to a "deep and fruitful vale, / With laurel crown'd and olive, / With

cypresses, oranges, and lofty pines," inviting her to enjoy with him
the newly discovered prospect:

> Now by these cooling shades,
> The beauty of these plants,
> By these delightful meadows,
> These variegated flowers,
> By the soft music of the rills and birds
> Let us sit down in joy![31]

The closest visual analogues to Milton's Eden are probably the
ideal landscapes of such painters as Giorgione, Titian,[32] Claude, and
Poussin[33] portraying an Arcadian landscape. The comparison seems
to me worth making, if only to suggest how pervasive the feeling for
an Arcadian world was. In certain landscapes of all of these painters
one seems to escape the actual countryside of the Roman campagna
into a timeless, extraordinarily peaceful world where goddesses
and nymphs do not seem out of place. In Giorgione's *Sleeping Venus,*
for example, the nude goddess reclines under a tree in perfect harmony with the landscape that extends behind her.[34] Milton's natural
world before the Fall is "a seat where Gods might dwell, / Or wander
with delight" (VII, 329–30)—not pagan gods, of course, but angels
and archangels. In short, Eden appears as a Christianized Arcadia.

The tranquillity of the landscape scenes of the painters I have
mentioned is sometimes on the verge of disruption, as in Giorgione's
The Tempest, in which a thunderstorm can be seen about to break
in the background. Poussin has a number of paintings in which an
Arcadian world is threatened: *Orpheus and Eurydice,* which shows
Eurydice about to be bitten by a snake; *Apollo and Daphne,* with
Cupid aiming an arrow at Apollo; *Landscape with a Snake,* in which
a snake is shown with its victim in one corner of the scene. The two
paintings on the theme *Et in Arcadia Ego* dramatically introduce
the presence of death into a tranquil pastoral world.[35] The elegiac
note in such paintings, and in *Paradise Lost,* where Eden is rarely
seen without ominous shadows, belongs to a more sophisticated
kind of pastoral than portrayals of simple, rustic life. Under the
threat of disruption or death the pastoral ideal can stand for more than
an escape from the strain and moral ambiguities of city or court.
It is not so much a pleasant fiction as a poignant image of what life
might have been.

The elegiac mood that so strongly colors our response to Eden extends to other descriptive passages in *Paradise Lost*. The vision of blissful life on the stars that Satan passes in his journey to the earth is powerful precisely because it is illusory—for him and, by implication, for anyone. The outline of an ideal landscape embodies general human yearnings for a simple happiness:

> Or other Worlds they seem'd, or happy Iles,
> Like those *Hesperian* Gardens fam'd of old,
> Fortunate Fields, and Groves and flourie Vales. (III, 567–69)

The sense of loss is like an undertow in the first book of the poem, strongest in the description of Satan's despair but reasserting itself in the catalogue of pagan gods. Having lost the "happy Fields" of heaven, the fallen angels will corrupt the appealing places of the earth, such as the "pleasant Vally of *Hinnom*" (I, 404), desecrated by the worship of Baal and transformed into "black *Gehenna*," the "Type of Hell." Fair Damascus, "on the fertil Banks / Of *Abbana* and *Pharphar*, lucid streams" (I, 468–69), becomes Rimmon's "delightful Seat." Even the reference to the "flowry Dale of *Sibma* clad with Vines" (I, 410) is elegiac, since these vineyards were destroyed as a punishment for Moab's pride (Isaiah xvi, 8).

The most alluring landscape of the first two books appears in the pastoral simile with which Milton marks the agreement of the fallen angels, beautifully evoking the harmony of nature after a storm:

> If chance the radiant Sun with farewell sweet
> Extend his ev'ning beam, the fields revive,
> The birds thir notes renew, and bleating herds
> Attest thir joy, that hill and valley rings.   (II, 492–95)

If the simile were merely an illustration of the concord of "Devil with Devil damn'd," its power would seem strangely out of proportion to the scene in Hell, but much more is involved. This moment of tranquillity, comparable to scenes of harmony in Eden, stands for a peace apparently beyond the reach of men, who, "though under hope / Of heavenly Grace,

> Yet live in hatred, enmity, and strife
> Among themselves, and levie cruel warres,
> Wasting the Earth, each other to destroy.   (II, 500–02)

And yet one ideal landscape in *Paradise Lost* suggests an attainable ideal. This is Milton's affirmation of his poetic power in the invocation to Book III:

> Yet not the more
> Cease I to wander where the Muses haunt
> Cleer Spring, or shadie Grove, or Sunnie Hill,
> Smit with the love of sacred Song; but chief
> Thee *Sion* and the flowrie Brooks beneath
> That wash thy hallowd feet, and warbling flow,
> Nightly I visit. (III, 26–32)

These scenes are more than a shorthand way of referring to places of inspiration. They are landscapes of the imagination where Milton finds something of the clarity and assurance suggested by the landscapes of Eden, though not the innocence. In this ideal world the poet has his bearings and can wander without fear of losing his way.

The true image of perfection in *Paradise Lost* is heaven. Although the landscape of Eden is much more fully and convincingly realized, it can only be regarded as a "shadow" of the hills and valleys of heaven, which stand for a bliss beyond the threat of change. The landscapes of heaven vary according to Milton's purposes. The region within the walls appears in one perspective as a vast plain, in another as a configuration of hill and valley. Still closer to the throne of God is the "river of Bliss," Milton's adaptation of the river of life briefly pictured in Revelation:

> [Immortal Amarant] there grows,
> And flours aloft shading the Fount of Life,
> And where the river of Bliss through midst of Heavn
> Rowls o'er Elisian Flours her Amber stream. (III, 356–59)

Although it threatens to become purely allegorical, this river, with its surrounding flowers, more nearly suggests a natural scene than the river of Revelation or Dante's river of light.[36] Where Dante emphasized the discontinuity between heaven and paradise, Milton in this scene, and in the one revealing the angels taking their supper while reclining on flowers, made the resemblances between the two places obvious enough for heaven to seem the model for Eden in significant ways. Since heaven has a visible and substantial landscape, however brief our glimpses of it, we can imagine the order and delight that Adam and Eve find in nature as a reflection of celestial harmony.

The celestial hills and valleys are more obviously symbolic than their earthly counterparts. The strongest image that Milton could find for the "horrible confusion" (VI, 668) introduced into heaven by war was the uprooting of these hills. The restoration of the landscape is proof of the Son's power to bring about a renewal of order:

> Heav'n his wonted face renewd,
> And with fresh Flourets Hill and Valley smil'd.
>
> (VI, 783–84)

As in the pastoral simile of Book II, the phrase "Hill and Valley" is a formula suggesting the return of harmony. Satan's reference to heaven's "happy Fields" (I, 249) and the "Vales of Heav'n" (I, 321) reflect visions of lost bliss and ease. In Eve's regret at losing the "happie Walks and Shades" (IX, 270) of the Garden and Adam's nostalgic account of the places where he saw God, landscape mirrors feelings in a similar way, reinforcing the sense that the bliss of paradise anticipates that of heaven.

Yet we can measure the landscape and the joys of paradise more readily than those of heaven. The immensity of heaven, as Milton pictures it, daunts the imagination. We know that heaven is traditionally square because Milton refers to it as God's "Quadrature" (X, 381), but Satan, who sees the wall in the distance "extended wide / In circuit, undetermind square or round" (II, 1048), cannot find its limits. The plain within the walls extends so far that Abdiel travels all night through "Heav'ns wide Champain" (VI, 2) returning from Satan's newly established kingdom in the "spacious North" (V, 726); on the following day the faithful angels make the same journey in reverse, marching over "many a Province wide / Tenfold the length of this terrene" (VI, 77). Even in the description of the angels at rest we are made aware of the vastness of heaven:

> Wide over all the Plain, and wider farr
> Than all this globous Earth in Plain out spred,
> (Such are the Courts of God) Th'Angelic throng
> Disperst in Bands and Files thir Camp extend
> By living Streams among the Trees of Life,
> Pavilions numberless.   (V, 648–53)

These incalculable numbers and distances suggest unbounded freedom and joy and a security that does not depend upon particular walks and bowers. It is meaningless to talk of angels losing their way in heaven.

These measurements invite comparison with the predominantly vertical measurements of hell, which indicate pride and ambition. The horizontal extension of heaven suggests that although Milton's cosmos has a ceiling, its size can no more be appreciated by the human mind than can the power and knowledge of God. We are not conscious of the size of the faithful angels because they are diminished by their environment. It is the self-assertive fallen angels who stand out against their background, in postures of defiance.

In its landscape as in so many other ways hell parodies heaven. Milton frequently refers to hell in terms that suggest moral and psychological rather than physical dimensions. As a "deep world / Of darkness" (II, 262–63), it seems impossibly removed from divine favor; as a "dark opprobrious Den of shame" (II, 58), it is a place where the unseemliness of rebellion can be kept from view; as the "infernal Vaile" (II, 742) it suggests a perversion of the repose of heaven. The external scene seems no more than a projection of spiritual realities when Satan first looks around him and sees "Regions of sorrow, doleful shades, where peace / And rest can never dwell" (I, 65–66). Yet Milton does give hell a discernible landscape, or rather a series of landscapes.[37] What Satan first sees as "The dismal Situation waste and wilde" (I, 60), he later refers to as "Yon dreary Plain, forlorn and wilde" (I, 180). This desolate plain, insofar as it is visible through the gloom, suggests that there is no relief or escape from their condition for Satan and his legions. When vistas open up in hell, they offer only more reasons for despair. The fallen angels can never lose for long the oppressive sense of confinement that Satan describes:

> Our prison strong, this huge convex of Fire,
> Outrageous to devour, immures us round
> Ninefold, and gates of burning Adamant
> Barr'd over us prohibit all egress. (II, 434–37)

Many of the features of the infernal landscape serve a specific occasion. A volcano provides gold for the building of Pandaemonium. A plain is available for the fallen angels who want to engage in heroic games while Satan is away; there are "Rocks and Hills" (II, 540) on which others can vent their rage; others can sing their own deeds in a "silent valley" (II, 547). Those who set out "On bold adventure to discover wide / That dismal world" (II, 571–72), proceeding away from the burning lake along the four rivers of hell, find no "easier habitation," of course, but a "Universe of death" (II, 622). Contrasts between the barrenness of hell and Eden's fertility are reinforced by topographical differences. The exploring angels pass through "many a dark and dreary Vale" and over "many a Frozen, many a fierie Alpe," but these have no relation to each other and seem a grotesque distortion of the hills and dales of the earth. There is no apparent order to the "Rocks, Caves, Lakes, Fens, Bogs, Dens, and shades of death" (II, 261) that make up this inhospitable world.[38] In the "frozen Continent" found in another part of hell the familiar landscape features are entirely obliterated:

> Beyond this flood a frozen Continent
> Lies dark and wilde, beat with perpetual storms
> Of Whirlwind and dire Hail, which on firm land
> Thaws not, but gathers heap, and ruin seems
> Of ancient pile; all else deep snow and ice,
> A gulf profound as that *Serbonian* Bog
> Betwixt *Damiata* and mount *Casius* old,
> Where Armies whole have sunk.   (II, 587–94)

In a poem about the loss of Eden the image of the "happie Garden" (III, 66) could not persist unchanged to the end, at least when landscape is never merely neutral background. The Garden itself does not change immediately, only Adam's perception of it in his new self-consciousness and guilt. In his imagination the place is not only disordered ("these wilde Woods forlorn" [IX, 910]) but diminished, shrunk to the "glade / Obscur'd" (IX, 1084–85) where he would like to live in solitude. In the broadest sense Eden ceases to exist from the moment it becomes for Adam a place to hide. The sudden transformation of the Garden in Adam's mind dramatically reveals how completely his original harmony with his surroundings depended upon harmony with God. As a consequence of his isolation from God, and from Eve, Eden loses its meaning.

Adam can renew his love for Eve and appeal to God for mercy, but the divorce between heaven and earth reflected in actual changes in the natural world is permanent. In his treatment of these changes, a standard theme of hexaemeral literature, Milton placed particular emphasis on the ravaging of the Garden. The most horrific image of change is that of Death ready to devour herb, fruit, flower, and "whatever thing / The Scythe of Time mows down" (X, 605–06). This is Milton's version of the tombstone in Arcadia, only his Eden, unlike the fictionalized world of shepherds and flocks, cannot absorb the presence of death. His pastoral world is devastated not only by time but by the winds, by the heat of the flaming sword, and ultimately by the flood. Adam actually sees the winds (which include *"Zephir,"* the normally gentle west wind always present in the earthly paradise) "shattering the graceful locks / Of these fair spreading Trees" (X, 1066–67). Michael's preview of the final destruction of paradise demonstrates to Adam as nothing else could that the bliss of Eden is irrevocably lost:

> then shall this Mount
> Of Paradise by might of Waves be moovd
> Out of his place, pushd by the horned floud,
> With all his verdure spoil'd, and Trees adrift
> Down the great River to th'op'ning Gulf,
> And there take root an Iland salt and bare,
> The haunt of Seales and Orcs, and Sea-mews clang. (XI, 829–35)

The lesson of the scene, as Michael expounds it, is that "God attributes to place / No sanctitie" (XI, 836–37). This is an essential part of Adam's education—if he is to create a new order for himself, he must not look back nostalgically to Eden—yet the vision is almost unendurable. The trees that formed stately alleys are set "adrift," as the hill of paradise is dislodged and swept away. Milton used a similar image and virtually the same rhythm in another powerful evocation of disorder, his description in *Lycidas* of the head of the murdered Orpheus being carried "Down the swift *Hebrus* to the *Lesbian* shore." The destruction is all the more frightening in *Paradise Lost* because it is unleashed by God. Paradise itself, by a kind of brutal realism that denies the validity of myth, is transformed from an ideal world into an actual place, an "Iland salt and bare" of the sort reported by travellers.[39]

Adam's first view of the world in which he finds himself before being taken up to Eden is a delightful scene of "Hill, Dale, and shady Woods, and sunny Plains / And liquid Lapse of murmuring Streams" (VIII, 262–63). While there is no reason to believe that this topography changes after the Fall, Milton could not very well picture again the interchange of hill and valley, with its connotations of pleasure and security. Instead he developed a contrast between the mount of paradise (and implicitly the delight, ease, and familiarity with God for which it stands) and a "lower World" (XI, 283), a "subjected Plaine" (XII, 640) where man dominates his surroundings instead of blending into them. Scenes of lust, ambition, and violence blot out the natural world, which Milton typically shows as a plain:

> So violence
> Proceeded, and Oppression, and Sword-Law
> Through all the Plain, and refuge none was found. (XI, 671–73)

This plain, into which Adam and Eve venture at the end of the poem, is sometimes the setting for pastoral scenes, but these are invariably disrupted: by Cain, or Nimrod, or by giants who attack the shepherds and scatter their flocks. Michael assures Adam that although he is "brought down / To dwell on even ground" (XII, 347–48) with his sons, God's presence will be found "In Vallie and in plaine" (XI, 349). Yet the overwhelming impression of the last two books is that man cannot look for any real refuge in the wilderness of this world; Milton's austere view of life after the Fall permits no more "happy Walks and Shades" (XI, 270).

The point of Michael's harsh lessons in history is not to intensify the memory of life in paradise but to wrench Adam's thoughts away from Eden. Michael's purpose is to bring Adam to accept the "lower World" and to recognize that henceforth struggle and not rest will be the basic condition of life in it. Adam must learn not to look to his natural surroundings for confirmation of God's benevolence and his own well-being as he did in the Garden. In his new understanding Eden is a type of the heavenly paradise that awaits the faithful. Meanwhile, he can find consolation, if he has faith and the strength to act upon it, in the "paradise within" that each individual can win for himself. Milton no doubt would agree with Richard Sibbes' assertion that "faith makes quiet the soul."[40] An inner peace, stronger than the peace of Eden because self-attained and independent of the external world, is the faithful man's reward in this life.

University of Michigan

NOTES

1. *Adventurer,* p. 101. Quoted in *Eighteenth-Century Critical Essays,* ed. Scott Elledge (Ithaca, N. Y., 1961), II, 713.

2. Cf. "A Note on the Verse of John Milton," *Essays and Studies,* XXI (1936), 32–40, and *Revaluation* (London, 1936), p. 47.

3. *A Preface to "Paradise Lost,"* (London, 1942), p. 51. See also Douglas Bush's similar defense, *"Paradise Lost" in Our Time* (Ithaca, N. Y., 1945), and J. B. Broadbent's commentary on Milton's paradise in *Some Graver Subject: An Essay on "Paradise Lost,"* (New York, 1960), pp. 173–84. The fullest treatment of the earthly paradise tradition is A. Bartlett Giamatti's *The Earthly Paradise and the Renaissance Epic* (Princeton, 1966).

4. Quotations of Milton's poetry are from *The Works of John Milton,* ed. Frank Allen Patterson et al. (New York, 1931–42).

5. *Purgatorio,* XXVIII.

6. *The Faerie Queene,* I, xii. Ernst Curtius defined the *topos* of the *locus amoenus* and enumerated the common characteristics of the ideal landscape. Cf. *European Literature and the Latin Middle Ages,* trans. Willard Trask (New York, 1953), chap. 10. Curtius does not distinguish between varieties of the *locus amoenus* in terms of their spaciousness. One of the most important panoramic, or broad, landscapes is Virgil's Elysium (*Aeneid,* VI, 637 ff.), in which the "locos laetos" include meadows, vales, groves, and fresh streams. The view that Musaeus shows Aeneas from a ridge—of gleaming fields, or plains ("camposque nitentis") extending below—gives a sense of the amplitude of the place. The descriptions of heaven, and paradise, that Howard Rollins Patch summarizes in *The Other World* (Cambridge, Mass., 1950) frequently involve a meadow or plain, often a plateau at the top of a mountain. Spenser associated delight with broad landscapes in *The Faerie Queene* on several important occasions, perhaps thinking of Virgil as well as traditional representations of paradise or false paradises. On the top of Mount Acidale is "a spacious plaine" (VI, c, 8). Guyon and the Palmer, once past the gate, emerge into "a larger space / That stretcht it selfe into an ample plaine" (II, vii, 20–21). Tasso's Armida is to be found on a "pian su l'monte ampio ed aperto" (*Gerusalemme Liberata,* XV, lii). Milton pictured his Garden as a "plain" at the top of a "woody Mountain" (VIII, 303) and emphasized its extent, but spaciousness is linked with delight most notably in the description of heaven, with its vast plains.

7. *FQ* III, vi. Quotations of Spenser's poetry are from *The Poetical Works of Edmund Spenser,* ed. J. C. Smith and E. De Selincourt (London, 1940).

8. *The Other World,* pp. 12–13.

9. *De Laudibus Dei,* I, 190–94, as translated by Eleanor S. Duckett in *Latin Writers of the Fifth Century* (New York, 1930), p. 85.

10. *Metamorphoses,* I, 107. Compare Avitus' "Hic ver assiduum coeli clementia servat," J. P. Migne, *Patrologia Latina,* LIX, 327, and Grotius' "Verque perpetuum gravem / Defendit hyemem," *Adamus Exsul,* in Watson Kirkconnell, *The Celestial Cycle* (Toronto, 1952), p. 100.

11. *The Descent from Heaven* (New Haven, 1963), p. 401.

12. Milton is more famous for his prospects that violate human scale to present immense vistas, as in Adam's view of "all Earth's kingdoms in thir Glory" (XI, 384) from the highest hill of paradise, or the prospect of cities and empires

that Satan shows Christ in *Paradise Regained*. The vogue of the prospect in the seventeenth century is discussed by B. Sprague Allen, *Tides in English Taste* (Cambridge, Mass., 1937) and more fully by Siegfried Korninger in *Die Natur-auffassung in der Englischen Dichtung des 17. Jahrhunderts* (Vienna, 1956), chap. 9.

13. *The Film Sense*, trans. Jay Leyda (New York, 1942), pp. 58–62.

14. *FQ* II, xii, 58. Compare the landscape before the Temple of Venus:

> Fresh shadowes, fit to shroud from sunny ray;
> Faire lawnds, to take the sunne in season dew;
> Sweet springs, in which a thousand Nymphs did play;
> Soft rombling brookes, that gentle slomber drew;
> High reared mounts, the lands about to vew;
> Low looking dales, disloignd from common gaze;
> Delightful bowres, to solace lovers trew;
> False Labyrinthes, fond runners eyes to daze;
> All which by nature made did nature selfe amaze. (*FQ* IV, x, 24)

15. *The Countesse of Pembrokes Arcadia*, ed. Albert Feuillerat (Cambridge, 1963), I, 13.

16. Robert Arnold Aubin, in *Topographical Poetry in XVIII-Century England* (New York, 1936), discusses the development of topographical poetry before the eighteenth century with particular attention to Denham and his immediate pre-decessors. In *Cooper's Hill* and the lesser known poems that anticipated it there is an attention to the outlines of particular scenes not to be found in Drayton's *Poly-Olbion*, where the topography of England is lovingly traced but never visualized. In the representation of ideal landscapes, Drayton's eclogues, William Browne's *Brittania's Pastorals*, and the works of Giles and Phineas Fletcher are not significantly different from Spenser.

17. *The Return of Eden* (Toronto, 1965), p. 31.

18. Arnold Stein has written suggestively on the order of the Garden, which he describes as "great variety fulfilling itself in greater harmony." *Answerable Style* (Minneapolis, 1953), pp. 64–66.

19. H. V. S. Ogden, in "The Principles of Variety and Contrast in Seven-teenth Century Aesthetics, and Milton's Poetry," *JHI*, X (1949), 159–82, has demonstrated with great thoroughness that an emphasis upon multiplicity of detail in both landscape painting and poetry gave way in the seventeenth century to a preference for variety ordered by contrast. He cites most of the passages quoted above, among others, to illustrate Milton's use of variety and contrast.

20. *FQ* II, xii, 59.

21. *Psyche* VI, 166, in *Complete Poems*, ed. A. B. Grosart, 2 vols. (Edin-burgh, 1880).

22. *Pastoral Poetry and An Essay on Criticism*, ed. E. Audra and Aubrey Williams (London and New Haven, 1961). Earl Wasserman sees in this passage "the ideal physical expression of Nature's one law of *concordia discors*, the active harmonizing of differences." See *The Subtler Language* (Baltimore, 1959), p. 103.

23. *Of Gardens* (1664).

24. *The Complete Works of Joshua Sylvester*, ed. A. B. Grosart (London, 1880), I, 104.

25. *A Reading of "Paradise Lost"* (Oxford, 1965), p. 79.

26. Cf. Bruno Snell's chapter, "Arcadia: The Discovery of a Spiritual Landscape," in *The Discovery of Mind*, trans. T. G. Rosenmeyer (Cambridge, Mass., 1953).

27. In *L'Arcadia* and *Gli Asolani*.

28. *European Literature and the Latin Middle Ages*, p. 191.

29. *Georgics* II, 467–71:

Yet theirs is repose without care, and a life that knows no fraud, but is rich in treasures manifold. Yea, the ease of broad domains, caverns, and living lakes, and cool vales, the lowing of the kine, and soft slumbers beneath the trees—all are theirs.   (Trans. H. R. Fairclough, *Loeb Classical Library*)

30. Spenser and Drayton provide characteristic examples of the motif:

The gentle shepheard satte beside a springe,
All in the shadowe of a bushye brere.
    "December," *The Shepheardes Calender*

In delights that never fade,
The Muses lulled be,
And sit at pleasure in the shade
Of many a stately tree.
    "The Muses Elizium"

31. Trans. William Cowper, *Complete Poetical Works* (New York, 1848), I, 767.

32. A. Richard Turner, in *The Vision of Landscape in Renaissance Italy* (Princeton, 1966), 119 ff., relates the pastoral landscapes of Giorgione and Titian to the contemporary literary vogue of Arcadia.

33. Poussin's landscapes are probably the most like Milton's. His *Spring* is unlike most representations of Eden in not being dominated by Adam and Eve and the serpent. Adam and Eve appear as relatively small figures set in a green world in which trees and open space alternate and several vistas open into the distance. Sir Kenneth Clark, in *Landscape into Art* (London, 1949), pp. 68–69, briefly compares Poussin with Milton and calls his *Spring* a "perfect illustration for *Paradise Lost*." Mario Praz's comparison of Milton and Poussin focusses on parallels in the artistic development of the two men: "Milton and Poussin," in *Seventeenth-Century Studies Presented to Sir Herbert Grierson* (Oxford, 1938), pp. 192–210.

34. See *The Vision of Landscape in Renaissance Italy*, pp. 94–95, for an excellent discussion of the "Arcadian mood" of this painting.

35. For Erwin Panofsky's explanation of the significance of the inscription see "*Et In Arcadia Ego*: Poussin and the Elegiac Tradition," *Meaning in the Visual Arts* (New York, 1955), pp. 295–320.

36. *Paradiso*, xxx.

37. Marjorie Nicolson, *John Milton: A Reader's Guide to his Poetry* (New York, 1963), pp. 193–200, distinguishes three hells: the landscape that Satan sees upon arising from the burning lake, which she suggests is based upon the Phlegraean Fields near Naples; Pandaemonium; and the world that the fallen angels explore in Satan's absence.

38. Marjorie Nicolson, *Mountain Gloom and Mountain Glory* (Ithaca, N. Y.,

1959), chap. 1, has shown that seventeenth-century English poets took their mountains from literary tradition, describing them as desolate and inhospitable in the manner of Roman poets. The mountains of hell are completely forbidding, as are the "Alpine mountains cold" of Milton's sonnet on the Piedmontese massacre. They are also monstrous in their asymmetry. As Miss Nicolson points out (p. 69), using Marvell's "Upon Appleton House" by way of illustration, beauty was at this time "a mean between extremes, appealing to Reason that recognized proportion, limitation, and restraint as qualities imposed by God upon Nature when he brought order out of chaos." In Milton's account of the creation the height of mountains is balanced by the depth of the seas:

> So high as heav'd the tumid Hills, so low
> Down sunk a hollow bottom broad and deep,
> Capacious bed of Waters.   (VII, 288–90)

The wild landscape of hell, though initially shocking to the fallen angels, seems an appropriate setting for demonic forces. Its affinities are with the more sinister haunted landscapes of epic and romance: meres, caves, deserts.

39. See Broadbent, *Some Graver Subject*, p. 273n., for examples.

40. Richard Sibbes, *Light from Heaven* (London, 1638), p. 138. In *Christian Doctrine, Works*, XVI, 49, Milton relates the "peace of God, which passeth all understanding" (Philippians iv, 7) to the individual's sense of justification: "From consciousness of justification proceed peace and real tranquillity of mind."

THE POET AND SATAN IN
PARADISE LOST

William G. Riggs

Realizing that the desire to achieve "Things unattempted yet in Prose or Rhyme" offers a potential for sin, Milton employs parallels between the narrator of *Paradise Lost* and Satan to indicate his awareness that great endeavors, even his own, may be pridefully motivated. But he defines carefully the difference between his "advent'rous" singing and satanic overreaching. The sharp contrast between the narrator's dependence on divine guidance and Satan's claims of self-sufficiency is repeatedly asserted within the context of striking similarities: both poet and Devil undertake great adventures; both, dwelling in hostile darkness, soar toward light; both, in need of direction, seek guidance from light (holy Light, Uriel) and primal sources of hexaemeral knowledge (Urania, Uriel). Milton supports such general parallels by the repetition of specific details and by numerous verbal echoes. But Satan lies to Uriel, curses the sun, and, inverting the poet's creative impulse, invokes his proper muse in Chaos. The devils can sing; they pursue the philosophical issues with which *Paradise Lost* is concerned; they build "Monument[s] / Of merit high." These satanic perversions of good mean more than that the devils are bad; they mean that man may be beguiled by some "fair appearing good." A Solomon may fall "To Idols foul." A poet exploring "things invisible to mortal sight" must humbly hope that he is not deluded, that all *is* "Hers who brings it nightly to [his] Ear."

I

A FAMILIAR GROUP of Milton's readers have not shared Adam's confidence that "Evil into the mind of God or Man / May come and go, so unapprov'd, and leave / No spot or blame behind" (V, 117–19);[1]

59

they have instead assumed, less charitably, that the impact of Satan's character in *Paradise Lost* implies an uncomprehended diabolical complicity on the part of the poet. Such readings have been vigorously rebutted,[2] but they manage to persist because they respond with appealing directness to what can hardly be missed: Satan is impressive. He impresses not just the romantic imagination and its offshoots; in seventeenth-century England the appeal of his heroics would have touched any admirer of Achilles or Hector or Aeneas. Of course most of Milton's first audience would have been willing, ultimately, to accept the poet's stated assessment of Satan's heroism, whereas Shelley, for instance, was not. But precisely because Milton's early readers knew the Devil was bad and did not, like C. S. Lewis, have to prove it, they could respond more openly to his admirable qualities, to his suffering fortitude and constancy of purpose. Much post-Romantic criticism has lost this sense of balance and has viewed *Paradise Lost* partially. Milton clearly intends to condemn Satan (who could doubt it?), but he just as clearly provides materials for the Satanist critique—a critique which offers us valuable intuitions: "Milton . . . was a true poet and of the Devil's party without knowing it."[3] Blake's notorious claim not only helps to suggest the complexity of Milton's struggle with evil; it also serves to isolate an important dimension of *Paradise Lost* by insisting that Milton's relationship as poet to the structure he created is a primary concern and that, in particular, the relationship of the poet to Satan is crucial. These are important considerations, but they remain distorted in Blake and those who subsequently have shared his attitude toward the place of Satan in Milton's poem. The reason for this distortion is plain: the Satanists, almost without exception, presume to know more than Milton about the workings of the creative imagination. I will be arguing that to so presume is usually to ignore the information Milton offers us concerning his own creative process. In his characterization of Satan, Milton leaves us little room for second-guessing about his unconscious sympathies. His poem demonstrates an acute sensitivity to both the appeals and the dangers of Satanism; his imagination is not covertly inflamed by fallen grandeur. In short, Milton knew exactly to what extent he was "of the Devil's party." In his epic he anticipates the Satanist response by repeatedly asking us to compare his portrait of the poet with his portrait of Satan. The similarities are not hidden; the differences are consciously and carefully defined.

That the description of the poet in *Paradise Lost* contributes significantly to the epic's total design has become a commonplace of recent commentary on Milton's poetry.[4] Milton, it is argued, presents the poet as a character within his own poem, a character whose fallen circumstances and aspirations to the knowledge of God mirror in several ways concerns central to the "argument" pursued in the epic's narrative. This sense of the poet's allusive participation in his own narrative has emerged from a view of the poem's structure which suggests analogical complexity as a principle of design. Since 1930 when E. M. W. Tillyard presented his first full-length study of Milton,[5] critics have been emphasizing that in *Paradise Lost* events in Heaven, on Earth, and in Hell correspond to each other by means of continually reverberating motifs. The poem repeatedly echoes itself, and the echoes serve to transform the chronologically transient occurrences of ordinary narrative into eternal paradigms. Milton, in this view, consistently unifies his narrative materials (and his ontology) by explicit comparisons between the divine, the human, and the infernal. While Adam's disobedience seems in part the result of Satan's fall, it is also an echo of Satan's sin. The Son's missions of creation are played against the backdrop of Satan's circumstantially similar voyages of destruction. The first council in Heaven pointedly recalls the consult in Pandaemonium. Heavenly paternity is parodied by Satan and his hellish offspring. To Milton's modern critics, the range of such analogies has appeared vastly extendible and has recently been seen to circumscribe the reader as well as the poet.[6] Milton's rhetoric may well be intended to draw the reader into an analogical participation in the story of the fall, but it seems to me that such participation, if it is to begin, begins at second hand with a view of the poet, a character clearly placed within *Paradise Lost* as an extended and concrete example of the relevance of Milton's cosmic drama to fallen man. My concern here, to consider the poet and Satan together, presents only a partial view of this relevance, but it is a good place to begin. Certainly for Milton the choices typical of Satan constituted the most radical agonies of our fallen world.

II

Denis Saurat has told us that "Milton had Satan in him and wanted to drive him out."[7] This is a blunt way to put things, but

Saurat would be close to the truth if he did not also insist that Milton
was unaware of his potential Satanism—in particular that he was
unaware of the potentially Satanic aspect of his aspiration to so
great a work as *Paradise Lost*. When in Book II we discover Satan
poised on the brink of Hell contemplating his flight into Chaos, his
"thoughts inflamed of Highest design" (II, 630), or when we are told
that Satan, "Thus high uplifted beyond hope, aspires / Beyond thus
high" (II, 7–8), we should not shy away from recalling the poet at the
outset desiring "with no middle flight . . . to soar / Above th' *Aonian*
Mount" (I, 14–15). Or again, when in Book I we hear Satan's prideful
self-justification, "till then who knew / The force of those dire Arms?"
(I, 93–94), and later find him once more willing to face an "unknown
Region . . ./ Unknown dangers" (II, 443–44), we should not, in supposed deference to the forgetful poet, refuse to recollect his initial
aspiration to try the unknown and achieve "things unattempted yet"
(I, 16). We should not, in short, smugly assume that Milton was miss-
ing the potential irony of such comparisons. By means of echoes
like these he intends us to ask a question, a question he himself was,
I think, the first to ask: is the attempt to write *Paradise Lost* presumptuous? Milton answers, "Yes, 'I have presum'd, / An Earthly
Guest, and drawn Empyreal Air'" (VII, 13–14); his constant hope,
however, is that the risk he runs is not prompted by self-justifying and
self-inflating pride.

In the invocation to Book I Milton's poet announces his subject,
"Man's First Disobedience" (I, 1), and proceeds directly to exalt its
importance—to make clear from the outset the audacity of his attempt
to explain to fallen men the justice of God's ways. He calls to a
heavenly muse:

> I thence
> Invoke thy aid to my advent'rous Song,
> That with no middle flight intends to soar
> Above th' *Aonian* Mount, while it pursues
> Things unattempted yet in Prose or Rhyme.   (I, 12–16)

There is no quibbling with greatness here. Milton is probably echoing
Ariosto, who at the beginning of *Orlando Furioso* had proudly in-
voked not a heavenly muse but his own mistress.[8] By ranking himself
beside the Italian poet, Milton may ultimately intend a contrast:
like Adam, Ariosto hearkened to the promptings of a mortal woman;

the poet of *Paradise Lost* looks to higher authority. Initially, however, the allusion serves simply to recall Ariosto's haughty tone ("I make no doubt but I shall have the skill / As much as I have promised to fulfill"),[9] and thereby to emphasize the hint of hubris latent throughout the first prologue to *Paradise Lost*. Less than twenty-five lines after this ambitious beginning Milton's epic voice sings of Satan:

> with all his Host
> Of Rebel Angels, by whose aid aspiring
> To set himself in Glory above his Peers,
> He trusted to have equall'd the most High.
> . . . .
> Him the Almighty Power
> Hurl'd headlong flaming from th' Ethereal Sky
> With hideous ruin and combustion down
> To bottomless perdition.   (I, 37–40; 44–47)

The immediate juxtaposition of the soaring ascent anticipated by the poet with the precipitous fall of the rebel angels suggests, at least, that Milton saw in his own circumstances as aspiring singer of divine epic the potential consequences of Satan's "ambitious aim." In viewing Satan and his cohorts we shall see this suggestion continually reinforced—for example, in the fall of Mulciber at the end of Book I. Here, specifically, an architect of things divine is cast down for his share in satanic overreaching.[10]

The initial invocation is not, of course, a cry of rebellion but a call for divine assistance:

> What in me is dark
> Illumine, what is low raise and support;
> That to the highth of this great Argument
> I may assert Eternal Providence
> And justify the ways of God to men.   (I, 22–26)

It should be clear that for Milton it is the poet's submission to the voice of his muse, to divine inspiration, which ultimately distinguishes the soaring creation of *Paradise Lost* from an act of blasphemous pride. Milton does not, however, present the invocation of a heavenly muse as his only defense against presuming too much. Throughout the narrative he remains sensitive to the relationship between himself as poet and his subject; he examines every implication of his creative act with a care which suggests a fear of self-delusion. While he insists on the pious intentions of what he undertakes, he never neglects to expose the satanic aspect of his poetic posture.

III

The mechanism of the poet's inspiration is based on a paradoxical pattern of outward darkness and inward illumination. In the prologue to Book III, Milton employs this paradox to express not only his humble dependence on God's grace but also the weakness and corresponding audacity of his presumptuous adventure beyond his own "Diurnal Sphere." Like fallen Satan, throwing round "his balefull eyes" (I, 56) in Hell, the poet, a fallen man, dwells in darkness:

> but thou [Light]
> Revisit'st not these eyes, that roll in vain
> To find thy piercing ray, and find no dawn;
> So thick a drop serene hath quencht thir Orbs,
> Or dim suffusion veil'd.   (III, 22–26)

To aim high from the depths of such obscurity is to echo Satan's despairing boast:

> From this descent
> Celestial Virtues rising, will appear
> More glorious and more dread than from no fall.   (II, 14–17)[11]

Throughout his prologues, the poet, "In darkness, and with dangers compast round" (VII, 27), repeatedly emphasizes the baseness of his condition; such an emphasis cannot exclude an awareness of the similarity between the poet's physical circumstances and those of his epic villain whose dwelling place is measured by its distance from light.[12] Indeed, in his second invocation Milton insists on this similarity by placing his narrator in a posture much more broadly reminiscent of Satan:

> Thee [holy Light] I revisit now with bolder wing
> Escap't the Stygian Pool, though long detain'd
> In that obscure sojourn, while in my flight
> Through utter and through middle darkness borne
> With other notes than to th' *Orphean* Lyre
> I sung of *Chaos* and *Eternal* Night.   (III, 13–18)

This passage follows *directly* the conclusion of Book II—over one hundred lines describing Satan's escape from Hell and labored flight up through Chaos. In a sense, of course, the epic narrator must trace

Satan's journey in order to describe it. But to take pains to visualize both the narrator and Satan struggling through "this wild Abyss / The Womb of nature" (II, 910–11)—Satan "Audacious" (II, 931), the poet "with bolder wing"—achieves nothing so much as to suggest an analogy between the two daring voyagers. The analogy is not simply glimpsed; Milton develops it in detail.

Just as the poet in the prologue to Book III has labored out of darkness to win the visionary illumination bestowed by God, so Satan's flight in Book II through the "darksome Desert" of Chaos is directed toward light. As the arch Fiend approaches the Sun, his "visual ray" is

> sharp'n'd . . .
> To Objects distant far, whereby he soon
> Saw within ken a glorious Angel stand
> The same whom *John* saw also in the Sun. (III, 620–23)

The poet has, at the beginning of this book, applied to holy Light for direction and increased clarity that he might "see and tell / Of things invisible to mortal sight" (III, 54–55). So here Satan, "Alone thus wand'ring" (III, 667), applies to the Regent of the Sun, Uriel, for assistance in his anti-creative task. His formal address to Uriel is an unmistakable, though bombastic, echo of a Miltonic invocation:

> *Uriel,* for thou of those sev'n Spirits that stand
> In sight of God's high Throne, gloriously bright,
> The first art wont his great authentic will
> Interpreter through highest Heav'n to bring,
> Where all his Sons thy Embassy attend;
> And here art likeliest by supreme decree
> Like honor to obtain, and as his Eye
> To visit oft this new Creation round. . . .
> . . . .
> Brightest Seraph, tell
> In which of all these shining Orbs hath Man
> His fixed seat, or fixed seat hath none
> But all these shining Orbs his choice to dwell;
> That I may find him, and with secret gaze,
> Or open admiration him behold. (III, 654–61; 667–72)

Satan, dissembling, does not simply adopt the supplicating posture of the poet: while his rhetoric is inflated and his periods suspended beyond anything the poet, speaking for himself, attempts, still the content and syntactic formulas of Satan's speech distinctly recall the voice of the poet invoking his muse. Satan's request for heavenly guidance ("Brightest Seraph, tell") is, of course, the keynote of Milton's first invocation ("Instruct me, for Thou know'st. . . . Say first" [I, 19, 27]). The compound string of eulogistic epithet and description through which Satan ingratiates himself with Uriel and Satan's cautious offering of alternatives ("In which . . . hath Man / His fixed seat, or fixed seat hath none / . . . with secret gaze, / Or open admiration") look back to the beginning of Book III and the poet's address to Light:

> Hail holy Light, offspring of Heav'n first-born
> Or of th' Eternal Coeternal beam
> May I express thee unblam'd? since God is Light,
> And never but in unapproached Light
> Dwelt from Eternity, dwelt then in thee
> Bright effluence of bright essence increat.   (III, 1–6)

Again in Book VII we find a similar suspended list of heavenly qualities and a similar offering of alternatives which here place Urania, like Uriel, "In sight of God's high Throne":

> Descend from Heav'n *Urania*, by that name
> If rightly thou art call'd
>   . . . .
>   for thou
> Nor of the Muses nine, nor on the top
> Of old *Olympus* dwell'st, but Heav'nly born,
> Before the Hills appear'd, or Fountain flow'd,
> Thou with Eternal Wisdom didst converse,
> Wisdom thy Sister, and with her didst play
> In presence of th' Almighty Father.   (VII, 1–2, 5–11)

Before the powers of heavenly instruction Satan, in his manner, resembles the poet, a humble servant of God—a resemblance good enough to fool Uriel. The likeness between the two is further suggested by the fact that Uriel, to whom the Devil looks for aid, shares with the poet's muse ("Thou from the first / Wast present" [I, 19–20]) special knowledge of the Creation: "I saw when at his Word the formless mass / This world's material mould, came to a heap" (III, 708–09). These multiple similarities do not seem random. That both Satan and the poet seek, in syntactically echoing passages, assistance from light and from sources of hexaemeral knowledge should appear striking. It should make clear that Milton is looking at the poet's situation in terms of Satan's fallen posture and wishes to communicate this perspective. The question, to repeat, is why Milton invites such a comparison, and the answer, again, is that recognizing the audacity of his own high poetic aspirations he wishes to distinguish them clearly from the kind of aspiring he sees as satanic. He is after the contrast, but he does not wish to gain it by slighting the similarities. On the contrary, the more clearly he can see and project the similarities between the poet and Satan, the more sure he can be that he has not been blinded by pride.

The crucial contrast is obvious but significant in that Milton employs it to speak for himself. Satan, unlike the poet, is lying. Uriel is persuaded to think that the Devil's purposes are exactly opposite to what they really are:

> Fair Angel, thy desire which tends to know
> The works of God, thereby to glorify
> The great Work-Master, *leads to no excess*
> *That reaches blame, but rather merits praise*
> *The more it seems excess.*   (III, 694–98; my italics)

The glorification of God is not what Satan has in mind, but it is precisely what the poet sees as the province of his own attempt. For the poet what "seems excess"—the attempt to discover "things invisible to mortal sight"—will, he hopes, "merit praise." Milton here seizes the occasion of the Devil's lie to define his own purposes.

Milton's use of Satan's stance as a foil to the poet's position is perhaps made most explicit at the beginning of Book IV. Here the Fiend, having landed on "Niphates top," turns his gaze toward Heaven and speaks directly to the Sun. The speech is roughly an inversion, perhaps a parody, of Milton's familiar "Hail holy Light":

> O thou that with surpassing Glory crown'd
> Look'st from thy sole Dominion like the God
> Of this new World; at whose sight all the Stars
> Hide thir diminisht heads; to thee I call,
> But with no friendly voice, and add thy name
> O Sun, to tell thee how I hate thy beams
> That bring to my remembrance from what state
> I fell, how glorious once above thy Sphere:
> Till Pride and worse Ambition threw me down.   (IV, 32–41)

The poet and the Devil again, in a warped glass, reflect each other, and latent in the fact that Milton's hymn to holy Light can be subjected to satanic parody is the suggestion that hubristic presumption lies close to the surface of the second invocation. But the poet has hesitated: "May I express thee unblamed?" Perhaps he may. In the most obvious sense the comparable addresses to light serve emphatically to demonstrate the difference between the poet and the Apostate. While the poet asks for assistance, humbles himself before holy Light, prays, Satan hurls envious defiance at a lesser luminary.

IV

As I have been suggesting, basic to this comparison of the poet and Satan is Milton's symbolic use of place and posture. The physical circumstances in which Satan and the poet find themselves often have clear moral equivalents. It is nothing new to notice that in *Paradise Lost* physical movement and physical placement frequently suggest moral states. Hell is a place as are Heaven and Eden; to sin is to fall. An aspect of this equation of physical and moral in which recent critics have shown interest is Milton's use of the verb *wander*. Isabel MacCaffrey, for one, documents the fact that "Not only moral values, but the intellectual values on which they depend, can be objectified, in Milton's topography, by the identification of physical and spiritual 'wandering.' *Error* is the linking word."[13] I have already cited Satan describing to Uriel his erratic and malicious voyage through Chaos, "Alone thus wand'ring." MacCaffrey lists additional instances of Milton's use of the verb, such as his description of the wandering pilgrims who sought Christ in Golgotha (III, 476–77), Adam's warning against "wand'ring thoughts, and notions vaine" (VIII, 187), Eve's recognition of loss ("From thee / How shall I part, and wither wander down / Into a lower World" [XI, 281–83]), and the poignant "wand'ring steps and slow," which completes Milton's picture of our fallen parents. Clearly *wander* is one of the several words in *Paradise Lost* to which the reader becomes sensitized through repetition. Recently Stanley Fish has added to MacCaffrey's list and has warned us against the attempt to read *wander* the same way in different contexts.[14] The relevance of context to meaning is, of course, crucial, but with a word used as Milton uses *wander*, repetition tends—as I think Fish would agree—to encourage a comparison of the very contexts within which the word appears. Discriminations, such as can be made, are the result of these comparisons.

What interests me here about *wander* is that it serves to relate the poet of the prologues to the characters of Milton's narrative. What we learn of the word in the poem proper lends a sense of human helplessness to the lyrical lines:

> Yet not the more
> Cease I to wander where the Muses haunt
> Clear Spring, or shady Grove, or Sunny Hill,
> Smit with the love of sacred Song.   (III, 26–29)[15]

Everywhere in the prologues Milton's description of the poet's creative song is seen metaphorically as a journey—a dark descent, a soaring flight. This spatial sense of human activity is, of course, informed by the Puritan preachers' favorite image of the Christian life: the wayfaring pilgrim, seeking Heaven, directed by light. As the pilgrims "stray'd so farr . . . / In Golgotha" remind us, such wayfaring was full of perils for frail humanity. In the prologue to Book VII Milton repeats the word *wander* to relate these perils specifically to the poet whose journey passes dangerously near the abyss of satanic aspiration:

> Up led by thee [Urania]
> Into the Heav'n of Heav'ns I have presum'd
> An Earthly Guest, and drawn Empyreal Air,
> Thy temp'ring; with like safety guided down
> Return me to my Native Element:
> Lest from this flying Steed unrein'd, (as once
> *Bellerophon,* though from a lower Clime)
> Dismounted on th' *Aeleian* Field I fall
> Erroneous there to wander and forlorn.   (VII, 12–20)

Here Milton's poet wishes to avoid the erroneous wandering of a Bellerophon (a type of Satan) by means of celestial assistance.[16] He asks Urania that he be "led" and "guided" in his epic wayfaring. The request parallels Satan's plea for assistance during his wandering flight through Chaos:

> Ye Powers
> And Spirits of this nethermost Abyss
> *Chaos* and *ancient Night,* I come no Spy,
> With purpose to explore or to disturb

The secrets of your Realm, but by constraint
Wand'ring this darksome Desert, as my way
Lies through your spacious Empire up to light,
Alone, and without guide, half lost, I seek
What rediest path leads where your gloomy bounds
Confine with Heav'n; or if some other place
From your Dominion won, th' Ethereal King
Possesses lately, thither to arrive
I travel this profound, direct my course.   (II, 968–80)

These passages, taken together, serve again to emphasize explicitly the difference between Satan's mission to falsify God's ways to man and Milton's task. In his attempt at ordered poetic creation Milton's epic voice directs its request to Heaven, the ultimate source of all creation; Satan, on the other hand, intending to destroy, to "Erect the Standard . . . of *ancient Night*" (II, 986) where God has built, applies for guidance to disorder itself.

It should by now be clear that in depicting Satan's effort to subvert God's providential ways Milton continually reminds us of the poet's own activity. In the description related by the epic voice, Satan's intention of beguiling mankind initially appears—not just to the devils—as an immense undertaking "Of hazard" (II, 453, 455). To the infernal host Satan's destructive journey is "th' adventure" (II, 474), Satan "their great adventurer" (X, 440); and when the Devil himself describes his "adventure hard" (X, 468) we are surely meant to recall that the poet's own voyaging in Hell and Heaven is "advent'rous" (I, 13). Yet here, so the poet hopes, the similarity ends. "Whom shall we find / Sufficient" (II, 403–04), Beëlzebub asks, and Satan answers, "this enterprise / None shall partake with me" (II, 465–66). The Devil deludes himself about his own self-sufficiency continually; in action he hopes to succeed through individual "strength," "art," and "evasion" (II, 410–11). The poet, by contrast, is weak ("fall'n on evil days / On evil days though fall'n, and evil tongues" [VII, 25–26]), artless ("my unpremeditated Verse" [IX, 24]), and completely open concerning the possibilities, dangers, and intentions of his song. While the poet aspires to "no middle flight," he is ultimately dependent for support on divine inspiration; the Devil, attempting "solitary flight" (II, 632), benightedly convinces himself that he is "self-begot, self-rais'd" (V, 860). In describing Mammon's proposal to found an empire in Hell after the pattern of Heaven the epic voice gives us the phrase which exactly describes the kind of comparison Milton is attempting between poet and devil: "emulation opposite" (II, 298).

v

The ways in which the poet of *Paradise Lost* "emulates" the devils may at first glance appear puzzling. Take, for example, a small detail from Book I—Satan's rousing of his troops from the burning lake:

> Yet to thir General's Voice they soon obey'd
> Innumerable. As when the potent Rod
> Of *Amram's* Son in *Egypt's* evil day
> Wav'd round the Coast, up call'd a pitchy cloud
> Of *Locusts,* warping on the Eastern Wind,
> That o'er the Realm of impious *Pharaoh* hung
> Like Night, and darken'd all the Land of *Nile.*   (I, 337–43)

In the standard Christian typology which controls most of *Paradise Lost,* Satan is placed at the head of a list of villains which prominently includes Pharaoh, not his opposite, Moses. But here it is primarily "*Amram's* Son" with whom Satan is compared—"That Shepherd, who first taught the chosen Seed, / In the Beginning how the Heav'ns and Earth / Rose out of Chaos" (I, 8–10)—that shepherd with whom Milton has compared the poet at the beginning of Book I. It should appear initially odd that Milton employs the figure of Moses to describe both the poet and the Devil. It should appear odd, that is, until it becomes clear that Milton is consistently laboring to place poet and devil in comparable contexts. For Milton the shape of good and evil could be paradoxically similar; both Moses *and* Pharaoh could, superficially, resemble Satan, as they do in this passage if we look at it closely. Not only does Satan, in summoning his fallen cohorts, appear as Moses calling forth the plague of locusts; he also resembles here his proper type, Pharaoh, in that the plague he calls forth, while it descends on a land of captivity, descends at the same time on his own land. The devils are both slaves and masters, both seraphic lords and locusts (a standard analogy);[17] they are their own Hell. This doubleness of reference with respect to Satan and the devils is picked up within a few lines and emphasized:

Till, as a signal giv'n, th' uplifted Spear
Of thir great Sultan waving to direct
Thir course, in even balance down they light.   (I, 347–49)

While the uplifted spear of Satan continues to resemble the "potent
Rod / Of *Amram's* Son," the appellation "great Sultan" simultaneously
identifies the Devil with Moses' enemy, Pharaoh. The complexity of
Milton's use of allusion here corresponds to his attitude toward the
infernal host. The devils are not simply monstrous. They incorporate
and reflect (and, of course, pervert) the world's magnificence, even,
in shadowing the chosen seed, its blessedness.

William Empson has provided some lively commentary on the
similarity between diabolical attitudes and the attitudes of men of
virtue as Milton saw them. Empson quotes Satan's address to the
rebel forces in Book V:

Thrones, Dominations, Princedoms, Virtues, Powers,
If these magnific Titles yet remain
Not merely titular. . . .

· · · · · · · ·

Will ye submit your necks, and choose to bend
The supple knee? ye will not, if I trust
To know ye right, or if ye know yourselves
Natives and Sons of Heav'n possest before
By none, and if not equal all yet free,
Equally free; for Orders and Degrees
Jar not with liberty, but well consist.
Who can in reason then or right assume
Monarchy over such as live by right
His equals, if in power and splendor less,
In freedom equal? or can introduce
Law and Edict on us, who without law
Err not? Much less for this to be our Lord,
And look for adoration to th' abuse
Of those Imperial Titles which assert
Our being ordain'd to govern, not to serve? (V, 772–74, 787–802)

It is startling to come to this passage directly from a reading of
Milton's prose controversy. Not only does Satan argue, like the
republican Milton, from a position which couples native liberty with
an insistence on degree and discipline; in writing this speech Milton
could hardly have escaped hearing the accents of his own voice:

Is it such an unspeakable joy to serve, such felicity to wear a yoke, to clink our shackles looked on by pretended law of subjection, more intolerable and hopeless to be ever shaken off than those which are knocked on by illegal injury and violence?[18]

. . . .

I find both in our own and foreign story, that dukes, earls, and marquises were at first not hereditary, not empty and vain titles, but names of trust and office; and with the office ceasing, as induces me to be of opinion that every worthy man in parliament . . . might for the public good be thought a fit peer and judge of the king. . . .Whence doubtless our ancestors, who were not ignorant with what rights either nature or ancient constitution had endowed them . . . thought it no way illegal to depose and put to death their tyrannous kings.[19]

Empson's estimate of the effect of Satan's republicanism on Milton's contemporaries should make any fair-minded reader pause:

Surely the first readers must have found this intriguing; the only good writer who had defended the regicide was ascribing to the devils the sentiments still firmly held by himself and his proscribed party. They would not find the speech particularly dull and cooked-up, as Mr. Eliot did; and they would not be at all sure how far the author meant the devil's remarks to be wrong.[20]

Empson is not concerned so much with the inconsistency of Milton's politics (they are not inconsistent here) as with the unattractiveness of his theology. He quite clearly sees the trouble with Satan's rebellion, which is, of course, that Satan is not simply opposing a "King anointed" (V, 777), an absolute monarch "upheld by old repute, / Consent or custom" (I, 639–40); he is rebelling against God, the source of all degree, a non-authoritarian, immanent deity.[21] What is interesting about Empson's exposition is that he displays broadly what no reader should miss: the subject of *Paradise Lost* is rebellion, rebellion faulted by an author who himself was for his own and subsequent ages the prime spokesman for "the good old Cause." Typically, Milton did not attempt to disguise this seeming paradox. Schooled in rebellion, he openly granted the Devil the advantage of what he had learned in defense of liberty. I am not as sure as Empson that Milton's contemporaries would have been confused as to "how far the author meant the devil's remarks to be wrong," but I think it undeniable that the politics of Hell are an instance of Milton's concern to demonstrate, both to his readers and to himself, how close in fact he was to a satanic position.

Other instances of the poet's proximity to satanism occur in Book
II—particularly in the passage describing Hell's Olympian games:

> Others more milde,
> Retreated in a silent valley, sing
> With notes Angelical to many a Harp
> Thir own Heroic deeds and hapless Fall
> By doom of Battel; and complain that Fate
> Free Vertue should enthrall to Force or Chance.
>
> . . . .
>
> Others apart sat on a Hill retir'd,
> In thoughts more elevate, and reason'd high
> Of Providence, Foreknowledge, Will and Fate,
> Fixt Fate, Free will, Foreknowledge absolute,
> And found no end in wandring mazes lost.
> Of good and evil much they argu'd then,
> Of happiness and final misery.   (II, 546–51; 557–63)

Dennis Burden is the most recent critic to observe that "this intellectual and poetic Hell is something with which the poem is deeply
concerned."[22] The poets of Hell sing epic ("Thir own Heroic deeds")
and tragedy ("complain that Fate / Free Vertue should enthrall to
Force or Chance");[23] the infernal philosophers reason "high / Of
Providence, Foreknowledge, Will and Fate"; and the song of the poet-
philosopher, Milton, is crucially involved in all of this. While he
aspires to sing Christian heroism, "argument / Not less but more
Heroic than the wrath / Of stern Achilles" (IX, 13–15); while his
tragic notes (IX, 6) are tempered by Providence, not ruled by
Chance; and while his explanation of "Free will" and "Foreknowledge
absolute" is not, like the devils' speculation, cut off from God; still
his consignment of the pagan precedents for his song to Hell argues
for his willingness to expose how close his hoped-for light is to darkness. Burden's sense of Milton's mind is, I think, correct: Milton's
experience in controversy made him instinctively seize upon the
counterargument. He wished to encompass his adversary, not ignore
him, and his encompassment of Satan made him fully aware of the
seductions the satanic posture had for a mind such as his own.

VI

Just as Milton allows the devils to engage in something like his
own poetic activity, so too he is willing to lay bare the dangers latent

in the fundamental source of this activity, his inspiration. The essential message of Milton's epic invocations is, to repeat, that everything, for the poet, depends upon his muse. The muse is both his support and his justification. Such support, such justification is not commanded by the poet; rather it is sought by prayer, the efficacy of which must remain in doubt. Milton's final prologue in *Paradise Lost* ends with the fear that "all [may] be mine / Not Hers who brings it nightly to my Ear" (IX, 46–47). This tenuousness as to the sources and effectiveness of the poet's inspiration is often implicit in the poem's "argument," and one place in which such an implication can be found is in Milton's treatment of topography.

Inspiration in *Paradise Lost* is almost inevitably associated with a physical setting. Milton's sense of place in this is traditional: he selects mountains and neighboring woods and waters as the sites of inspirational vision. His classical precedents for such settings, which he names outright or suggests by description, are the haunts of the Homeric muses: "th' *Aonian* Mount" (I, 15), "th' *Olympian* Hill" (VII, 3), and the Castalian Spring on Mount Parnassus (III, 28). Yet while he does not cease "to wander where the Muses haunt / Clear Spring, or shady Grove, or Sunny Hill" (III, 27–28), he wishes to soar above "th' *Olympian* Hill" and therefore prefers the biblical counterparts to these places of inspiration. He calls the Mosaic Muse "Of *Oreb*, or of *Sinai*" (I, 7) and the spirit dwelling in "*Sion* and th' flowery Brooks beneath" (III, 30).

"*Sion* Hill / . . . and *Siloa's* Brook" (I, 10–11) represent for Milton and his Christian contemporaries archetypal settings for the manifestations of God's grace. In Book III Satan views "Direct against" the magnificent stairs which Jacob will see ascending to Heaven

> A passage down to th' Earth, a passage wide,
> Wider by far than that of after-times
> Over Mount *Sion*, and, though that were large,
> Over the Promis'd land to God so dear,
> By which, to visit oft those happy Tribes,
> On high behests his Angels to and fro
> Pass'd frequent.   (III, 528–34)

As these lines suggest, Sion Hill, on which David built his altar, Solomon, the Temple, constituted in Milton's traditional thought a

focal point of communication between man and God. Milton's translation of Psalm lxxxiv puts it this way:

> 1 How lovely are thy dwellings fair!
>   O Lord of Hosts, how dear
>   The *pleasant* Tabernacles are
>   Where thou dost dwell so near!
>
> . . . .
>
> 4 Happy who in thy house reside
>   Where thee they ever praise,
> 5 Happy whose strength in thee doth bide,
>   And in their hearts thy ways!
> 6 They pass through Baca's *thirsty* Vale,
>   *That dry and barren ground*
>   As through a fruitful wat'ry Dale
>   Where Springs and Show'rs abound.
> 7 They journey on from strength to strength
>   With joy and gladsome cheer,
>   *Till* all before *our* God *at length*
>   In Sion do appear.
>
> (1–4; 17–28; Milton's italics indicating his additions.)

This psalm displays the typological dimension of Sion, the first
among God's "dwellings fair." In *Paradise Lost* we frequently see
types of Sion Hill: Mount Sinai is clearly one; in respect to inspiration
Milton seems to have considered Olympus and Parnassus pagan
shadows of God's holy hill; Michael, descending from Heaven to
instruct fallen Adam,

> on a Hill made halt
> A glorious Apparition, had not doubt
> And carnal fear that day dimm'd *Adam's* eye.
> Not that more glorious, when the Angels met
> *Jacob* in *Mahanaim,* where he saw
> The field Pavilion'd with his Guardians bright;
> Nor that which on the flaming Mount appear'd
> In *Dothan,* cover'd with a Camp of Fire
> Against the Syrian King.   (XI, 210–18)

To administer Adam's vision of the future, the archangel ascends with
our first father "a Hill / Of Paradise the highest" (XI, 377–78), and
Raphael, sent by God to instruct unfallen man, alights upon "th'
Eastern cliff of Paradise" (V, 275), itself a promontory from which

our fallen parents must "wander down / Into a lower World" (XI, 282–83).

Paradise, of course, is not simply one of the fair dwelling places of God. It is also the site of Satan's fatal deception. Similarly the mount of speculation on which Adam learns from Michael "the sum / Of wisdom" (XII, 575–76) is compared by Milton to a place of Satanic temptation:

> Not higher that Hill nor wider looking round,
> Whereon for different cause the Tempter set
> Our second *Adam* in the Wilderness,
> To show him all the Earth's kingdoms and thir Glory.
>
> (XI, 381–84)

If we look back at the roll call of devils in Book I, it becomes clear that this double aspect—sacred and profane—consistently characterizes Milton's conception of the places of inspiration. In such settings men have heard infernal as well as heavenly voices:

> The chief were those who from the Pit of Hell
> Roaming to seek thir prey on earth, durst fix
> Thir Seats long after next the Seat of God,
> Thir Altars by his Altar, Gods ador'd
> Among the Nations round, and durst abide
> *Jehovah* thund'ring out of *Sion*, thron'd
> Between the Cherubim; yea, often plac'd
> Within his Sanctuary itself thir Shrines,
> Abominations; and with cursed things
> His holy Rites, and solemn Feasts profan'd
> And with thir darkness durst affront his light.   (I, 381–91)

From Sion Hill itself, a dwelling place of the poet's muse, Milton moves to its environs and in so doing continues to convey the impression that divine inspiration can be confused with abomination by the unwary:

> Nor content with such
> Audacious neighborhood, the wisest heart
> Of *Solomon* he [Moloch] led by fraud to build
> His Temple right against the Temple of God
> On that opprobrious Hill, and made his Grove
> The pleasant Valley of *Hinnom, Tophet* thence
> And black *Gehenna* call'd, the Type of Hell.   (I, 399–405)

Here "that opprobrious Hill," which appears twice more in the following fifty lines as "that Hill of scandal" (I, 416) and "th' offensive Mountain" (I, 443), is, strictly considered, Mount Olivetti and represents, like Sion Hill, a frequently profaned site of God's condescension to men. (The "Hill of scandal" could in one sense actually be called Sion Hill since, for Milton, all Jerusalem's hills were the hills of Sion.)[24] The settings Milton associates with his Christian muse are further recalled in this passage by "the Type of Hell." A reader familiar with the geography of the Holy Land would notice that this same "pleasant Valley of *Hinnom*" is, as described by Jerome, "watered by the fountains of Siloam" (*In Jeremiam*, vii, 31)—by the "*Siloa's* Brook" of Milton's initial invocation.[25] There is no real need to spend more time looking at a map of the Holy Land. My point is this: in the catalogue of devils Milton locates the fallen angels, emerged from Hell, in landmarks similar or identical to the places of inspiration mentioned by the poet at the beginning of *Paradise Lost,* and this placement suggests the dangers of hearkening to a voice speaking out of Sion. The poet runs a risk. Even the classical muses whom he refuses to ignore out of hand (III, 27–28; his debt to former epic is, he realizes, immense) are here emphatically consigned to Hell (I, 508–21).

It is, of course, true that Milton did not invent the geography of his infernal roll call, that his purpose was not simply to provide a contrasting echo to the landmarks of his first invocation. Nevertheless in his continued emphasis on the fact that the worship of God can be twisted and perverted into the adoration of Satan, he could hardly have missed the implication that the holiest of men must constantly be wary lest, blinded, their devotions degenerate to fume. The Devil was, in Milton's mind, constantly ready to deceive the proud man, and in this passage describing Sion's descent to idolatry, Milton's primary example of a man so deceived is Solomon "whose heart though large / Beguil'd by fair Idolatresses, fell / To Idols foul" (I, 444–46). I would like to suggest that the figure of Solomon had a particular exemplary significance for Milton. Solomon's name was, of course, associated with divine poetry, and Milton clearly saw himself as writing in the tradition of Sion's singers. At the same time Solomon's uxoriousness certainly represented for Milton—as both his life and his great epic testify—a crucial source of human error. But most significantly, I think, Solomon had built, under the guidance of God, the greatest religious monument of the Mosaic world, the Temple— a structure which, in medieval and Renaissance theories of artistic creation, constituted the ultimate model for all artistic endeavor.[26] Solomon, building after the divinely revealed fabric of God's world in "Measure, Number, and Weight" (Wisdom of Solomon xi, 21), had served for ages since Augustine as the archetypal example of the human artist working in imitation of God's creative act. Milton and his readers would not have missed the implication that, as a divinely inspired work, *Paradise Lost* was obviously comparable both to the Temple and to the world itself. Marvell, in his dedicatory poem, assumes these analogies to be commonplace:

> Thy verse created like thy theme sublime
> In Number, Weight, and Measure needs not Rime.

Milton seems to be underscoring this connection between Solomon and the poet when he emphasizes by repetition that it was Solomon's "heart though large," his "wisest heart" which was "led by fraud to build / His [Moloch's] Temple right against the Temple of God." The emphasis recalls the poet of the first invocation whose Muse prefers "Before all Temples th' upright heart and pure" (I, 18). While the poet is praying that his own heart will not be deceived, "led by fraud," that he will not build an idolatrous temple, the example of Solomon remains before him as a warning that those once confident of God's blessing can still fall from grace.

While the example of Solomon's idolatrous building casts a warning shadow over Milton's own "advent'rous" (I, 13) attempt at a poetic monument to God, it also serves as a mundane type of Hell's infernal arts—of Pandaemonium, "Built like a Temple" (I, 713) which far surpasses the world's "greatest Monuments of Fame, / And Strength and Art" (I, 695–96), and of the "Advent'rous work" (X, 255) undertaken by Sin and Death, the causeway from Hell, "a Monument / Of merit high" (X, 258–59) which, like all infernal creations, parodies God's own building in Chaos. In the case of Solomon's idolatrous works, we are dealing with an instance of human history reflecting the play of forces and events in the cosmos at large. Such a view of history was orthodox, and, as many have recognized, such a view is central to the unity of Milton's epic. In *Paradise Lost*

Milton repeatedly exploits cosmic polarity to project on a grand scale the predicament of man and the choices available to him: man should, as one of the multitude of God's servants, obey the Almighty and magnify Him through works; like a devil man may disobey God and fall, his life and works then becoming dross for the hellhound Death. The cosmic tensions of *Paradise Lost* reflect in particular the situation of the poet who, as a member of a fallen race, precariously attempts to counter the potential pride of his artistic aspirations with the humility of selfless intentions and dependence on God. Viewed with reference to the poet's own artistic predicament, the examples of negative creativity which extend from Pandaemonium to the song which ravishes Hell (II, 546–55) seem continually to suggest that the infernal aping of heavenly artistry is dangerously similar to Milton's effort in *Paradise Lost* to build, like Solomon, in imitation of the divine creative acts. My argument has been that the explicit comparison of poet and devil in *Paradise Lost* are intended by Milton to demonstrate an undeluded recognition of the satanic potential of his poetic act. Within the epic, ambition and presumption dog the poet in the form of satanic resemblances to his attempt to understand and give poetic shape to the pattern of God's ways with men. But, by the very act of objectifying such resemblances in infernal analogies to the poet's aspiring flight, Milton is able to keep differences clearly in sight. When in Hell the devils ask, "As he our darkness, cannot we his Light / Imitate when we please?" (II, 269–70), an analogy to the poet's own undertaking is clearly in view. At the same time, however, the difference between poet and devil is here equally plain. The poet cannot imitate God's light *at will*. Like the earthly and heavenly opposites of sin—the prophets, the angels, the Son—Milton labors to express God's will, not his own. He rejects satanic self-sufficiency; he invokes the muse.

Boston University

NOTES

1. All citations of Milton's poems refer to *John Milton: Complete Poems and Major Prose*, ed. Merritt Y. Hughes (New York, 1957).

2. Prominent voices here are C. S. Lewis, *A Preface to "Paradise Lost"* (London, 1942) and Douglas Bush, *"Paradise Lost" in Our Time* (New York, 1948).

3. William Blake, *The Marriage of Heaven and Hell* in *The Complete Writings of William Blake,* ed. Geoffrey Keynes (Oxford, 1966), p. 150.

4. See in particular Anne Davidson Ferry, *Milton's Epic Voice* (Cambridge, Mass., 1963); Isabel Gamble MacCaffrey, *"Paradise Lost" as "Myth"* (Cambridge, Mass., 1959); Jackson I. Cope, *The Metaphoric Structure of "Paradise Lost"* (Baltimore, 1962); Joseph H. Summers, *The Muse's Method* (Cambridge, Mass., 1962); Louis L. Martz, *The Paradise Within* (New Haven, 1964); Dennis H. Burden, *The Logical Epic* (Cambridge, Mass., 1967).

5. E. M. W. Tillyard, *Milton* (London, 1930).

6. See Stanley Eugene Fish, *Surprised by Sin* (New York, 1967) and Jon S. Lawry, *The Shadow of Heaven* (Ithaca, N. Y., 1968).

7. Denis Saurat, *Milton, Man and Thinker* (New York, 1925), p. 220.

8. The "things unattempted yet" topos has a long history, for a summary of which see Ernst Robert Curtius, *European Literature and the Latin Middle Ages,* trans. Willard Trask (New York, 1953), pp. 85–86. Milton was surely aware of this tradition, as he was also undoubtedly aware that his most recent significant predecessor in the use of this topos was Ariosto. See Hughes' note to I, 16 and IX, 29–31 of *Paradise Lost.*

9. Harington's translation.

10. For a discussion of satanic artistry see pp. 79–80.

11. This also imitates the pattern of paradox inherent in the fortunate fall. Milton continually shows us that the shape of good can be imitated by evil.

12. Note Sin's description of Hell: "With terrors and with clamors compasst round" (II, 862). In addition to being "In darkness, and with dangers compast round" (VII, 27), the poet is plagued by "the barbarous dissonance / Of Bacchus and his Revellers" (VII, 32–33).

13. *"Paradise Lost" as "Myth,"* p. 190.

14. *Surprised by Sin,* pp. 130–41.

15. For a similar comment on these lines see Ferry, *Milton's Epic Voice,* p. 41.

16. See J. B. Broadbent, *Some Graver Subject: An Essay on "Paradise Lost"* (London, 1960), p. 235: ". . . but why Bellerophon? It can only be because the invocation intrudes into the poem's structure the poet's anxiety about the presumptuous heroics of Book VI and the cosmography of Books VII and VIII. Bellerophon insures Milton against the sin of Adam and Eve, curiosity." See also Summers, *The Muse's Method,* p. 137: "The poet contrasts his own presumption in composing what we have read thus far with Satan's; but he faces the possibility that he may fall, to wander in madness like Bellerophon, if divine wisdom does not attend him in his descent to our 'Native Element.'"

17. The analogy is based on Revelation ix, 1–6.

18. *The Tenure of Kings and Magistrates* (Columbia edition, V, 25).

19. *The Ready and Easy Way to Establish a Free Commonwealth* (Columbia edition, VI, 136).

20. William Empson, *Milton's God* (London, 1961), p. 82.

21. Ibid., p. 75.

22. *The Logical Epic,* p. 58.

23. See Howard Schultz, *Milton and Forbidden Knowledge* (New York, 1955), p. 90. In a discussion of this passage similar to Burden's, Schultz assures

us that Milton is referring to tragedy here by comparing lines 550–51 with *Paradise Regained* IV, 261–66.

24. See, for evidence of this, Milton's version of Psalm lxxxvii.

25. See Allan H. Gilbert, *A Geographical Dictionary of Milton* (New Haven, 1919), p. 145. Gilbert believes that Milton's description of the valley as "pleasant" depends on Jerome.

26. For discussions of the relevance of Solomon's Temple to medieval and Renaissance theories of art see, in addition to Curtius, Rudolf Wittkower, *Architectural Principles in the Age of Humanism* (London, 1952) and Otto von Simson, *The Gothic Cathedral* (New York, 1954).

THE NARRATOR AS INTERPRETER
IN *PARADISE REGAINED*

Roger H. Sundell

The speaker of *Paradise Regained* not only relates but interprets as well the speeches and events of the poem. This interpretive commentary begins in the single prologue, where the
speaker explicitly introduces elements of plot, character, and
theme, and where he identifies himself, declares the divine
authority by which he speaks, and thus establishes with his
reader an appropriate mode of communication. His methods of
guiding the reader through the intricate events and arguments
of the poem vary according to the nature of individual episodes. Those methods range, as in the opening episodes of
Book I, from overt judgment of character to the most subtle
intimation of theme, and they include the provision of multiple
perspectives on major events. Another significant method of
internal commentary involves the presentation of the Son of
God as the definitive interpreter of demonic temptation and,
more generally, of the human condition. In the temptation
episodes, then, the narrator shares with the hero the role of
interpreter.

I

A MONG THE finest displays anywhere of Milton's poetic virtuosity,
and among the clearest examples of the Miltonic speaker defining
himself and the poem he is about to present, the prologue to Book I
of *Paradise Regained* explicitly introduces the main themes of the epic
in a series of bold antitheses:

> I who erewhile the happy Garden sung,
> By one man's disobedience lost, now sing

At an early stage, work on this essay was supported by a Summer Faculty
Fellowship granted by the University of Delaware.

Recover'd Paradise to all mankind,
By one man's firm obedience fully tried
Through all temptation, and the Tempter foil'd
In all his wiles, defeated and repuls't,
And *Eden* rais'd in the waste Wilderness.
  Thou Spirit who led'st this glorious Eremite
Into the Desert, his Victorious Field
Against the Spiritual Foe, and brought'st him thence
By proof th'undoubted Son of God, inspire,
As thou art wont, my prompted Song, else mute,
And bear through height or depth of nature's bounds
With prosperous wing full summ'd to tell of deeds
Above Heroic, though in secret done,
And unrecorded left through many an Age,
Worthy t' have not remain'd so long unsung.[1]   (I, 1–17)

Milton begins here that orientation and guiding of the reader of *Paradise Regained* that will continue through the poem.[2] The speaker proclaims immediately the poem's "title theme"—the recovery of Paradise by one man's obedience following its loss by another man's disobedience. Involved in this theme, he informs us, are the contrasts between the two Adams and between the original Eden, the "happy Garden," and the new Eden "rais'd in the waste Wilderness" —a garden that blooms in the physical desert of Israel and in the spiritual desert of fallen mankind. The fact that one man's disobedience has led to the loss of Eden for *all* men, but now will lead to the recovery of Paradise by one man's firm obedience, looks back to Adam's recognition of *felix culpa* at the end of *Paradise Lost*. Emphasis, moreover, falls upon both the singularity of Christ's achievement and its universal significance, the magnitude of that achievement being underlined by the speaker's repeated use of the word "all" in describing Christ's trial "Through *all* temptation" and his triumph over *all* the Tempter's wiles.

The second theme set forth in the prologue concerns a transformation of the character of Christ that takes place during the course of the poem. Christ enters the desert a "glorious Eremite," the latter word signifying a religious recluse and emphasizing the human side of Christ's dual nature. But the speaker emphasizes the divine side of Christ's nature when he tells of the Spirit's bringing Christ out of the Wilderness, "By proof th'undoubted Son of God."

The alteration, then, involves the manifestation of Christ's divinity and his preparation for public life through the triumph over Satan which we will witness.

The speaker also provides, at the outset, pertinent information concerning the poem itself. The first word of the opening verse paragraph, "I," stands in marked contrast to that of the second paragraph, "Thou," calling attention to the nature of the narrator and to his relationship with the Spirit who inspires his song. We quickly become familiar with the speaker of *Paradise Regained,* who identifies himself as the singer of *Paradise Lost;* and we understand the authority with which he speaks, for before the narration begins we hear him claim the Holy Spirit as his sole and necessary source of inspiration. Secondly, echoing the prologue to Book IX of *Paradise Lost,* the speaker describes Christ's deeds in the poem as "Above Heroic," asserting that the subject of the poem is different in kind from, and worthier than, the subjects of previous heroic poems. He further describes these deeds as "in secret done," and accomplished thus without the motivation of fame, "That last infirmity of Noble mind." The narrator thus comments both on his own nature and on that action which distinguishes the poem from all others.

In this richly textured introduction to the brief epic, the speaker orients his reader by setting forth an extraordinary amount of useful information about the poem and its singer. He unveils the two great themes of Christ's recovery of Paradise and of the manifestation of his divinity. Two technical matters revealed are the speaker's own nature as a singer inspired by the Spirit of God and the uniqueness of the poem's subject. The poet's methods of introducing these interpretive materials have involved, first, the exposition of content through explicit declaration and through deliberate and repeated focusing upon key words; and, second, the self-conscious calling of attention to the nature of the speaking voice itself, to its experience and authority and purpose. Before events of the poem begin, the speaker economically but lucidly creates for the reader a framework for understanding the poem.

II

Extensive interpretive commentary appears next in the narration of episodes other than the temptations. The first of these episodes is the briefest and in some ways the simplest; yet it is also one of the few spectacular moments in the poem. In one long, heavily conjunctive sentence, beginning with the awesome voice of John the Baptist and concluding with the Father's approving voice from Heaven, the baptism of the unknown Christ (I, 18–32) opens the poem with an appropriate sense of new and unique beginnings. Louis Martz has suggested that it may be looked upon as a memory in the meditative mind of a narrator who "roams freely over the past, present, and future life of its hero."[3] It is as valuable, perhaps, to see the episode simply as the first and most immediately engaging in a sequence of brief, independent, introductory actions.

In this episode (including the closing description of Satan as an observer), the narrator introduces all the major characters, both human and supernatural, but the episode remains focused pointedly on the human participants. For it reveals a *human* audience responding with awe to an extraordinary *human* voice. The audience then witnesses a single *man* declared by that voice to be the Messiah. This declaration is confirmed from Heaven by means which are visible, audible, and most meaningful to the *human* observers. Even the great Proclaimer, divinely warned of Christ's coming, responds to his presence in a markedly human way, by demonstrating humility— he "would have resign'd / To him his Heavenly Office." Herein lies one of the principal functions of the episode—to convey attitudes appropriate to fallen man as he views events which will lead directly to the possibility of *his* redemption. The episode of the baptism presents, in short, the human perspective within which the reader will naturally view the poem's events, regardless of the availability of additional perspectives.

A second narrative function is to develop major themes set forth in the prologue. In contrast to the prologue, this episode expands those themes less through explicit statement than through suggestive description. In the course of relating the events, the speaker picks up from the prologue and weaves into his narration first of all the important contrast between Christ the *one man*, and the multitudes, the "Regions round." Secondly, he emphasizes dramatically the change that will take place in Christ. The man "deem'd" the Son of Joseph arrives at the Jordan "unknown," but he leaves having experienced publicly the proclamation on earth and in Heaven of his divine identity. Finally, in the Baptist's opening words, "Heaven's Kingdom nigh at hand," we discover further elaboration on the theme of "Recover'd Paradise" and an anticipation of what will become the principal concern in the second and longest of the temptations— the concern with Christ's "discovery" of his role as "Israel's true King" (III, 441).[4]

In the episode of the baptism, then, we witness events which initiate Christ's role on earth as Savior. We are introduced, however briefly, to the major characters of God, his Son, and Satan. We recognize in the narration of the episode the development of the major themes of the poem. And finally, we become aware of the perspective of fallen man towards divine events which are of vital importance to him. Now, by virtue of the shift in the narrator's focus of attention, we are led into the demonic realm of Satan and his "mighty Peers."

As onlooker at the "assembly fam'd," Satan is bewildered by "th'exalted man, to whom / Such high attest was giv'n." In a phrase which plays upon the epithet "thunderer" (used throughout *Paradise Lost* in reference to God), the narrator describes the "Adversary" as "Nigh Thunderstruck" by the voice of God confirming the identity of his Son. Thus begins the first of two demonic councils in *Paradise Regained*, the second introductory episode in which the narrator advances a second, Satanic perspective on the impending events of the poem, and introduces what one might call a Satanic syndrome of narrative commentary on the poem's antagonist.

In a typically instructive narrative framework enclosing the first long speech of *Paradise Regained*, the interpretive aids are sometimes explicit, such as the indications of Satan's state of mind, and sometimes oblique, such as the suggestion of his uncertainties and ignorance in the description of the setting of the council "Within thick Clouds and dark tenfold involv'd" (I, 41). The direct, evaluative reference to Satan's "envy" upon witnessing the baptism indicates the narrator's predictably unsympathetic point of view towards Satan. The reader's responses to Satan's fallacious logic and heavy rhetoric, conditioned by the narrative point of view and the human perspective already established in the preceding episode, will be likewise largely unsympathetic. Nonetheless, this episode is devoted solely and intensively to the deep concern of the newly-threatened fallen angels and to the tortured mind of their leader. The poem offers, thus, a second, demonic perspective within which the reader perceives and comprehends more fully the poem's antagonistic forces without shifting his allegiance. This perspective is introduced in the narrator's revelations of Satan's state of mind as he leaves the scene of the baptism in agony and fear and prepares to invoke his "mighty Peers." It is sustained, obviously, by Satan himself in his long speech. The Satanic perspective becomes dramatically clear, for example, in Satan's unique, uncomprehending version of those events at the baptism which we have already witnessed.[5]

In relating the episode of the demonic council, the narrator uses a limited number of descriptive words in his commentary and, significantly, they and their synonyms recur throughout *Paradise Regained* in reference to the speeches and actions of Satan. For example, the words which frame Satan's speech merit special attention, for they not only define the posture, tone, and frame of mind of the Tempter as we see him first, but they form as well a descriptive study of the antagonist which will not alter noticeably for the remainder of the poem: "Nigh Thunderstruck," "aghast," "Distracted," "much Amazement," "wonder," "nor rests," "sad," "envy," "rage," "girded with snaky wiles," "all guile."[6] Many of these terms, associated in *Paradise Lost* with specific kinds of events, helped convey the moral judgments of the narrator. They recur in *Paradise Regained* for the same purpose, but in a manner comparatively unelaborated and even formulaic.

The second episode needs little further comment here. The long speech of Satan functions as exposition and development of his character and immediate concerns. The council likewise functions as preparation for Satan's journey into the wilderness to tempt with "well couch't fraud, well woven snares" the "man of men . . . whom he suspected rais'd / To end his Reign on Earth so long enjoy'd" (I, 124–25).

In the temptation episodes of *Paradise Regained* Milton transfers to the divine and exemplary character of Christ the interpretive role of the narrator. Perhaps by way of introduction to this method of internal commentary, the poet abruptly reduces the amount of narrative commentary in the next and third introductory episode, the council in Heaven. One-third of the episode of the demonic council (thirty-one of ninety-three lines) is spoken by the narrator. The narrative of the council in Heaven consists of less than one-fifth commentary (ten of fifty-seven lines). A strong and appropriate emphasis thus falls on the authority of the words of God. And the reader may recognize, even at this early point in the poem, a conjunction of the point of view of the poem (as continuously supplied by the inspired narrator) with the divine perspective on the events of the poem (embodied, of course, in the speech of the Father).

Commentary in the third episode differs in kind as well as in degree from that in the preceding episodes. Whereas the narrative frame enclosing Satan's long speech presents to the reader a descriptive study of the state of mind of the antagonist—anxieties, fears, motivations all clearly and explicitly interpreted—the introduction to the speech of the Father, by contrast, consists simply of the single word "smiling," conveying to the reader the serenity and conclusiveness of the divine pronouncements. Thus the narrator has only to introduce the episode and to describe the reactions of the unfallen angels to God's assurances of his Son's impending victory over Satan. His introduction is a brief, transitional statement which, through a simple shift from the demonic to a divine perspective, reveals that Satan's carefully formed and malevolent plans all fall ironically within the divine plan.[7] The temptations, in short, will facilitate and hasten Satan's own defeat: "But contrary unweeting he fulfill'd / The purpos'd Counsel pre-ordain'd and fixt / Of the most High" (I, 126–28). The second narrative passage (I, 168–72) is also brief, involving simply a description of the angels responding in admiration to the words of God and then dancing and singing a hymn of triumph. Thus, the appearance of the narrator is abbreviated and his methods of narration are altered to conform with the presentation of the guiding, interpretive voice of God.

The speech of God serves as a second prologue to *Paradise Regained*, in the sense that it reintroduces, from the new, divine perspective, many of the major elements of the poem. Most importantly we discover the great theological framework within which the events of *Paradise Regained* exist—the divine plan for the redemption of man, the "winning by Conquest what the first man lost / By fallacy surpris'd" (I, 154–55). God begins by alerting Gabriel to a "verification" of the message Gabriel had delivered to Mary. His emphasis is not upon the birth of Christ, but upon the phrase "Son of God" and its significance for mankind.[8] The attention is to Christ's divine nature. We are alerted, then, with Gabriel, to the fact that events soon to take place will demonstrate to us, as they will reveal to Christ, what roles must be fulfilled and what demands must be answered by the "Son of God."

Serving to interpret for Gabriel, and the reader, the nature and meaning of Christ's mission, God continues by asserting that, in order to show his Son worthy of his divine nature, he will "expose" him to Satan in the wilderness, where Christ "shall first lay down the rudiments / Of his great warfare" (I, 157–58). We will witness Christ's discovery of the way he will save mankind. The last portion of the speech makes that way clear and, recalling the references in the prologue to deeds "Above Heroic," places Christ's actions not only within their vast theological context, but also within the Western tradition of heroic action:

> His weakness shall o'ercome Satanic strength
> And all the world, and mass of sinful flesh;
> That all the Angels and Ethereal Powers,
> They now, and men hereafter, may discern
> From what consummate virtue I have chose
> This perfect Man, by merit call'd my Son,
> To earn Salvation for the Sons of men.   (I, 161–67)

The first two lines delineate the three forces with which Satan will tempt Christ—the strength of the devil, the world, and the flesh. The remaining lines, focusing persistently on the human side of Christ's nature and on the mission he undertakes for humanity, prepare for his appearance in the poem as a man who already knows his duty, but who does not yet know the means of performing it. In short, we have in the speech of God a valuable, interpretive introduction to the protagonist, Christ, and clear indications of the poem's plot and themes.

The opening episodes of *Paradise Regained*, then, reveal a rich variety of methods used by the poet not only to relate a series of interconnected events, but also to convey a considerable amount of interpretive information. The themes announced explicitly in the prologue by the narrator have been redefined and developed by direct and indirect means in each of the episodes. Three distinct and significant perspectives on the events of the poem—the perspectives of fallen man, of Satan, and of God—have been introduced in order that the reader may recognize the manifold implications of each word and action in the temptations of Christ. Interpretive comments on the character of Satan have formed a study of the Tempter which remains as unaltered throughout the poem as Satan himself, and the character of the Son has likewise been helpfully described. We have been introduced, finally, to a transference of the interpretive role itself from the narrator to a character whose authority within the poem cannot be challenged, and whose words define the plot and significance of the entire poem.[9]

III

The first meditation of Christ follows the "introductory" three episodes and while it is, in a sense, the fourth such episode, it is distinguishable from the others for several reasons. Two later events in the poem (Christ's second meditation in Book II and the night of terror in Book IV) are structurally parallel to the first meditation; they immediately precede the other temptations, they share with the temptations such elements as time and place, and they involve only the character of the protagonist. Each of these episodes performs analogous interpretive functions as well, serving to orient the reader both in terms of the character of Christ and in terms of the specific temptation he is about to encounter. The first meditation of Christ, then, is illustrative of these preliminary episodes and their interpretive functions.

Perhaps the most useful information conveyed in the description of Christ entering the wilderness (I, 183–95) is the narrator's commentary on the form and content of the ensuing meditation. The narrator indicates that Christ "muses" and "revolves in his breast" two critical questions: "How best the mighty work he might begin / Of Savior to mankind," and "which way first / Publish his Godlike office now mature." Contemplative and uncertain, Christ also demonstrates absolute reliance upon his Father, for he follows unquestioningly, we are informed, the "Spirit" who directs his steps now to the desert, the scene of temptation. The narrator thus carefully prepares the reader to hear Christ himself by describing in advance of the meditation much that, indeed, takes place. For we overhear the words of the young Christ now deeply concerned with the discrepancy between what he feels and has heard about himself and what he has done. He reviews every event pertinent to this discrepancy, arriving finally at a fuller understanding of his need to act, yet discovering no sure way to begin. He must no longer "live obscure,"

> But openly begin, as best becomes
> The Authority which I deriv'd from Heaven.
> And now by some strong motion I am led
> Into this Wilderness, to what intent
> I learn not yet; perhaps I need not know;
> For what concerns my knowledge God reveals.   (I, 288–93)

In the brief descriptive passage that opens the episode, then, the narrator points out to the reader the main concerns of the meditation, which themselves reveal key traits of the character of Christ: his pensiveness, uncertainty of knowledge, and absolute trust in the Spirit who leads him. And in using the terms "musing," "revolving," and "Meditations," the narrator indicates that the form of Christ's thoughts will remain exploratory and tentative rather than rigidly analytical and conclusive. Christ's musings on his most recent experience, the baptism, follow precisely such a form.

In addition, a new perspective on the impending events of the poem is presented by the narrator and then clarified and enriched in the meditation. This, of course, is the unique perspective of Christ himself, which Milton differentiates from those perspectives already revealed. In contrast with the divine perspective in which the impending events are foreknown and in which the roles Christ must fulfill are theologically set forth, the perspective of Christ is significantly limited. But in contrast with the Satanic perspective, warped by self-deception and clouded by fears and envy, the perspective of the Son of God is clear. He is fully aware of his mission, the narrator insists, and in the meditation itself he reveals precisely the ways in which he has come to understand that mission. His retelling of the episode of the baptism (which has become a useful point of reference) contrasts sharply, for example, with Satan's, and reveals to the reader a mind which must orient knowledge and experience in terms of a unique identity and mission. For Christ, the baptism is the last in a series of divine revelations of identity and clarifications of duty. It serves as a heavenly signal to him that the time has come when he "no more should live obscure, / But openly begin" to save mankind.

We may turn now to another method of internal commentary used by Milton in the first meditation of Christ and in the later two preliminary episodes as well. This method, familiar to readers of narrative poetry, also occurs more frequently than any other in the numerous transitional passages of narration scattered through the poem. It involves simply describing the setting of an event in such a way that significant aspects of character, plot, and theme are clearly revealed or anticipated. I have already noted the suggestions of Satan's ignorance and confusion conveyed in the narrator's description of a setting for the demonic council "Within thick clouds." The description of the wilderness Christ now enters is even more revealing than these.

The narrator first describes the desert as "wild / And with dark shades environ'd round" and then elaborates at the close of the meditation:

> So spake our Morning Star then in his rise,
> And looking round on every side beheld
> A pathless Desert, dusk with horrid shades;
> The way he came not having mark'd, return
> Was difficult, by human steps untrod;
> And he still on was led, but with such thoughts
> Accompanied of things past and to come
> Lodg'd in his breast, as well might recommend
> Such Solitude before choicest Society.   (I, 294–302)

The phrase "our Morning Star then in his rise," itself richly suggestive, echoes from the meditation Mary's quoted reference to "A Star, not seen before in Heaven." And the phrase refers directly to the beginning of Christ's mission on earth—a beginning that happens as the poem "happens." (Even as the poem closes, the angels conclude their final hymn of praise and triumph by singing, "Now enter, and begin to save mankind.") The "Star" of Christ is, of course, both the light he brings to a spiritual wilderness and also the light of divine wisdom that shines within him. Though the desert is "pathless," his way unmarked, and return "difficult," Christ will return; having discovered by virtue of his wisdom the "way," he will make possible a corresponding return for all men lost in the spiritual wilderness.

Moreover, the "horrid shades" of the fraud, the guile, the evil of the "Spiritual Foe" will be dispersed by the light of "our Morning Star." The phrase may suggest as well a contrast between the true light of Christ and a deceptive light of Satan, the former Lucifer. Finally, we should note that the solitude of the wilderness, a characteristic the narrator twice calls attenion to, is both threatening and comforting for Christ. We know that the temptations are imminent, but we know also of "things past and to come" that occupy Christ's mind as he begins the forty days of fast which terminate with his triumph over temptation. The suggestions one thus discovers in the narrator's description of Christ entering the pathless wilderness are extraordinarily rich, and illustrate yet another form of interpretive guidance present in the poem.

IV

Throughout the greater part of *Paradise Regained,* Christ and Satan, exemplifying, respectively, divine wisdom in man and "hellish wiles" in man's enemy, match insight, wit, and rhetoric as they confront each other in a series of verbal battles for the souls of all men. During the course of these extended conflicts the commentary of the narrator is abbreviated. His "interventions" often take the form of curt phrases which simply move the dialogue from one speaker to another. Such relatively uninformative comments as "he uttered thus" and "The Son of God replied" contrast sharply with the richly informative commentary of the early episodes and with the interpretive commentary on much of the dialogue in *Paradise Lost.* Most characteristic of the narrator's comments is phraseology in which a single word or a brief epithet indicates the posture of a character or the general tone of a speech. Such phrases as the following emphasize a single interpretive insight, and, as numerous scholars have noted, are typical narrative comments in the dialogue of Christ and Satan: "To whom our Savior answer'd thus *unmov'd,*" "To whom thus Jesus *temperately* replied," "To whom our Savior *with unalter'd brow,*" and "To whom thus answer'd Satan *malcontent*" (my emphasis). We can account for such a marked decrease of narrative commentary simply by recognizing that Christ himself, throughout the temptations, is fulfilling not only the role of the protagonist in a narrative comprised mainly of dialogue between him and his adversary, but also the role of divine interpreter of a series of experiences applicable both to himself and to all men.[10]

The first temptation begins with a short description of Satan appearing to Christ as a shepherd (I, 314-20) and the passage clearly emphasizes problems of deception and perception relevant to the major theme of the temptation. The aged man followed "as seem'd" the quest of a ewe. As Christ "saw" him, Satan "Perus'd" Christ "with curious eye." This focus upon seeing and perceiving recalls the preliminary episode of Christ's meditation with its emphasis on the revealing light of divine wisdom entering the dark wilderness. Both the preceding episode (the meditation) and the initial description of the temptation itself focus, then, upon perception, and, in so doing, anticipate Christ's impending discovery of his role as prophet, one who sees and reveals and serves, thus, as God's "living Oracle."[11]

We know that the force which has led Christ into the wilderness is the "Spirit." Satan begins his temptation by casting doubt on the benevolence of that force in asking "Sir, what ill chance hath brought thee to this place . . .?" Christ's response is abrupt and clear: "Who brought me hither / Will bring me hence, no other Guide I seek" (I, 335-36). Recalling the profound faith in the wisdom of God which he expressed in his meditation, Christ demonstrates in his opening words his confidence in the light within him. But Satan's reply ignores the significance of Christ's brief answer. It focuses initially upon the problem of seeing or understanding ("By Miracle he may, replied the Swain, / What other way I see not.") and then, with subtle appeal to a sense of social as well as personal welfare, introduces the temptation to turn stone into bread: "So shalt thou save thyself and us relieve / With Food, whereof we wretched seldom taste" (I, 344-45). Christ's answer to this request for a miracle performed upon physical reality, partly for apparently charitable purposes, constitutes the first in a long series of reorientations from the material concern of Satan to a spiritual concern appropriate to Christ's mission and instructive for all mankind. The answer concentrates heavily on seeing and interpreting *rightly:*

> Think'st thou such force in Bread? is it not written
> (For I discern thee other than thou seem'st)
> Man lives not by Bread only, but each Word
> Proceeding from the mouth of God, who fed

> Our Fathers here with Manna? In the Mount
> *Moses* was forty days, nor eat nor drank,
> And forty days *Eliah* without food
> Wander'd this barren waste; the same I now:
> Why dost thou then suggest to me distrust,
> Knowing who I am, as I know who thou art?   (I, 347–56)

Christ thus interprets Satan's temptation by isolating and revealing in the subtle words of the Tempter the identity of their speaker, their misleading emphasis upon material concern, and their implication of distrust of God.

Christ's role as interpreter of the words of Satan is even more clear at the end of the first temptation. Satan, "now undisguis'd," suggests that he has served both man and God by revealing valuable wisdom to man through "presages and signs . . . answers, oracles, portents and dreams" which he has inspired (I, 394–95). Christ's reprimand is spoken "sternly." Comprehending fully, perhaps for the first time, the prophetic nature of his mission, he declares

> God hath now sent his living Oracle
> Into the World to teach his final will,
> And sends his Spirit of Truth henceforth to dwell
> In pious Hearts, an inward Oracle
> To all truth requisite for men to know.   (I, 460–64)

Within the narrative context of the poem, these words are directed to Satan. But the explanation of the bases of true and false prophecy is also directed "beyond the poem." Christ's words comprise an authoritative interpretation of an epistemological problem facing all men. It is divine wisdom in man, he explains, that makes possible knowledge of all necessary truth.

Examples of Christ's role as interpreter of the temptations he faces are as numerous as his speeches to Satan. One further example, from a passage discussed perhaps as often as the poem itself, may suffice in this exploration of his interpretive role. The temptation of the kingdoms, as Lewalski has shown, reveals in great detail to Christ the nature of his Messianic role as Israel's King.[12] The temptation extends through the greater portions of three of the four books of the poem and involves Satan's offers and Christ's rejection of numerous expediencies appropriate to the acquisition and retention of a kingdom "of this world." Having tempted Christ unsuccessfully with wealth, honors, arms, and empires themselves, Satan, spending his last "darts," as the narrator notes, offers to make Christ "famous then / By wisdom." Concluding his temptation with a catalogue of the intellectual and artistic accomplishments of Greece, Satan urges Christ to study classical learning:

> These here revolve, or, as thou lik'st, at home,
> Till time mature thee to a Kingdom's weight;
> These rules will render thee a King complete
> Within thyself, much more with Empire join'd. (IV, 281–84)

Christ's thorough dismissal of Satan's temptation is more often read as a commentary on Milton than as an interpretation of the content and manner of a specific temptation. That temptation, prompted by malice and appealing explicitly to the acquisition of fame and political power, is clearly an attempt to divert Christ into valuing above all else—specifically above divine insight and Biblical revelation—the accomplishments of a great culture. The clearest interpretive judgments in Christ's answer to Satan focus upon this point. Notice, in the following quotations, the reorientation of the content of Satan's temptation toward spiritual rather than political light and Judeo-Christian rather than pagan light:

> he who receives
> Light from above, from the fountain of light,
> No other doctrine needs, though granted true.   (IV, 288–90)

> Alas! what can they teach, and not mislead;
> Ignorant of themselves, of God much more,
> And how the world began, and how man fell
> Degraded by himself, on grace depending?   (IV, 309–12)

> In [our Prophets] is plainest taught, and easiest learnt,
> What makes a Nation happy, and keeps it so,
> What ruins Kingdoms, and lays Cities flat;
> These only, with our Law, best form a King.   (IV, 361–64)

So emphatic a series of judgments and so authoritative a series of interpretations needs no further interpretation by a narrator. Christ's answer stands sufficient for any man who would *substitute* for the values of divine truth the pleasures of learning and art. The intensity of Christ's judgments, so often found out of tune with his character and with the poem, is warranted by the necessity for Christ to withstand at this point as insidious a temptation as Satan has yet devised. Coming at the end of a long series of temptations, inspired by Satan's near desperation, and involving a force—the intellect and its achievements—which we have found to be heavily emphasized in Milton's portrait of the youthful and contemplative Christ, such a strongly argued and rhetorically devastating answer is necessary at this point in the poem and wholly appropriate to the character of Christ. Recognizing him as the interpreter here, we discover as well an answer directed towards a "fit audience" of readers who might well find Satan's temptation far more difficult to overcome than does Christ.

Though the interpretive role of the narrator of *Paradise Regained* is greatly reduced by the presence of the divine commentator, the narrator's words are nonetheless useful. For example, the single descriptive term "sagely," which prefaces the denunciation of classical learning, serves to temper the effect on a reader of Christ's forceful, outspoken answer to Satan, for it points to the wisdom embodied in both the content and the method of Christ's words. The word "sagely" is consistent, moreover, with the pattern of narrative responses to the speeches of Christ established early in the opening temptation and extending through Christ's quiet, calm triumph at the close of the poem.

The great majority of terms the narrator applies to Christ's speeches connote emotional tranquillity or intellectual control. Such words and phrases as "unmov'd," "patiently," "calmly," and "with unalter'd brow" recur so frequently and contrast so sharply with the Satanic syndrome of narrative comments that the reader, even in the first, short temptation, begins to anticipate their recurrence. Thus, the three descriptive terms "sternly" (I, 406), "fervently" (III, 121), and "with disdain" (IV, 170) emphasize the only three instances in the entire poem where Christ is noticeably disturbed by Satan. (In each of these instances, Satan directly insults either Christ or God: in the first, he deviously suggests that he is serving God by doing evil; in the second, he accuses God of seeking glory; and in the third, he bluntly asks Christ to worship him.) Thus, the narrator's limited role as interpreter of the words of Christ is nonetheless useful in calling attention to significant general characteristics of Christ's words and in pointing out variations from their typical content or tone.

The narrator pays more attention to Satan's speeches of temptation than to Christ's responses; yet it too is limited in comparison with the narrative commentary in the introductory episodes. The relatively brief descriptions of Satan take several forms (which, of course, often overlap). In phrases such as *"Perplex'd* and *troubl'd"* (IV, 1), "inly *rackt"* (III, 203), and "with fear *abasht"* (IV, 195), the narrator reveals the mental anguish which is characteristic of Satan's state of mind throughout the poem. The phrases "inly stung with *anger* and *disdain"* (I, 466), "stood struck / With *guilt* of his own sin" (III, 146–47), and "now swoln with *rage"* (IV, 499) point, on the other hand, to a specific emotion that motivates the words of Satan. Finally, the narrator, as in the following phrases, points to the deceptive rhetoric and misleading logic which are Satan's characteristic techniques of temptation: "This answer *smooth* return'd" (I, 467), "with *fair speech* these words to him address'd" (II, 300), and "With *soothing words* renew'd, him thus accosts" (III, 6). Filled with confusing rhetoric and fallacious logic, and motivated by a complex of emotions such as envy, fear, and anger, the words of Satan demand and receive from the narrator a degree of commentary greater than the clear, authoritative, and exemplary words of Christ. To an extent, then, the narrator and Christ share the role of internal commentator on the dialogues of the temptations. Yet the great and most significant portion of that role is assumed and fulfilled by the character of Christ, whose words repeatedly illuminate both for himself and for the reader the fraudulence and malice of the Tempter.

Milton employs, then, various methods of internal commentary in *Paradise Regained* for the purpose of guiding his reader towards appropriate responses to major elements of the poem. The scope of this rhetorical method is indeed broad, ranging from very simple, direct statements of theme and purpose in the prologue, through more subtle kinds of suggestion and anticipation, to highly sophisticated and complex interpretation of events by a character both involved in those events and able as well to act, speak, and, in both ways, interpret definitively.

University of Wisconsin–Milwaukee

NOTES

1. All citations for Milton are to Merritt Y. Hughes, ed., *John Milton: Complete Poems and Major Prose* (New York, 1957).

2. The epic poet's conventional privilege to provide an interpretive and evaluative perspective on the action of the poem, though occasionally a matter of dispute in Milton criticism, is now generally recognized and acknowledged. Appropriate commentary on such "intervention" may be found in Wayne Booth's *The Rhetoric of Fiction* (Chicago, 1961), pp. 3–16, and in Robert M. Durling's *The Figure of the Poet in Renaissance Epic* (Cambridge, Mass., 1965), pp. 5–10. Among recent studies of Milton's poems (especially *Paradise Lost*) with explicit emphasis on the narrator are Frank Kermode's "Adam Unparadis'd" in *The Living Milton* (London, 1960), Anne Davidson Ferry's *Milton's Epic Voice* (Cambridge, Mass., 1963), and Stanley Fish's *Surprised by Sin* (New York, 1967).

3. Louis L. Martz, *The Paradise Within* (New Haven, 1964), p. 178.

4. As elsewhere in this essay, I refer to the scheme of the three mediatorial offices of Christ (as prophet, priest, and king) delineated in Chapter XV of the *Christian Doctrine* and most valuably applied to the poem by Barbara Lewalski in "Theme and Structure in *Paradise Regained*," SP, LVII (1960), 186–220 and again in *Milton's Brief Epic* (Providence, 1966).

5. The several perspectives on the action constitute an aspect of Milton's narrative method in this poem that has received little attention. The interaction of multiple perspectives or points of view in the earlier epic has been briefly treated by Joseph H. Summers in *The Muse's Method* (Cambridge, Mass., 1962), p. 122 ff., and by Arnold Stein in *Answerable Style* (Minneapolis, 1953), p. 123 ff.

6. Readers of *Paradise Lost* will readily associate many of these words with specific dire events in the earlier poem. Eve, for example, was "not unamaz'd" (IX, 552) at the sound of the Serpent's voice as the temptation in Eden began. Increasingly susceptible to the "guileful Tempter" and increasingly off balance, she soon thereafter replied to him "Yet more amaz'd unwary" (IX, 614). And Satan's methods of temptation and persuasion in *Paradise Lost* are frequently described in terms of wiles, guile, and subversion. Satan himself, in moments of self-torturing confession, was filled with rage; and in moments of recognition of God's good and beautiful creation, he was racked with envy and despair. The evaluative force of these words is neglected in studies of *Paradise Regained*, though many writers have noted the evaluative commentary presented in *Paradise Lost*. See, for example, Isabel MacCaffrey, *"Paradise Lost" as "Myth"* (Cambridge, Mass., 1959), p. 102.

7. This narrative method of abrupt transition is familiar, of course (cf. *Paradise Lost*, X, 610–15); but the simultaneous shifting of a reader's perspective—of his knowledge, values, and sympathies—which the transition tends to encourage has received little attention.

8. As Louis Martz has noted, this phrase significantly "resounds throughout the poem" (*The Paradise Within*, p. 180), signalling always the theme of identity.

9. The remaining four episodes which stand apart from the temptations are: the doubting of Andrew and Simon (II, 1–59); the troubled thoughts of Mary (II, 60–108); the second demonic council (II, 115–241); the receiving of Christ by the angels (IV, 581–639). In regard to the nature and function of narrative commentary they are similar to, though as one would expect hardly identical with,

those examined here. In particular, the closely connected episodes of Book II, which tell of the disillusionment of Andrew and Simon and of the maternal concern of Mary with the disappearance of her son, constitute an extremely revealing introduction to the longest of the temptations.

10. Both Arnold Stein in *Heroic Knowledge* (Minneapolis, 1957) and Howard Schultz in *Milton and Forbidden Knowledge* (New York, 1955) emphasize the exemplary nature of Christ's words and actions in the poem, though neither relates them clearly to the interpretive role of the narrator. Barbara Lewalski briefly notes (*Milton's Brief Epic*, pp. 327–28) that the presence in the poem of the Redeemer, who comments upon and evaluates Satan's activities, renders "additional narrative evaluation superfluous."

11. Lewalski, *Milton's Brief Epic*, pp. 193 ff.

12. *Ibid.*, pp. 256 ff.

CHRIST'S NATIVITY
AND THE PAGAN DEITIES

Lawrence W. Hyman

In reading the *Nativity Ode*, the sense of loss that we feel at
the disappearance of the pagan gods is genuine, but it does
not interfere with the unity of the poem. For the coming of
Christ is also presented in a paradoxical manner: the Prince
of Light comes to us in darkness, the all-powerful God in a
"house of mortal clay." We should therefore not be surprised
that the arrival of Christianity, which will eventually make
all life divine, has as its first result the banishment of what
men had thought of as divine—the false gods. The ambivalent
attitude towards the pagan gods is thus continuous with the
paradox of Christ; and the poem, although complex in bringing together contradictory feelings, is unified in tone.

THE RELATIONSHIP between dogma and poetry, between Milton's
desire to argue and his desire to harmonize conflicting beliefs and
feelings, which is to become so complex in his later poems, is quite simple in the early poems, particularly in the *Ode on the Morning of
Christ's Nativity*. There is no doctrine or belief that must be argued.
But a directness and simplicity in the action of a poem does not result
in a simple or direct response. We respond to the entire imaginative experience, not only to the theme. And this complexity of tone in the
Ode has been felt by many critics, particularly when they deal with
the banishment of the pagan gods. Why in a poem dedicated to the
birth of Christ does Milton place so much emphasis on these pagan
gods? How are we to feel about the disappearance of these gods who
are presented with so much imaginative power? And even if we give
a doctrinal answer—that we are to rejoice in their disappearance—how
are we to relate this negative feeling to the dominant mood of the
poem?

Most readers are convinced that Milton is successful in maintaining a unified mood, and I agree with this conclusion. No reader is really troubled by the apparent shift in emphasis from Christ to the pagan gods who are displaced by him. What has not been seen, however, is the continuity between the two worlds. The regret at the disappearance of the pagan deities—Pan, Osiris, Isis and Orus—does not in any way contradict the joy at the birth of Christ, for Christianity itself is marked by an ambivalent mood, a mood that is complex enough to embrace regret as well as joy. Instead of a shift in mood in the last section of the poem, there is a continuity. The ambivalent feeling at the departure of the pagan gods is part of the ambivalence which is intrinsic to the advent of the true God. The structure of this poem is more unified than has generally been recognized, but the feeling towards the Nativity is more complex.

For sixteen of its thirty-two stanzas, the movement of the poem is a steady one. We go from the "rude manger" covered with snow to the "globe of circular light," which breaks forth into a celestial music of "such holy song" as will make us believe that "Time will run back and fetch the age of gold." The movement is forward and upward, literally—that is, geographically—as well as emotionally, until we feel that heaven itself "Will open wide the gates of her high palace hall." But we are then quickly reminded that we are anticipating, that the Second Coming, the return of the golden age, although implicit in the coming of the infant Christ, will actually occur only at the end of time. The immediate effect of the Nativity is the destruction of Satan's kingdom on earth—or rather, the beginning of that destruction, since it will be completed only at the Last Judgment. But it is the beginning of that destruction that the poet is interested in. After a brief reference to the Day of Judgment, stanzas 19–25 are devoted to the immediate manifestation of the destruction of Satan's kingdom: the disappearance of the pagan gods.

The oracles are silenced; Apollo, Peor, Ashtoreth, Moloch, Isis and Osiris are banished, or at least no longer appear at their usual haunts, while "With flow'r-inwoven tresses torn / The nymphs in twilight shade of tangled thickets mourn." The gods are banished with such lovely images and such gentle sorrow that many readers have wondered whether the poet himself is also mourning for the loss of these gods and goddesses of the classical world. Why, some critics have asked, does the poet celebrate the coming of Christ by dwelling, particularly in the closing movement of the poem, on such a beautiful aspect of the pagan world?

> The lonely mountains o'er
> And the resounding shore.
> > A voice of weeping heard and loud lament;
> From haunted spring and dale
> Edged with poplar pale
> > The parting Genius is with sighing sent;
> With flow'r-inwoven tresses torn
> The nymphs in twilight shade of tangled thickets mourn.

This banishment of the classical deities who haunt the springs, dales, mountains, and shores has an obvious relationship to Milton's own decision to turn away from classical poetry, much as he admired it, in order to become a Christian poet. As he said some years later, he wished to write poetry which had the "power, beside the office of a pulpit, to inbreed and cherish in a great people the seeds of virtue and public civility, to allay the perturbations of the mind and set the affections in right tune."[1] The biographical critics, most notably James Hanford, Arthur Barker and A. S. P. Woodhouse, have therefore related this passage in the *Ode* to important decisions in Milton's own life. Woodhouse points out how much Milton rejoices in these pagan deities in the *Elegia Quinta*, yet is ready to banish them in the *Ode* "because he is ready to accept the supremacy of the order of grace over nature herself."[2] Arthur Barker, also relating the conflict in the poem to a similar conflict in Milton's early life, finds that the poem transcends "the conflict between the two traditions" to bring about a "harmonious perfection symbolized by the music of the spheres."[3]

Critics who tend to look more closely at the text than at Milton's life have also tried to reconcile the heavenly light and heavenly music which dominate the first half of the poem with the plaintive tone and the dark shadows of the second half. Rosemond Tuve, who offers us the most thorough analysis of the imagery, denies that there is any conflict between the pagan and the Christian elements in the poem. "It is not the war between these two principles to which we must attend, but the seed of a peace between them in that the Light, being love, took on the Darkness to bring it back to His own nature:

> That glorious Form, that Light unsufferable
> And that far-beaming blaze of Majesty, . . .
> He laid aside; and here with us to be,
>   Forsook the Courts of everlasting Day,
> And chose with us a darksom House of mortal Clay."[4]

The "peace" which Miss Tuve finds in the poem is between Nature and the Light brought by Christ; for Nature, however sinful it may be, is redeemable. With the pagan deities, however, Miss Tuve has more difficulty. She at first is willing to admit that they must be banished because, unlike Nature, "they do not acknowledge" their "inferiority" to Christ. But she soon realizes that the banishment of the deities might bring her up against the old problem, and she is determined not to "be caught into thinking that Milton stood on the brink of a Puritanical antipathy, to become worse later, toward pagan thought—nymphs, fays, Apollo and the rest" (p. 64). We are told that Milton could accept the beauty of these nymphs and fays as long as they were not worshipped as gods. We can thus banish the "sacredness" of these gods without at the same time banishing their loveliness.

But realizing, perhaps, that if these gods are banished they are banished as indivisible entities with their true "loveliness" as well as their false "sacredness," Miss Tuve proceeds to distinguish between Satan (or Leviathan in this poem), who deceived us into worshipping the false gods, and the gods themselves, and between some of the gods, who reveal the loveliness of truth, and others who "are vicious and savage." The further we go into these subtle discriminations the further we get from the poem, and also from Miss Tuve's determination to deny any conflict between Milton's Christianity and his love for the pagan gods.[5] It would be much simpler to admit that there is a conflict inherent in any action which banishes a world which we also find beautiful. And there is nothing to detract from Milton's greatness as a poet or as a man in allowing him to express this conflict. We should not, as critics of Milton's poetry, be concerned with Miss Tuve's desire (shared by a number of critics) to keep Milton firmly within a medieval tradition of untroubled Christian orthodoxy.

What is justified, however, in Miss Tuve's intentions, is her desire to see the poem as a unified composition, for most readers feel this unity as they read the poem—rather than a tension between pagan and Christian sympathies. But the unity in the poem is a different matter from the unity in Milton's own conception of how a love of the classical past can be made logically consistent with a rather Hebraic concept of Christianity. The unity of the poetic experience does not depend on a logically coherent compromise between contrary attitudes. On the contrary, the unity in art is richer and more interesting when it can accept attitudes and beliefs which are contradictory in everyday experience, and when it fuses them into the kind of unity which can be attained only in art. Contradictions have to be resolved when we have to act, to take a stand one way or the other. But in art we do not take a stand; instead we are concerned with exploring the complex interrelationship of our feelings, particularly those feelings which move in different directions.

Some sense of such a unity is described by Cleanth Brooks and J. E. Hardy, who find that Milton "does not emphasize this element [the contrast between the two halves of the poem] to the point of making a contradiction between such regret and the great joy caused by Christ's birth. The tone of the poem is too simple to admit of such tensions." And this lack of tension is explained by a kind of aesthetic distance. "We are never close up to the scene. This sense of distance and detachment is achieved in part by the cosmic sweep of the Hymn."[6] Brooks and Hardy are right, I believe, in looking for the unity within the poem in the way that the poem is composed, rather than in a logical coherence between the conflicting feelings. And there is undoubtedly some truth in their remark about the "sense of distance and detachment" that Milton is able to achieve in his depiction of both the coming of Christ and the disappearance of the classical gods and goddesses. But this sense of detachment must *not* be interpreted so as to indicate that Milton is not deeply involved in both the celestial music which announces the Nativity:

> Ring out, ye crystal spheres
> Once bless our human ears
>
> . . . .
>
> And let the bass of heaven's deep organ blow

and in the desolation which is felt at the disappearance of the old gods:

> In consecrated earth
> And on the holy hearth
> The Lars and Lemures moan with midnight plaint.

Whatever may be said about detachment and impersonality, we must certainly be careful to distinguish the "detachment" of poetry from the meaning of this word in ordinary experience. In any case the unified tone of the poem can be explained more simply and directly by looking again at the imagery. Despite the excellent analyses of the language by the previously mentioned critics (as well as by others), it has not yet been pointed out that the departure of the deities is emotionally related to the advent of Christ. For regret and joy experienced simultaneously, so that one feeling cannot be separated from the other, is inherent in the paradox of the Christian myth.

Miss Tuve has already pointed out that "Light" (in the second stanza), the image which is most closely related to divinity, is brought to earth in "a darksom House of mortal Clay." This paradox is continued in the "Hymn" itself by the emphasis on "winter," "midnight," and the cold snow, all of which prevent the sun from giving life to the earth. The bringer of eternal life comes to mankind in a scene which seems to deny all life. The "universal peace" which follows represents, it is true, the final victory *over* death. But at this point even this "peace" is presented by the absence of all sound, which seems to be in contrast to the celestial harmony that it suggests. The silence is in contrast to the heavenly music just as the darkness is in contrast to the celestial light. Of course we realize that the sun "withheld his wonted speed" because "He saw a greater Sun appear / Than his bright throne and burning axletree could bear." But we are not to forget the darkness that is the immediate result of the advent of the Prince of Light.

Thus the paradox inherent in the Christian story—the fact that the power and the glory of heaven is brought to us by an infant who, in contrast to the "angelic symphony," cannot even speak, and who in contrast to the celestial light is surrounded with darkness—prepares us for the final section of the poem. For at this point we are told that the advent of God, who has come to redeem the earth and its inhabitants, brings about, as its very first consequence, the disappearance of those gods who for thousands of years infused Nature with divinity. The fact that this divinity is false is not relevant here since man felt them to be divine, and the poem is concerned not with the validity of beliefs outside of the poem but with feelings within the poem. This disappearance of the pagan gods is continuous with the first part of the poem, for Milton reminds us that the glory and joy that Christ will bring must come about through his suffering on the Cross, and that the celestial harmony will be ushered in by the Last Judgment when

> The aged Earth, aghast
> With terror at the blast,
>   Shall from the surface to the center shake.

If the Prince of Peace must be crucified by the hatred of men and the celestial harmony brought in with a terrifying "blast," we are prepared for the fact that the divinity which shall one day bathe all earth in a heavenly light must first banish those gods which have heretofore allowed man to feel at one with Nature.

The regret that we feel at the departure of the divinities is therefore a genuine regret. The loss of the old divinities as a prelude to the coming of the true Divinity is thus comparable to the contrast between the rude manger in which Christ appears and the kingdom of earth and heaven which he will inherit. When we know what will occur as a result of the immediate action, when we know that this cold dark night will usher in a greater light than the sun could ever give, our attitude towards the immediate scene is changed. But not completely; for we do not erase the immediate sensation of darkness or of helplessness or of pain. The "bitter grief" which we feel at the crucifixion is part of the joy that we feel at the eventual triumph over death. The ecstasy of the Christian is made up of both the pain and the triumph. It is not the negation of one feeling by a contrasting feeling but the fusion of both that creates the distinctive quality of Christian ecstasy.

Once we recognize these contrasts in the advent of Christ, we can see that there is no real change in mood when we are told that the first step in bringing about an age of gold is the removal of the pagan gods. We know that in the future

> Truth and Justice then
> Will down return to men,
>   Orbed in a rainbow; and like glories wearing,
> Mercy will sit between,
> Throned in celestial sheen,
>   With radiant feet the tissued clouds down steering.

But such knowledge does not negate the sense of loss that we feel at the present moment when we no longer have the presence of any gods to bring us close to the natural world:

> Nor is Osiris seen
> In Memphian grove or green,
>   Trampling the unshow'red grass with lowings loud;
> Nor can he be at rest
> Within his sacred chest,
>   Naught but profoundest hell can be his shroud;
> In vain with timbreled anthems dark
> The sable-stoled sorcerers bear his worshipped ark.

The similarity between the feelings towards the coming of Christ and the departure of the false gods is strengthened by these images of darkness. Just as the Prince of Light came to us in the darkness of winter only to bring about a greater light, so he now inaugurates a heaven on earth by causing Osiris, the god of green groves, to disappear into "profoundest hell." Everything that is good, everything that reaches to the light of heaven, is first brought into the poem by what is cold and dark here below. Even the music of the spheres has as its prologue the "timbreled anthems dark"; while in the following stanza the celestial brightness brings about darkness: "The rays of Bethlehem *blind* [the] dusky eye" of another pagan god. The paradox of the infant who becomes king, of the darkness that brings light, permeates the entire poem, and thus allows us to feel as well as see this aspect of Christianity which brings us to ecstatic joy by means of loss and suffering.

It is not only by imagery but, more subtly and more strikingly, by his use of time that Milton enables us to experience, simultaneously, the immediate sense of the action and its future significance. As a number of critics have already noted, the poem constantly brings together the future and the past within the present moment. "Indeed the Christian ideas of the circularity of time and the simultaneity of all moments under the aspect of eternity underlie the inmost structure of the poem."⁷ We are in the presence of the young poet on Christmas morning in 1629, at the nativity 1629 years earlier, and with the quiring angels as they bring in a new heaven and a new earth at the moment when time comes to an end. For this reason we are emotionally able to experience the painful effect of the birth, the crucifixion, and the Last Judgment at the same time as we experience the ecstatic joy of the marriage of heaven and earth. By allowing us to experience the future and the past in the present moment, the poem also allows us to experience simultaneously the contrary emotions that are associated with the different events. Everything comes together at the moment of Christ's birth; it is "a moment of astonishment," to use the phrase of one sensitive critic.⁸

The harmony that pervades this poem is, therefore, not the result of the Christian attitude overcoming the love for the classical gods, or the result of some logical reconciliation between Milton's regret at the departure of these gods and his Christian faith. The beliefs and feelings that Milton had as a man certainly go into the poem; but their function is not to convince us of anything but to allow us to see how contrary feelings brought to the surface by the Nativity can be reconciled into a harmony. And the harmony is not brought about by the objectivity of an essayist or an historian, who allows us to see what is good or bad in both Christian and non-Christian beliefs. It is brought about by a poet who can fuse both a sense of loss and a sense of triumph in the imagery and structure of the poem.

We are thus unable to answer the old questions as to whether Milton, at the time he wrote the poem, was turning away from the pagan spirit, or whether he was doing so with regret or with untroubled joy. For although these personal feelings enter into the poem, the feelings created by the poem are something else, and go beyond any personal belief on the part of the poet or the reader. There is nothing *in* the poem to agree or disagree with. The beliefs are used by Milton to show the complex emotions that they can bring forth. We are asked, therefore, not to move in any particular direction—to rejoice or to mourn for the loss of the pagan gods—but simply to join the poet in a growing awareness of how contradictory feelings are brought into a harmony. And this harmony is brought about by the power of poetry to make us experience diverse events simultaneously.

Fortunately, such harmony, unlike that described in the poem, can be heard by mortal ears.

Brooklyn College

NOTES

1. *The Reason of Church Government Urged Against Prelaty*, Book II, *John Milton: Prose Selections*, ed. Merritt Y. Hughes (New York, 1947), p. 107.

2. "Notes on Milton's Early Development," *University of Toronto Quarterly*, XIII (1943), 77.

3. "The Pattern of Milton's *Nativity Ode*," *University of Toronto Quarterly*, X (1941), 180.

4. *Images and Themes in Five Poems by Milton* (Cambridge, Mass., 1957), p. 47. Except for this stanza, taken directly from Miss Tuve, all quotations from the poem are taken from the modernized edition of Douglas Bush, *The Complete Poetical Works of John Milton* (Boston, 1965).

5. To prove, as Miss Tuve does, that the love of pagan gods, or a certain kind of regard for them, is consistent with the doctrines of Lactantius or Prudentius, does not prove that there was no conflict in Milton. And it certainly does not tell us anything about the conflict in the poem, where the harmony is of a different kind than is reached by theology.

6. *Poems of Mr. John Milton* (New York, 1951), p. 103.

7. Lowry Nelson, Jr., *Baroque Lyric Poetry* (New Haven, 1961), p. 51.

8. Lawrence Stapleton, "Milton and the New Music," *University of Toronto Quarterly*, XXIII (1953–54), 226.

PARODY OF STYLE
IN MILTON'S POLEMICS

D. M. Rosenberg

Because Milton believed language to be an external manifestation of inner spirit, he exposes his political and religious
adversaries' corruptions of style by impersonating them. By
parodying their linguistic abuses, he supports his assertions
about their dishonesty and ignorance. His verbal range is
broad and various, shifting from mockery of High-Church
grandiloquence, to burlesque of commercial jargon, to rough
satire. He uses his own plain, concrete diction, however, as a
moral and stylistic norm. Ridicule of Bishop Hall's peculiar
diction and aphoristic phrasing plays an important part in
Animadversions and *An Apology*. Through parody, Milton
awakens his readers' perceptions, persuading them to participate with him in the controversy over church reform and
religious liberty.

MILTON BELIEVED that the vicious attitudes of his eminent adversaries could best be exposed through their own language. Style
for him was an outward testimony of man's wisdom and goodness. In
his *Apology*, he writes: "So that how he should be truly eloquent who is
not withall a good man, I see not."[1] A bad style, then, could reveal
hypocrisy, or ignorance, or pretentiousness. In *Of Reformation*, for
instance, Milton lays open the language of prelatical apologists. Arguing against the need for biblical commentary by the Church Fathers,
he writes:

But let the Scriptures be hard; are they more hard, more crabbed, more
abstruse than the Fathers? He that cannot understand the sober, plain,
and unaffected stile of the Scriptures, will be ten times more puzzl'd with
the knotty Africanisms, the pamper'd metafors; the intricat, and involv'd

sentences of the Fathers; besides the fantastick, and declamatory flashes; the crosse-jingling periods which cannot but disturb, and comes thwart a settl'd devotion worse than the din of bells, and rattles.   (I, 568)

Style is a central thematic problem in his polemics. Understanding that values are implicit in a writer's manner of expression, the parodist impugns what he believes to be corruptions of style. Then, through an exaggeration of the erudite and affected style of his religious and political adversaries, he evokes their characteristic idiom and tone in order to exploit it. He contends that the style itself contains the issues. Believing that clarity of diction is a principle of moral significance, he argues that the prelatical tradition has raised a barrier of words between men and the truth of Scriptures. "Now sir, for the love of holy *Reformation*," he continues, emphasizing his exasperation,

What can be said more against these importunat clients of Antiquity, then she her selfe their patronesse hath said. Whether think ye would she approve still to dote upon immeasurable, innumerable, and therfore unnecessary, and unmerciful volumes, choosing rather to erre with the specious name of the Fathers, or to take a sound Truth at the hand of a plain upright man, that all his dayes hath bin diligently reading the holy Scriptures, and therto imploring *Gods* grace, while the admirers of Antiquity have bin beating their brains about their *Ambones*, their *Diptychs*, and *Meniaia's?*   (I, 568)

By using simpler, more concrete diction, he defines his own relationship both with the language and the reader. He juxtaposes the excessively Latinate style of the church against the biblical simplicity of his own diction. The sentence opens with Milton's mimicry of the weighty and polysyllabic idiom of the church, emphasizing its difficulty as well as its drone. Just as the diction is alien and obscure, so his own phrase, "to take a sound Truth at the hand of a plain upright man" is familiar and transparent. By drawing upon the monosyllabic words of Anglo-Saxon stock, Milton speaks as the plain upright Englishman. His is the language of living speech. Playing the part of the honest and straightforward speaker, he employs the appropriate style. Imaginatively giving expression to his position, he has made the reader participate in the language and therefore in the controversy. Rather than relying on conventional dialectic alone, Milton has awakened his reader's perceptions through his diction.

In his imitations and parodies, Milton was alert to the demands of literary propriety. Styles should be appropriate to place, time, person, and especially subject. He assimilated these elements of decorum and used them to his rhetorical advantage. His parodic diction, for instance, depending on occasion and subject, is characteristic of a grandiloquent style, or, at the other extreme, in more explicitly satirical passages, the low language of dialect forms and cant.

In a satirical passage in *Areopagitica* (II, 544–45), related to the character writings of the time,[2]. he imitates the mercantile jargon of the middle class. Borrowing from the realistic homilies of the pulpit, Milton manipulates the vernacular of worldly merchants in order to criticize them. Close to daily experience, in the world of "piddling accounts" and trading, Milton interprets through language the reality of the religious hypocrite. Through the incongruity of a mercantile idiom in a religious context, he wittily caricatures the spiritual triviality and absurdity of applying the values of commerce to religion. The wealthy businessman thinks he can speculate by shrewdly investing in "som Divine of note" who would function as a middleman. The "whole ware-house of his religion" operates as a homely metaphor which suggests the stockpiling of spiritual deadwood. In contrast to the worldly bourgeois comforts of entertainment, gifts, and feasts, he places the grand but ascetic figure of Christ. The effect of the abrupt shift is shocking, and renders the satirical figures of the bribed pastor and self-deceiving merchant as not only coarse but corrupt.

In a second character sketch which immediately follows, Milton makes the commercial idiom even more extravagant:

Another sort there be who when they hear that all things shall be order'd, all things regulated and settl'd; nothing writt'n but what passes through the custom-house of certain Publicans that have the tunnaging and poundaging of all free spok'n truth, will strait give themselvs up into your hans, mak'em, & cut'em out what religion ye please.

Spiritual values are here indecorously demeaned by the cumbersome trade jargon of "tunnaging and poundaging." The language is further reduced in the callous slang of "mak'em, & cut'em out what religion ye please," as Milton histrionically recreates the banality of the worldling and materialist.

By impersonating the characteristic idiom of his enemies, he corroborates his assertions about their dullness and stupidity. Had he restricted himself to a highly mannered style, his arguments would have appeared too remote from the realities of the subject. Keeping his style as flexible as possible, he can employ it with the immediacy of a destructive satirical instrument. Through mimicry of their language, he caricatures the attitudes of his opponents by exploiting the very expression of what he exposes.

Milton had been nurtured on the various tactics of rhetoric. As a student, he was taught to write in styles which were adapted to imaginary characters. *Ethopoeia* and *prosopopeia,* as these pervasive declamatory exercises were called, permitted young writers to feign both persons and lines, as in the composition of dramatic monologues.[3] Cultivating this art of impersonation, Milton was able to caricature with dramatic diversity. For the satirist, imitations of style and tone constitute a literary refinement of oratorical or histrionic delivery.

Adopting the rhetorical concept that style should be appropriate to the subject, he discovered those particular idioms which blend expression and idea. In his satirical attacks, he often sacrifices formal diction for low language if his subject necessitates bluntness and simplicity. Not only can he destructively mock the self-deceiving jargon of the church or of commerce, but in his impersonation of the plain-speaking man, he descends, if need be, to billingsgate and scatology. Satire thrives on moral extremes, and Milton uses the extremes of language as a satirical weapon.

"There may be a sanctifi'd bitternesse against the enemies of truth," Milton explains in his defense of low language, and then he alludes to Luther, Erasmus, David, and Solomon—great men, who, in their righteous indignation, used "tart rhetorick" (I, 901). If Christ Himself speaks of "unsavory traditions" and "scruples not to name the Dunghill and the Jakes" (I, 895), then Milton will not eschew the coarseness of "honest words" (I, 902). In his dedication to truth, the dramatic speaker aggressively fills his vituperative passages with rowdy and indecent references, to overturned urinals in *Animadversions,* or bordelloes, stinking bishops' socks, and old vomit in *An Apology.* He continually pursues his enemies "with bad words, who persecuted others with bad deeds" (I, 907).

Given "the will, the Spirit, and the utterance" (I, 875), his boisterous diatribe rides full tilt against those he sees as enemies of truth. Assuming the posture of rage, Milton's language reflects his fierce joy in it. He draws upon the conventional notion that satire originated with satyr plays, and that the language of satire, therefore, is rough and uncouth. When he calls admirers of the Remonstrant, "grosse-headed, thick witted, illiterat, shallow" (I, 873), his vehement expressions reinforce the rough-speaking satirist's claim to bluntness and honesty. His cultivated scorn sometimes emerges as mockery in the sounds themselves: "The time is taken up with a tedious number of Liturgicall tautologies, and impertinencies" (I, 684). Verbal jeering such as this demonstrates Milton's conscious attempts in satirical art. His joy in abusive virtuosity is reminiscent of the coney-catching pamphlets of Greene, the lampoons of Nashe and Harvey, or the tracts of Martin Marprelate.

Though his satirical rage and low language are at variance with rationality, Milton reconciles them. As satirist, he stresses the importance of maintaining reason, and he argues that it is reasonable to express "indignation, or scorn upon an object that merits it" (I, 899). Disdaining "the affected name of moderation" (I, 868), he rejects the decorous externals of propriety. Employing his own kind of rhetoric to attack rhetoric, he subverts the conventions of Anglican decency in all its forms, verbal as well as liturgical.[4]

In both *Animadversions* and *An Apology*, Milton dissects the mannered style and literary affectation of his opponent. With mocking particularity, he criticizes Bishop Hall's writing, referring to his incoherent organization, weak syntax, odd phrasing, ambiguous and superfluous diction, and feeble similitudes. One of the recurrent tactics in *Animadversions* is for Milton to counterattack by impairing, through distortion, his opponent's word choice, thereby ridiculing it. Disfiguring Hall's rhetorical devices, he gibes, "And thus you throttle yourselfe with your own Similes" (I, 687). Accusing him of sophistry, he replies to a remark of the Remonstrant, "O rare suttlety" (I, 671). As the artless, honest spokesman, he reproves the Remonstrant for calculated evasiveness: "If you have no grounde-worke of Logick, or plain-dealing in you, learne both as fast as you can" (I, 695). In *An Apology*, Milton takes the English Seneca to task for his hopping aphoristic style, with its "quips and snapping adagies" (I, 872). Condemning "this babler"

(I, 871) of dishonest words, he breaks down Hall's stylistic mannerisms, describing his "coy flurting stile . . . to be girded with frumps and curtall gibes, by one who makes sentences by the Statute, as if all above three inches long were confiscat" (I, 873). Clearly, Milton's disapproval of Hall's writing is more than superficial faultfinding. Believing in the organic relationship between inner spirit and outward manifestation, he interprets the styles of his adversaries as revelations of their pedantry, affectation, and dullness.

In the Nonconformist tradition, Milton gives particular prominence to the Word of God. If the spirit of the word is central to Milton's belief, he applies it as well to the words of men. Accordingly, a language which is self-consciously mannered, ambiguous, or obscure, betrays an inner spirit which is dishonest. Milton's plain speaking, then, is a satirical technique rising from his conviction that rhetoric is a vehicle for social morality.

Michigan State University

NOTES

1. *Complete Prose Works of John Milton,* ed. Don M. Wolfe, et al. (New Haven, 1953—), I, 874. Hereafter cited in the text with volume and page number.
2. Benjamin Boyce, *The Polemic Character, 1640–1661* (Lincoln, Nebraska, 1955), p. 24.
3. Donald Leman Clark, *John Milton at St. Paul's School* (New York, 1948), p. 190.
4. Thomas Kranidas, *The Fierce Equation: A Study of Milton's Decorum* (The Hague, 1965), p. 87.

RETRIBUTIVE JUSTICE IN *LYCIDAS:*
THE TWO-HANDED ENGINE

Kathleen M. Swaim

In the image of *Lycidas* 130 Milton conflates "th' abhorred shears" of Atropos and St. Peter's two keys. *Two-handed* is ambiguous, held with two hands or composed of two portions. *Engine* covers both keys and shears, and perhaps also sheephook. The fateful shears invoke the ritual harvest of "the shearers feast" (117). "Blind Fury" similarly conflates a Fury and Fate (Atropos). The ambiguity of image and phrasing in "two-handed engine" accommodates a combination of pagan and Christian instruments of final justice, as so much of *Lycidas'* thought and imagery interweaves humanistic and Christian material, especially pastoral, while building toward a new revelation of triumphant Christian truth. Structurally, the engine image concludes the second movement of *Lycidas* with emphasis on punishment imposed from above according to human deserts, as the first movement ends with emphasis on reward ("meed") imposed, and as the third ends with Grace that uplifts beyond human deserts.

IN MOST of the vast commentary on Milton's "two-handed engine" (*Lycidas*, 130–31)[1] critics have searched out sources and analogues and contemporary artifacts as a way of securing a precise equivalent for the poet's ambiguous phrase and image. I would like to offer yet another observation on this much exercised engine, but one that takes its method and aim from the context of the image, themes, and artistry of *Lycidas* as a whole, rather than from theology, literary history, or the history of ideas and culture. In brief, it is my contention that in the "two-handed engine" Milton is conflating two images employed earlier in the poem—"th' abhorred shears" of Atropos and St. Peter's two keys—and that what looseness there is in the image exists to accommodate a combination of these pagan and Christian instruments of final judgment, as so much else in the poem interweaves humanistic and Christian material while building toward a new revelation of the triumph of Christian truth.

Tracing through the various and wide-ranging critical suggestions of the past provides an exercise in patience and a lesson in ingenuity. Sources and analogues of the "two-handed engine" have been uncovered in Ezekiel, Psalms, Jeremiah, and Revelations,[2] as well as in Dante, Savonarola, Jehan Gerard, John of Salisbury, Du Bartas, Sir Thomas Smith, Thomas Adams ("the Shakespeare of Puritan Theologians"), John Donne, Phineas Fletcher, and Edmund Spenser.[3] Among the various mechanical instruments which have been suggested are: a mace or club, an executioner's axe, a sheephook or pastoral rod, Time's scythe, Death wielding Time's scythe, the lock of St. Peter's door, two massy keys, the "temple of Janus and the two doors that were open during peace and closed in a time of war," and most recently a turret-clock.[4] Interpretations shift among *two-handed, two-handled,* and even *two-edged.* The most frequently mentioned instrument is a sword, whose forms include a one-edged sword, a two-edged broadsword of heroic combat, a sword of war as wielded by the Scots, a two-handed sword typifying revolution or civil war, a two-edged sword as scriptural symbol for the word of God, and the sword of God's justice.[5] These critics tend to recall Milton's only other use of the adjective "two-handed," in *Paradise Lost* VI, 251, where "the Sword of *Michael*" is brandished "with huge two-handed sway." When the adjective is stressed, interpretive ingenuity ranges very widely indeed, discovering such abstract equations for this double image as: the two houses of Parliament (the engine being liberty); the combined power of Spain and France; the two nations of England and Scotland; the Court of High Commission with its ecclesiastical and temporal powers; "twin superstitious appeals to hope of gain and fear of consequence" of Roman Catholicism (i.e., the engine); the two aspects of the Word of God, the Law and the Gospel; and Man "in his dual capacity of labour and prayer."[6] Several writers have suggested looking at contemporary painting, woodcuts, and monuments.[7] A few have noted, then quickly dismissed, the possibility of ambiguity in the image.[8] The basic fault of most of these commentators is that they indulge in narrow guessing games while disregarding the context of the poem as a whole.

That Milton can control a wide range of suggestion within a brief phrase or image no one would deny, but individual images and phrases must be measured by the controlling center of the poem. A review of the structure of *Lycidas* lets us glimpse this controlling center. *Lycidas* consists of three major movements enclosed within a framework of the pastoral and the poet's consciousness of himself and his role.[9] Each movement begins with a formalized call to the Muses and moves outward from the security of pastoral convention in quest of present answers to the questions that have most troubled thoughtful men in all ages: questions of justice, the function of evil and the nature of death, the value of dedication and labor, the validity of the search for spiritual order, and the place of creativity in a universe visibly organized only arbitrarily and incomprehensibly. Each of the three quests—lines 15–84, 85–131, and 132–85—explores a combination of such questions, and each concludes with a startling penetration to a new perception of order. The progression of thought is generally increasingly elevated, within each quest moving upward and outward from the merely conventional, and in the threefold sequence moving from humanistic or rational answers toward the mystery of Christian faith.

More specifically, the first quest begins with an invocation to the "Sisters of the sacred well" (15) and concludes with faith in "all-Judging *Jove*" (82) and the assurance of heavenly fame and meed. The second unit begins in a consciously lower mode—with less intense expression and a retreat into the security of the conventional—and invokes another form of the Muses' inspiration, this form also associated with a water source:

> O Fountain *Arethuse*, and thou honour'd floud,
> Smooth-sliding *Mincius*, crown'd with vocall reeds,
> That strain I heard was of a higher mood:
> But now my Oat proceeds.   (85–88)

This second unit concludes with the image of the "two-handed engine" ready to smite irrevocably. It achieves a perception of the certainty of retributive justice—punishment balancing the earlier assurance of reward from Jove. The third unit—like the second—begins with an invocation to a form of the Muse (again a water source) and again with an evaluation of the preceding conclusion. "Dread" com-

ments on the end of the second quest as "higher" did on the end of
the first. Beginning with

> Return *Alpheus,* the dread voice is past,
> That shrunk thy streams; Return *Sicilian* Muse   (132–33)

the third movement progresses to the apotheosis of Edward King /
Lycidas, to the ecstatic vision of salvation and beatitude for the
dead hero, King as poet, priest, shepherd, and dedicated pilgrim,
and the consequent redemptive energy for those of us who still "wander
in that perilous flood" (185). By contrast with the first and second
quests, the third movement provides an answer that is free from
limitations and more than satisfying to the poet and believer. The
difference may be seen in the contrast of the rewards that conclude
the first unit and the punishments that conclude the second—both
of these answering human deserts and standards though seen as
imposed supernaturally from above—with the Grace that concludes
the final movement. Grace is by definition beyond the deserving of
even the most dedicated or perfect mortal and beyond human com-
prehension and measurement, as it comes without measure.

With this review of the structure and several of the major themes
of *Lycidas* in mind, we may now proceed to observe how "that two-
handed engine" of line 130 functions within the larger design. "The
Pilot of the *Galilean* lake" (109)—the last to give deposition in the
court of inquiry after "the Herald of the Sea," "sage *Hippotades*,"
and Camus—contrasts the lost Lycidas with the rotten remaining
clergy, whose chief care is "how to scramble at the shearers feast, / And
shove away the worthy bidden guest" (117–18):

> The hungry Sheep look up, and are not fed,
> But swoln with wind, and the rank mist they draw,
> Rot inwardly, and foul contagion spread:
> Besides what the grim Woolf with privy paw
> Daily devours apace, and nothing sed,
> But that two-handed engine at the door,
> Stands ready to smite once, and smite no more.   (125–31)

The engine is the final image of the second movement of *Lycidas;* it
embodies the answer of the "dread voice," promising retributive
justice to "our corrupted Clergy."

Twenty lines before the two-handed engine is mentioned, "the

Pilot of the *Galilean* lake," whom I take to be St. Peter,[10] keeper of the keys of the kingdom of heaven, is pictured with his proper engine of judgment:

> Two massy Keyes he bore of metals twain,
> (The Golden opes, the Iron shuts amain).   (110–11)

With these, according to the orders of Christ in Matthew xvi, 19, Peter's power is defined: "Whatsoever thou shalt bind on earth shall be bound in heaven: and whatsoever thou shalt loose on earth shall be loosed in heaven." Traditionally, St. Peter stands with his keys at the door of heaven and determines whether a soul proceeds to the realms of gold or the infernal pit. This tradition is familiar to Milton and turns up elsewhere in his work.[11] In *Lycidas* the keys present alternatives of value and opportunity: grace or imprisonment, treasure or weight, everlasting salvation or everlasting damnation.[12]

Since the "two-handed engine" concludes a verse paragraph that introduces a figure with two keys, it seems a natural expectation that the reader equate the two double instruments. That the "two-handed engine" is *at a door* makes keys an insistent interpretation. We have to do with a question of ultimate judgment and, in the tradition thoroughly familiar to Milton, St. Peter is an ultimate judge and his keys the universally acknowledged instrument of that judgment. St. Peter's judgment—administered by keys at the door or gate of heaven—permits the saved to enter, but shuts off the damned from salvation. Whether or not keys may be said to *smite*, the repeated action of line 131, is a question I take up below, but it seems to me that, given the concept of judgment and the figure of St. Peter just preceding, the image of line 130—"But that two-handed engine at the door"—demands interpretation, on one important level, as keys.

St. Peter begins speaking with line 113, and it is not clear precisely where his speech ends—whether, that is, it ends with line 118 or with line 131. The speech gradually shifts away from the Pilot's point of view and—like so much else in the poem—achieves the distancing and the personal passion that characterize the poet's view. St. Peter would not himself speak of "that two-handed engine at the door" meaning himself and his burden, but the poet might well do so, a poet, that is, who is moving away from the ancient vision persuaded of the certainty of his faith in retributive justice and a right-

eous universe. Other sections of the poem face other major questions
and achieve the certainty of faith in other ideas. The leap of faith
to the vision of a "*Lycidas* sunk low, but mounted high" (172) and
received into "the blest Kingdoms meek of joy and love" (177)
shows a similar pattern of ratified Christian faith, in this case in the
paradox of heaven's salvation. The distancing in this penultimate
paragraph of the poem comes with the shift to perception of Lycidas' "large recompense" or—in other words—to perception not of
salvation, but of the redemptive energy that sparks and guides men
on earth to salvation. The final glimpse of St. Peter at the end of the
second movement of *Lycidas* provides the same sort of distancing—
a shift to the human point of view of the poet.

Given the poem's richly patterned ambiguity and its movement
toward triumphant paradox, the double possibilities in *two-handed*
(meaning either held and wielded with two hands or composed of
two portions or hands) encourage us to look more closely at other
images. Another two-handed or perhaps two-handled instrument, the
shears of Atropos, is mentioned in the final verse paragraph of the
first movement of the poem, where earthly fame is contrasted with
heavenly praise and the judgment of the classical Fates with the
"perfet witnes of all-judging *Jove*" (82). The image is found in lines
73–76:

> But the fair Guerdon when we hope to find,
> And think to burst out into sudden blaze,
> Comes the blind *Fury* with th' abhorred shears,
> And slits the thin spun life.

Although Milton's epithet is *Fury*, the details of the shears and the
"thin spun" thread of life assure us that we have to do here with
Atropos.[13] Milton's conflation of a Fate and a Fury combines two
very rich concepts: associated with Atropos is the fact of arbitrary
death and the view of life as merely time on earth, and associated
with the Furies is the suggestion of a supernatural agency of justice
within a morally directed scheme. The conflating of these two
highly suggestive images within a word here demonstrates another
form of what Milton does in both *two-handed* and *engine* and their
conflations of shears and keys.[14]

The blindness is, of course, characteristic of the inflexible Atropos,
but the trait signals also lack of vision as vision is largely defined

throughout *Lycidas*. In brief, blindness is failure to see Christian truth or the confinement of sight to the merely earthly or even the merely classical. It is worth noting too that we have to do here with one of the Furies rather than one of the Eumenides, but at this point in the poem and from the speaker's point of view death seems arbitrary and justice absent. In the course of the poem what we might call the Eumenides vision is achieved; justice becomes mercy—positive, regenerative, ordered, and ultimately Christian.

Northrop Frye is one of several commentators to remark that the engine cannot be interpreted as keys, since keys cannot be said to *smite*,[15] though no one would deny that St. Peter "stands ready" "at the door" or that his judgment is both single and irrevocable—the ideas conveyed by line 131. According to the *OED*, the range of the verb *smite* covers more than a score of meanings, and one of the most prominent of the intransitive ones, with uses dating from ca. 1150 to 1843, has special theological import: "Of the deity, in or after Biblical use: To visit with death, destruction, or overthrow; to afflict or punish in some signal manner." Surely this meaning covers the action of both the shears and St. Peter's keys. The *smiting* of line 131 acts upon those shut out from salvation, hence afflicted, punished, and visited with damnation. Although Milton does not use the word *smite* in describing the action of Atropos' shears, this definition is certainly also appropriate for the supernatural agent who "slits the thin spun life" and shapes each mortal's career by what is, like Peter's, a unique and irrevocable act. To conceive of *smite* as striking a blow in either attack or punishment is too narrow and simple, and disregards Milton's thorough Biblical grounding.

"Two-handed engine" I believe includes the two primary instruments of justice described above, the keys and the shears. Another mechanical object mentioned in the St. Peter passage may be included within the connotational range of the ambiguous engine. The sheephook of line 120, as several commentators have noted, may be two-handed—that is, carried with two hands—if not an instrument for smiting, and may be linked with the execution of justice, particularly if the sheephook is viewed as the symbol of a bishop's powers, analogous to a king's sceptre. "A pastoral staff or crosier" wielded by bishops of the Middle Ages signified "their power to administer correction as well as to guide and sustain the flock. This dual function was sometimes materially symbolized by tipping the lower end with iron and ornamenting the crook with ivory or precious metal."[16] As the "Miter'd locks" of line 112 of *Lycidas* reminds us, Peter was the first bishop.[17] The classical and Christian dimensions of pastoral imagery, so important in the total conception of *Lycidas*, enforce each other in this view of the "two-handed engine."

Also conflating classical and Christian pastoralism is "the shearers feast" (117) at which the ravenous clergy show themselves. In the rural mode, the shearer's feast would celebrate the triumphant completion of a round of the natural cycle. I believe "the shearers feast" in *Lycidas* includes echoes of the shears mentioned in line 75 as "abhorred" and provides further overtones for the interpretation of the two-handed engine. Atropos' office and instrument, of course, mark the completion of a different kind of natural cycle—that spun by Clotho and measured by Lachesis. But the inflexible finality of "th' abhorred shears" has given way to a new vision of shearing—as harvest valued from on high and celebrated ritually by a community or fellowship—and thus has moved us significantly toward the entertainment of "all the Saints above . . . and sweet Societies" (178–79) that signals the triumphant transcendence of spirit and grace over matter and fate, the highest theme of the whole poem.[18] The escapes from weight, isolation, and the arbitrary and accidental into purified spirit, the community of faith, and the orderly and harmonious, mark the achievement of the quest of *Lycidas* as a whole—whether one views that quest as traditionally elegiac or as satisfying Milton's more private poetic needs.

This review of the structure of *Lycidas* and of one thread in its patterned imagery has served to place a troublesome and ambiguous phrase and image within the larger context of the poem's themes and art. An *engine* is defined as something made with ingenuity, a contrivance, instrument, or means. The present essay has considered the famous "two-handed engine" as a poetic "engine" or a contrivance of Milton's to set forth and open up the idea of retributive justice through the conflation of several mechanical instruments. The ambiguity of the image here for one brief occasion solves what was a constantly engaging challenge to Milton: the quest for the right relationship of classical and Christian imagery and experience. A more precise phrase than "two-handed engine" might have cut off the multiple suggestions of shears, pastoral and ritual shearing, and keys. A less ambiguous phrase might also have upset the progressive building of themes and images toward the paradoxical Christian transcendence of the poem's climax.

University of Massachusetts
Amherst

NOTES

1. Quotations from *Lycidas* refer to the text in *Milton's "Lycidas": The Tradition and the Poem*, ed. C. A. Patrides (New York, 1961). Quotations from other poems by Milton are taken from *John Milton: Complete Poems and Major Prose*, ed. Merritt Y. Hughes (New York, 1957). My sizable debts to the essays collected in the Patrides volume are general rather than specific.

2. William H. Ward, *Athenaeum*, April 14, 1906, pp. 451–52, and Edward Chauncey Baldwin, *MLN*, XXXIII (1918), 211–15; R. E. Hughes, *N & Q*, n.s. II (1955), 58–59; Maurice Kelley, *N & Q*, CLXXXI (1941), 273; and A. F. Pollard, *TLS*, August 29, 1936, p. 697. These critics tend to look for equivalents of *engine*, especially *sword*; Biblical concordances reveal suggestive data under *smite* also, e.g., I Samuel xxvi, 8: "Now therefore let me smite him, I pray thee, with the spear even to the earth at once, and I will not smite him the second time." Peter *smites* with a sword in John xviii, 10.

3. Kenneth McKenzie, *Italica*, XX (1943), 121–26; Edward S. LeComte, *SP*, XLVII (1950), 589–606, and *SP*, XLIX (1952), 548–50; John M. Steadman, *N & Q*, n.s. III (1956), 249–50; R. J. Shoeck, *N & Q*, n.s. II (1955), 235–37; H. L., *Athenaeum*, June 30, 1900, p. 815; George G. Loane, *N & Q*, CLXXXI (1941), 320; Maurice Hussey, *N & Q*, CXCIII (1948), 503; E. S. Fussell, *N & Q*, CXCIII (1948), 338–39; Thomas B. Stroup, *N & Q*, n.s. VI (1959), 366–67; and C. W. Brodribb, *TLS*, June 12, 1930, p. 496.

4. Nowell Smith, *TLS*, December 6, 1928, p. 965; G. H. Powell, *Athenaeum*, May 5, 1906, p. 547, and H. Beckett, *TLS*, July 3, 1943, p. 319; C. W. Brodribb, *TLS*, June 12, 1930, p. 496, and *TLS*, June 5, 1943, p. 271, and Lowell W. Coolidge, *PQ*, XXIX (1950), 444–45; M. D., *Athenaeum*, April 28, 1906, p. 515, and Kathleen Crighton Tomlinson, *TLS*, June 12, 1943, p. 283; Katharine A. Esdaile, *TLS*, June 19, 1943, p. 295; W. Arthur Turner, *JEGP*, XLIX (1950), 562–65; J. Milton French, *MLN*, LXVIII (1953), 229–31; N. W. Hill, *TLS*, July 28, 1927, p. 520; and Claud A. Thompson, *SP*, LIX (1962), 184–200. J. Max Patrick has suggested privately to me that the engine may be the cross: "an upright stick crossed with a bar . . . gives two handles which may be grasped by two hands; and, of course, the cross does deliver the definitive and final blow." The cross thus viewed fits in with the ambiguities of *Lycidas* in that swords regularly have cross heads, keys are (or used to be) cross-shaped, and in heraldry keys are often crossed (though in an $\times$ shape). He notes also that "the crossed keys of St. Peter in the papal arms approximate the shape of shears or scissors."

5. In addition to the notes already cited, by Smith, Steadman, Hughes, Baldwin, and Kelley, see Leon Howard, *HLQ*, XV (1952), 173–84, H. Mutschmann, *TLS*, April 25, 1936, p. 356; A. H. T. Clarke, *TLS*, April 11, 1929, pp. 295–96; and Mindele C. Treip, *N & Q*, n.s. VI (1959), 364–66.

6. G. M. Trevelyan, *TLS*, April 25, 1929, p. 338, and Donald C. Dorian, *PMLA*, XLV (1930), 204–15; George MacLean Harper, *TLS*, June 16, 1927, p. 424; Donald A. Stauffer, *MLR*, XXXI (1936), 57–60; K. N. Colville, *TLS*, November 22, 1928, pp. 909–10; William J. Grace, *SP*, LII (1955), 583–89; G. W. Whiting, *Milton and This Pendant World* (Austin, Texas, 1958), pp. 29–58, and the notes by Stroup and Fussell cited previously. It may be aesthetically pertinent to observe that much of *Lycidas* moves in pairs: "once more . . . and once more" (line 1), Myrtles and Ivy (2), "harsh and crude" (6), etc., culminating in the double placement of the hero at the end of the poem.

7. Beckett, *TLS*, July 3, 1943, p. 319; Brodribb, *TLS*, June 12, 1930, p. 496; and Esdaile, *TLS*, June 19, 1943, p. 295.

8. LeComte, *SP*, XLVII (1950), 595; Stauffer, *MLR*, XXXI (1936), 57; Dorian, *PMLA*, XLV (1930), 213; Hill, *TLS*, July 28, 1927, p. 520; Beckett, *TLS*, July 3, 1943, p. 319; Treip, *N & Q*, n.s. VI (1959), 365–66; Tomlinson, *TLS*, June 12, 1943, p. 283.

9. My review of the structure of *Lycidas* builds upon that supplied by Arthur Barker in "The Pattern of Milton's *Nativity Ode*," *UTQ*, X (1941), 171–72.

10. Ralph E. Hone, *SP*, LVI (1959), 55–61, is often persuasive in arguing that the Pilot is properly Christ. C. A. Thompson, *SP*, LIX (1962), 186, agrees with Hone. I suggest that the Pilot image may be another example of conflation, i.e., the simultaneous suggestion of several possibilities, here Peter and Christ. The Warburton-Newton notes to the poem observe that "the making [Peter] the minister is in imitation of the Italian poets, who in their satiric pieces against the church always make Peter the minister of vengeance." See Scott Elledge, *Milton's "Lycidas": Edited to Serve as an Introduction to Criticism* (New York, 1966), p. 294. See also *De Doctrina Christiana*, I, xxix, especially pp. 226–33 in the Columbia edition of *The Works of John Milton*, vol. XVI.

11. In the description of the arrival of late Friars in Limbo in *Paradise Lost*, III, 484–85, Milton says:

> And now Saint *Peter* at Heav'n's Wicket seems
> To wait them with his Keys.

Several passages in the poems suggest that the distinction in the metals of the keys has spiritual significance. In *Comus*, 13–14, the Attendant Spirit speaks of "that Golden Key / That opes the Palace of Eternity." The atmosphere of hell is defined by weight, specifically by iron; keys are prominent in Satan's encounter with Sin and Death in Book II of *Paradise Lost*. Sin's engine is "the fatal key" (725), "the powerful key" (774), "the key of this infernal pit" (850), and again "the fatal Key, / Sad instrument of all our woe" (871–72). Standing before "the adamantine Gates" (853) and after raising "the huge Portcullis," Sin

> in the key-hole turns
> Th' intricate wards, and every Bolt and Bar
> Of massy Iron or solid Rock with ease
> Unfast'ns.   (876–79)

The *mass* of the keys in *Lycidas* 110 makes them heavy enough to *smite* with.

12. Thomas B. Stroup, who equates the "two-handed engine" with keys and the two keys with the Law and the Gospel, adds: "one of the keys opens the Kingdom to the true believers; the other shuts it to the unfaithful"—*N & Q*, n.s. VI (1959), 366.

13. The Fates are described as "those that hold the vital shears" in *Arcades*, 65. In *John Milton: "Paradise Regained," The Minor Poems, and "Samson Agonistes"* (New York, 1937), p. 922, Merritt Y. Hughes notes: "The two hands may represent the two Houses of Parliament. The engine seems like a symbol of its power to establish true liberty, like the 'wholesome and preventive Shears' which Milton foresaw the Long Parliament using against 'The New Forcers of Conscience.'"

14. In *N & Q*, n.s. II (1955), 58, R. E. Hughes describes an additional instance of conflation in lines 130–31 of *Lycidas:* " 'At the door' contains three previous details of the poem and resolves all three. These three details are: the Golden door which Peter opens, the entrance to the sheepfold, and the entrance to the shearer's feast. All three are reflected in 'door' which thus becomes the inclusive image for salvation."

15. In his edition of *"Paradise Lost" and Selected Poetry and Prose* (New York, 1951), p. 581.

16. L. W. Coolidge, *PQ*, XXIX (1950), 444. Earlier C. W. Brodribb had interpreted Milton's engine as a sheephook in *TLS*, June 12, 1930, p. 496, and June 5, 1943, p. 271.

17. Perhaps there is a pun intended in the *locks* of 112 and the *keys* of 110, and we may recall the scissors as *engine* in *The Rape of the Lock.*

18. The parable of the marriage of the king's son, Matthew xxii, 1–14, provides a view of judgment and fellowship interestingly analogous to that developed here.

MILTON AND THE ANCIENTS
ON THE WRITING OF HISTORY

Irene Samuel

Milton's views on the writing of history develop from an early
acceptance of rhetorical commonplaces to independent judgments not only on how history should be written but on what
history is worth writing. This development was produced by
his experience as a historian and controversialist and by his
study of classical works, notably Lucian's satiric *How to Write
History*. He goes beyond the ancients—and his contemporaries
—in removing all "set speeches" from proper historiography;
he speaks with Lucianic bite on the fabulous in history; despite
his lifelong regard for Sallust, he repudiates Sallust's comment
that a nation depends for greatness on its historians. Ultimately
he applies a single standard to all mankind's doings, and concludes that nations get the historians they deserve. By the
time he rejects the suggestion that he write the story of his
own troubled times he has reached convictions like those
written into *Paradise Lost* on the worthlessness of recording
what does not merit praise.

FOR A writer who—whatever his purposes[1]—undertook two historical
works, the *History of Britain* and *A Brief History of Moscovia*, Milton has little to say of historiography.[2] In the planned curriculum of
his tractate *Of Education* he prescribes "choice histories" only for the
advanced course in literature along with "heroic poems, and Attic
tragedies of stateliest and most regal argument, with all the famous
political orations" (*Works*, Columbia edition, IV, 285—cited throughout by volume and page number). As for his teaching practice, Edward
Phillips gives no complete list of the works read under his uncle's tute-
lage, but it is astonishing that the one history Phillips names was evi-
dently studied less for its substance as history than as an introduction

to the Italian language: "Giovan Villani's History of the Transactions between several petty States of Italy" is paired with "Pierre Davity, the famous Geographer of France," who served as the introduction to French.[3] Yet Milton, for all his preference for poetry, philosophy, and theology, had enough interest in history to make some pungent comments on how it should be written. Indeed his scattered remarks on the writing of history furnish something like a paradigm of his developing views on rhetoric and poetics, as he moves from casual acceptance of academic commonplaces to his own independent verdict.

Classical rhetoric treated history either as a branch of epideictic oratory or under the division of *narratio*.[4] The persuasive effect on readers was to be the historian's primary concern in shaping his style. And young Milton at Cambridge had clearly assimilated the main lines of classical rhetoric when he opined in his Third Prolusion: "History, nobly ordered, now soothes and composes the restless agitation of the mind, now causes anointment with joy, anon it produces tears, but these gentle and quiet, which even though moist bring with them something of pleasure" (XII, 163). History is thus a part of literature, to be so ordered that it induces the pleasure of emotional response. Sir Philip Sidney had managed a clearer distinction between the two in his *Defense of Poesy*, starting from Aristotle's familiar dictum that poetry is more philosophical than history. He, to be sure, had measured the value of the discipline by the examples it furnishes; its examples failing to support precept, their truth has less cogency than the poet's feignings.

With his growing involvement in the affairs of his time Milton looked to history for something other than mental soothing. But his concern in the *Reason of Church-Government* is with what the historian may do for his country, debasing or ennobling its story in the eyes of mankind. He adapts to England the comment of Sallust on the recorded story of Rome:

The acts of the Athenians, in my judgment, were indeed great and glorious enough, but nevertheless somewhat less important than fame represents them. But because Athens produced writers of exceptional talent, the exploits of the men of Athens are heralded throughout the world as unsurpassed. Thus the merit of those who did the deeds is rated as high as brilliant minds have been able to exalt the deeds themselves by words of praise. But the Roman people never had that advantage.[5]

Milton writes: "if the Athenians, as some say, made their small deeds great and renowned by their eloquent writers, England hath had her noble achievements made small by the unskillful handling of monks and mechanics" (III, 237). History still owes its importance to the rhetorician's art, belongs to literature.

Yet his own study of history, as far back as his letter to Diodati dated September 23, 1637, concerned its substance. He gives an account of his progress: "I have by continuous reading brought down the affairs of the Greeks as far as to the time when they ceased to be Greeks. I have been long engaged in the obscure business of the state of Italians under the Longobards, the Franks, and the Germans, down to the time when liberty was granted them by Rodolph, King of Germany: from that period it will be better to read separately what each city did by its own wars" (XII, 29). And he asks to be sent "Justiniani, the historian of the Venetians" (ibid.). True, a year later, asking Buommattei's advice for his further reading in Italian, his phrasing again suggests that history is a branch of literature, along with tragedy, comedy, epistles, and dialogues, and that the requisite of its style is that it be "noble" (XII, 37).

Within twenty years his notions changed. The experience of using historical evidence in controversy as well as his own writing of history clarified his requirements. Two letters to Henry de Bras written in 1657 declare, along with his continued preference for Sallust as the best of the Roman historians, his later view on historiography. On July 15 he writes: "I prefer Sallust to any other Latin historian; which also was the almost uniform opinion of the Ancients" (XII, 93); and on December 16:

Respecting him I would venture to make the same assertion to you as Quintilian made respecting Cicero,—that a man may know himself no mean proficient in the business of History who enjoys his Sallust. (XII, 101)

In the earlier letter, as he explains the grounds of his preference, he reveals to what extent his view of the writing of history has remained under, to what extent shifted from, the influence of rhetoric:

You ask me, with reference to what he has said, in the introduction to his Catilinarian War—as to the extreme difficulty of writing History, from the obligation that the expressions should be proportional to the deeds—by what method I think a writer of History might attain that perfection. This, then, is my view: that he who would write of worthy deeds worthily must write with mental endowments and experience of affairs not less than were in the doers of the same, so as to be able with equal mind to comprehend and measure even the greatest of them, and, when he has comprehended them, to relate them distinctly and gravely in pure and chaste speech. That he should do so in ornate style, I do not much care about; for I want a Historian, not an Orator. Nor would I have frequent maxims [sententias], or criticisms [judicia] on the transactions, prolixly thrown in, lest, by interrupting the thread of events, the Historian should invade the office of the Political Writer: for, if the Historian, in explicating counsels and narrating facts, follows truth most of all, and not his own fancy or conjecture, he fulfils his proper duty. I would add also that characteristic of Sallust, in respect of which he himself chiefly praised Cato,[6]—to be able to throw off a great deal in few words: a thing which I think no one can do without the sharpest judgment and a certain temperance at the same time. There are many in whom you will not miss either elegance of style or abundance of information; but for conjunction of brevity with abundance, i.e., for the despatch of much in few words, the chief of the Latins, in my judgment, is Sallust. Such are the qualities [virtutes] that I think should be in the Historian that would hope to make his expressions proportional to the facts he records.　　　　　　　　　　　　　　　(XII, 93–95)

In fact, Sallust's remark demands less of the historian than Milton suggests; he says only: "And for myself, although I am well aware that by no means equal repute attends the narrator and the doer of a deed, yet I regard the writing of history as one of the most difficult of tasks: first, because the style and diction must be equal to the deeds recorded . . ." (The War with Catiline III, 2, tr. J. C. Rolfe). He requires only a style proportional to the deeds.

Milton's repudiation of the ornate style for history reads more like an explicit denial of the recommendation in Cicero's Orator xx, 66: "History involves a narrative in an ornate style, with here and there a description of a country or a battle. It has also occasional harangues and speeches of exhortation. But the aim is a smooth and flowing style, not the terse and vigorous language of the orator" (tr. H. M. Hubbell, Loeb Classical Library, 1939). It denies also the view he had earlier shared that history, like epideictic oratory, is to entertain its audience, who will be grateful for a style designed to please (Orator lxi, 207–08). Milton now favors the terse style for the historian. Except on that point he agrees with the opinions assigned to Antonius in Cicero's De Oratore: the first law for the historian is that

he tell the truth and the whole truth, using a chronological arrangement and giving some estimate of the plans, deeds, speeches, causes,
persons involved (see *De Oratore* II, xii, 51–xv, 64). Unlike Cicero's
Antonius, he now specifically warns against the historian's preempting
the role of political philosopher; he does not want *sententiae* and
judicia any more than fancies and conjectures,[7] but only the most accurate possible account. And here his taste for Sallust conflicts in a
measure with his enunciated standard; Sallust, highly sententious, fills
his work with maxims and pronounces judgments at every turn. It is
presumably his "conjunction of brevity with abundance" that Milton
commends when he praises him above Tacitus, whose greatest merit
to Milton's mind "is that he imitated Sallust with all his might" (XII,
93), and again when he makes a taste for Sallust a measure of the
reader's understanding of "the business of History" (XII, 101). Yet
surely Sallust's political philosophy, his staunch republicanism, was
what chiefly won him Milton's high praise. Not many years back Milton had coupled "grave orators and historians" in his *First Defense*
(VII, 39).

In his second letter to Henry de Bras Milton confirms what he has
said about the use of *sententiae* by the historian. To his young
friend's query about Aristotle's precept in *Rhetoric* III he replies:

As for that precept . . .—'Use is to be made of maxims both in the narrative
of a case and in the pleading, for it has a moral effect'—I see not what it
has in it that much needs explanation: only that the narration and the
pleading (which last is usually also called the proof) are here understood
to be such as the Orator uses, not the Historian; for the parts of the Orator
and the Historian are different whether they narrate or prove, just as the
Arts themselves are different. What is suitable for the historian you will
have learnt more correctly from the ancient authors, Polybius, the Hali-
carnassian, Diodorus, Cicero, Lucian, and many others, who have handed
down certain stray precepts concerning that subject.   (XII, 101–03)

To turn to the ancient authors whom Milton names for their precepts on the writing of history may suggest how far he has in fact
struck out a new vein. The reference to Cicero may be to *Brutus* lxxv,
262: "in history there is nothing more pleasing than brevity clear and
correct," or to the *Orator* xxxvi, 124, which distinguishes the style of
narratio from that of history: "The narrative will be credible, clearly
expressed, not in the style of history but almost in the tone of everyday

conversation." Clearly, in Cicero's view,[8] the historian is to aim at loftiness as well as succinctness and clarity. But essentially Milton is repudiating rhetorical precepts for the writing of history. His reference to Dionysius of Halicarnassus is probably to two assertions in *The Roman Antiquities*: "we do not deem it fitting that the histories of renowned cities and of men who have held supreme power should be written in an offhand or negligent manner" (I, i, 4, tr. Earnest Cary, 1937); and "truth and justice . . . ought to be the aim of every history" (I, vi, 5). The absence of reference to the practice of Herodotus and Thucydides, highly praised for their style in Dionysius' work *On Literary Composition* (22, 24), suggests that Milton's concern here is less with style itself than with the method appropriate to the historian. And hence it is less from rhetoricians than from historians that the passage derives.

Polybius is certainly one of Milton's chief sources;[9] for although he is himself occasionally sententious, his "stray precepts" on the historian's duties and functions consistently argue against an epideictic use of maxims, narrative, and proof. He opens his *Histories* by agreeing with "previous chroniclers" that "there is no more ready corrective of conduct than knowledge of the past" and that "the surest and indeed the only method of learning how to bear bravely the vicissitudes of fortune is to recall the calamities of others" (I, 1, 1–2, tr. W. R. Paton, Loeb, 1922). But as he proceeds, his insistence that the historian must not be a partisan (I, 14, 1–9), that he must not invent material in order to make his narrative sensational (II, 8, 10–11), that his concern must be with the causes of what happened (III, 7, 5), with facts, and not with who reports them (III, 9, 3), that he must so far as possible himself examine the scene of events and compare the testimony of living witnesses (III, 33, 17–18; 48, 12), not merely repeat hearsay evidence (IV, 2, 3–4)—his insistence on all these matters relegates moral effects to a minor role in his work. True, the "vicissitudes of fortune" provide a recurrent theme. And his statement of plan even suggests a concern with literary unity: "The subject I have undertaken to treat, the how, when, and wherefore of the subjection of the known parts of the world to the dominion of Rome, should be viewed as a single whole, with a recognized beginning, a fixed duration, and an end which is not a matter of dispute . . ." (III, 1, 4–5; cf. Aristotle, *Poetics* VII, on unity of plot in tragedy and Plato, *Phaedrus* 264c, on unity in a discourse). But even if his purpose was rather, as restated in the fragment from the Preface to Book VI, "that readers of my work may gain a knowledge of how it was and by virtue of what peculiar political institutions that in less than fifty-three years nearly the whole world was overcome and fell under the single dominion of Rome" (VI, I, 2, 3), he avoided the pitfalls common to historians with a theory to demonstrate. He may have believed that the constitutions of states determine their success and failure (VI, I, 2, 8–9), but his work shows rather his effort to achieve certainty in his judgments and assertions (IV, 2, 3–4). Given that primary concern to avoid falsifying the facts, his comments on the inventions of other historians have added weight.

Close to Milton's view of the distinction between oratory and history is Polybius' condemnation of the historian Timaeus for "having made up his mind as to what ought to have been said" and then composed "public speeches, harangues to soldiers, discourses of ambassadors," and the like as if he were "a man in a school of rhetoric attempting to speak on a given subject" so that he "shows off his oratorical power, but gives no report of what was actually said" (XII, fragment VI, 25a, 1–5). So again he condemns Zeno "because he is not for the most part so much concerned with inquiry into facts and proper treatment of his materials, as with elegance of style . . ." (XVI, fragment II, 17, 9; cf. 18, 1–3). He recurs to the theme when he urges the historian to take due precautions, studying and comparing documents, examining the scene of events for himself, reviewing the course of political developments, and consulting living witnesses, "the most important part of history" (XII, fragment VI, 25c, 1–7, 27), lest he merely produce "false rhetorical exercizes" (25b, 5).[10] Closer still to Milton's requirement for the adequate historian is his adaptation of the famous "great wave" of Plato's *Republic* on philosophers and kings to the relation between the making and writing of history:

I would say that it will be well with history either when men of action undertake to write history, not as now happens in a perfunctory manner, but when in the belief that this is a most necessary and most noble thing they apply themselves all through their life to it with undivided attention, or again when would-be authors regard a training in actual affairs as necessary for writing history.   (XII, fragment VI, 28)

Here is a parallel not only to Milton's assertion in the letter to de Bras on the historian "who would write of worthy deeds worthily" but to his earlier assertion in the *Apology for Smectymnuus* on the poet who ought "not presum[e] to sing high praises of heroic men or famous cities unless he have in himself the experience and practice of all that which is praiseworthy" (III, 304).

Diodorus Siculus in his *Library of History* similarly combines a large didactic purpose with a sense of the scrupulousness with which history should be written and a contempt for those who confuse it with rhetorical display. As C. H. Oldfather writes in the introduction to his edition and translation (Loeb, 1933), "More often than any extant ancient historian Diodorus stresses the view that history should instruct in the good life"(p. xx). The whole eulogy of history with which Diodorus begins (I, 1–2) reaches its climax when he declares: "it is ever to be seen urging men to justice, denouncing those who are evil, lauding the good, laying up, in a word, for its readers a mighty store of experience" (I, 2, 8). And Diodorus does not declare more than he performs: he deliberately appends passages of praise and blame (as in XI, 46 and XV, 88). Yet he is equally concerned to avoid turning history into a species of epideictic oratory. In Book XX, he writes a long passage censuring "those who in their histories insert over-long orations or employ frequent speeches": they merely disrupt the narrative and lose the reader's interest; they would do better if they "wish to display rhetorical powers to compose by themselves public discourses and speeches for ambassadors" or perhaps "orations of praise and blame and the like." The literary kinds ought to be kept distinct. Instead, "writers by excessive use of rhetorical passages have made the whole art of history an appendage of oratory" (XX, 1, 1–3, tr. Russel M. Greer, Loeb).

Diodorus too applies the Platonic–Aristotelian doctrine of unity to history: "the genius of history is simple and self-consistent and as a whole is like a living organism" (XX, 1, 5); to confuse it with the genius of oratory is to lose the proper charm of each. Yet Diodorus does not entirely ban either speeches of the historian's composition, since "history needs to be adorned with variety," or the aid of rhetoric in composing such speeches. He too is unwilling "when the subject matter is great and glorious" that "the language appear inferior to the deeds" (XX, 2, 1–2). Diodorus' "stray precepts" thus confirm Polybius' and support Milton's contention, in the second letter to de

Bras, that history is not a branch of oratory, as well as his requirement, in the first, that the worthy subject be given worthy treatment. He does not come as close as Polybius to Milton's view that only the man of worth can write history properly.

But, unquestionably, it was less the "stray precepts" of Polybius and Diodorus Siculus than the wit and wisdom of Lucian in *How to Write History* that stayed with Milton and helped determine his standards for the historian. The whole amusing account of everyone turning historian and of the absurdities to which they sink, together with the precepts on what to avoid, what to aim at, shows just the combination of good sense with astringent criticism of folly that delighted Milton. Back in *Animadversions* he had alluded to a passage in this work of Lucian's to mock his adversaries as "like that doughty centurion Afranius in Lucian" (III, 141; see *How to Write History,* 26). The detail with which he there applied the reference shows how he relished the passage. His own mockery of opponents is often Lucianic in tone and technique. And, as we shall see in his *History of Britain,* he has an amused contempt for the fabulous and fanciful equal to Lucian's own.

The precepts of *How to Write History* are easily summarized, and the resemblance to Milton's will be apparent. (The tone and the illustrations make the essay vastly different, of course, from what such a summary suggests.) But if Milton had not been concentrating on the virtues of Sallust, we may surmise that he would simply have told young Henry de Bras if he wanted to know how history should be written he need only go and reread Lucian.

The first fault of historians that Lucian names is that instead of recording events they turn flatterer, praising their own side and slandering the enemy, forgetful that "the dividing line between history and panegyric is . . . a mighty wall," since history "cannot admit a lie" (7). History is unlike poetry too, since the poet, "inspired and possessed by the Muses," may say what he will, whereas the historian must tell the truth and not indulge in "a sort of prose-poetry" or use myths, eulogies, exaggerations (8). History has only one end: the utility of truth; it may not aim at giving pleasure except as an adequate presentation of truth is pleasing (9–13). A variety of errors in arrangement, proportion, use of models, diction is possible; but none of these is so bad as downright errors of fact, especially avoidable errors (14–33).

The good historian starts with two gifts, "political understanding and power of expression," the first of which can come from nature alone, the second from practice, effort, and imitating the ancient models; and while advice cannot replace natural gifts, it can show the naturally gifted what to aim at (34–36). The would-be historian should be "one who could handle affairs if they were turned over to him" (37), independent-minded, fearless, incorruptible, impartial, outspoken (38–41). His aim in writing should be exactness and lucidity, his diction neither highflown nor vulgar (43–44). Poetical touches he must reserve for passages that warrant them, prudence rather than enthusiasm determining their use (45). Accuracy in collecting the facts, impartiality in judging what is credible, orderliness in following a chronological sequence—these must be his aim (47–49), and a mind like a clear mirror that reflects without distorting (50). Unlike the orator, he must let the facts speak for themselves, content to arrange and explain them so that their pattern comes clear (51). He will therefore use a preface proportionate to the subject he treats, to clarify what is to come, not as the orator does to win his hearers (52); in his narrative he will aim at a smooth consistent continuity, proportioning his treatment to the importance of the matter (53–56), avoiding long descriptive passages that merely display eloquence, preferring rapidity to prolixity (57). If he must introduce a speech, he may play the orator a little but should always keep the invented discourse appropriate to the person and the occasion (58). Passages of praise and blame should be brief, just, and based on evidence (59). If fabulous matter gets involved, the wise historian will relate it, but not as though he believed it (60). Above all he will bear in mind the great rule that posterity determines: posterity will favor the impartiality of truthfulness (61–63).

In his insistence on the distinction of the historian from the orator as well as the poet, on the style proportionate to the matter, on the statesmanlike nature of the fit historian, and on rapidity, clarity, accuracy as the virtues of his style, Lucian comes closest of the ancients Milton names to the positions Milton takes. His emphasis on independence and outspokenness is like Milton's in the narrative passages of his controversial prose and in his attacks on the distorted *narratio* of his opponents. On impartiality and detachment, controversy, naturally enough, permitted Milton to say nothing. Political disputes hardly permit discussion of all the virtues of the historian. Still, within the limits set by controversy Milton applies standards like those of Lucian for history. *Eikonoklastes* and the *First Defense* are especially rich in their use of the topics suggested by what historical narrative should be: Milton belabors the *narratio* of his adversary as a tissue of fictions, absurdities, interrupted and repetitious discontinuities, and pseudo-oratorical irrelevances.

Whatever lingering tolerance for oratorical effects in history Milton's earlier experience with *narratio* as a source of arguments may have left him, the experience of writing history finally removed. Presumably he came to his work on *The History of Britain* still prepared to find in England's distant past matter for epic and tragic poems. He not only had once thought the legends of Arthur and his knights likely subjects (*Mansus* 81–83); he had noted in his *Commonplace Book* (XVIII, 241–45) a variety of matters for possible treatment from British and Scottish story. The effort to compile a rational history from the sources at his disposal was surely among the many experiences that changed his mind.

He sets out bravely enough to deal with the fabulous, giving as grounds for its inclusion that it may have some vestige of truth and, perhaps more important, that it may prove useful to literature:

Nevertheless there being others besides the first supposed author, men not unread nor unlearned in antiquity,[11] who admit that for approved story which the former explode for fiction, and seeing that ofttimes relations heretofore accounted fabulous have been after found to contain in them many footsteps and relics of something true, . . . I have therefore determined to bestow the telling over even of these reputed tales—be it for nothing else but in favor of our English poets and rhetoricians, who by their art will know how to use them judiciously.   (X, 2–3)

The suggestion that poetry and oratory may find an appropriate use for such materials marks a shift from his earlier view of history as itself a branch of literature and suggests his later strictures on the historian's not confusing himself with the orator. Now the historian may serve orator and poet by reporting what he doubts the historicity of. He must, of course, label it dubious.

So Milton speaks his doubts as he compiles his history. Yet sometimes he includes dubious matter rather as occasion for pungent comment than because it may prove of service to poets and orators. He could hardly have expected to contribute to either group when he remarks on

twenty kings in a continued row that either did nothing or lived in ages that wrote nothing, at least a foul pretermission in the author of this, whether story or fable, himself weary, as seems, of his own tedious tale.
    But to make amends for this silence, Blegabradus, next succeeding, is recorded to have excelled all before him in the art of music—opportunely, had he but left us one song of his twenty predecessors' doings.   (X, 29)

And on the legends of Arthur, whose "wars beneath the earth" along with "the magnanimous heroes of the table" the young Milton had hoped to sing (*Mansus* 81–83, tr. Hughes), he comments scathingly:

Arthur . . . made great war, but more renowned in songs and romances than in true stories.   (X, 123)

And further:

he who can accept of legends for good story may quickly swell a volume with trash and had need be furnished with two only necessaries, leisure and belief, whether it be the writer or he that shall read.   (X, 128)

Of the various achievements attributed to Arthur he asks:

When should this be done? From the Saxons till after twelve battles, he had no rest at home.   (X, 131)

    On the whole, he apparently decides, not even poets and orators will find value in much of these materials. And after pronouncing William of Malmesbury the best for "style and judgment" of the writers he has had to peruse, he names another purpose for his own work:

what labor is to be endured turning over volumes of rubbish in the rest . . . is a penance to think. Yet these are our only registers, transcribers one after another for the most part, and sometimes worthy enough for the things they register. This travail, rather than not know at once what may be known of our ancient story, sifted from fables and impertinences, I voluntarily undergo, and to save others, if they please, the like unpleasing labor, except those who take pleasure to be all their lifetime raking the foundations of old abbeys and cathedrals.   (X, 180)

Of antiquarian zeal Milton shows no trace. Not that he is unwilling to search out facts, but the labor of the search and the sense of meeting alien ways give him no delight. His remark recalls Sir Philip Sidney's in *The Defense of Poesy* on the historian,

laden with old mouse-eaten records, authorizing himself for the most part upon other histories, whose greatest authorities are built upon the notable foundation of hearsay, having much ado to accord differing writers and to pick truth out of partiality, better acquainted with a thousand years ago than with the present age . . . , curious of antiquities and inquisitive of novelties.

Mere antiquities appeal little to the poet whose concern is, as Sidney's and Milton's was, with the exemplary and doctrinal.

One decision that Milton arrived at in working on *The History of Britain* reverses a habit of all ancient historians, including his favorites, and a doctrine of ancient rhetoricians and historians on the art of writing history, including those he names in his letter to de Bras:

I affect not set speeches in history, unless known for certain to have been so spoken in effect as they are written, nor then unless with rehearsal; and to invent such, though eloquently, as some historians have done, is an abuse of posterity, raising in them that read other conceptions of those times and persons than were true. Much less therefore do I purpose here or elsewhere to copy out tedious orations without decorum, though in their authors composed ready to my hand.   (X, 68)

Even Lucian allowed rhetoric to aid the historian when he had to compose a speech for one of the persons involved in events, reminding him only to keep it appropriate to both person and subject (*How to Write History*, 58). But Milton has gone beyond Lucian and all other ancient historiographers in his demand for factual truth.

He has gone indeed beyond the practice of historians of the Renaissance too. Machiavelli, from whose *Discorsi* on Livy Milton quotes many passages in his *Commonplace Book*, permitted himself considerable leeway in inventing speeches, as Allan Gilbert remarks in an introductory note to his translation of *The History of Florence*:

Avowedly fictitious are the frequent orations in the Thucydidean manner of the Florentine historians before Machiavelli. These are developed beyond dramatic requirements into expositions of social and political truths suggested by Florentine events. (*The Chief Works and Others*, III, 1027)

Thucydides himself had of course justified the practice:

It was difficult for me to recall precisely what was said in the speeches which I heard myself, and difficult for my informants from elsewhere; but I have represented each speaker as presenting, on a given issue, the case which I thought him most likely to have presented, while keeping as close as I could to the argument, as a whole, of what was actually said.

(*Thucydides*, i, 22, 1, tr. K. J. Dover [Oxford, 1965])

And the practice can be further justified by a variety of arguments, some of which K. J. Dover elaborates in his introduction (p. xi). Mrs. Raina Fehl, who has given thought to the matter, writes me: "Events in war are, if anything, less predictable than others, accidental, and in that sense of secondary importance. Secondly, in the mind of a person who attaches moral responsibility to utterances, particularly public utterances, what a man said is an important index of the meaning of affairs. Such speeches are not ornament at all then. They are rather essential—or would be if they were indeed the speeches made by the speakers."[12]

But Milton, for all his familiarity with the practice and presumably with its grounds, will have none of it. History is not to seek the aid of rhetoric in the invention and arrangement of its materials, nor to claim a greater validity by thus inventing and arranging instead of reporting fact. Even setting apart "tedious orations without decorum," he puts his finger on the precise error of the most eloquent and appropriate of such invented speeches: they mislead as they suggest misconceptions of the times and persons they are supposedly reporting, and thus "abuse . . . posterity." The appeal to posterity, though on a different ground, again recalls Lucian.

On one major point the experience of working on *The History of Britain* completely reversed Milton's earlier agreement with ancient historians and rhetoricians. Now the stylistic art that rhetoric teaches cannot, to his mind, determine how well a nation's history fares in the opinion of mankind. In the *Reason of Church-Government* he had adapted Sallust's words to lament that "England hath had her noble achievements made small by the unskillful handling of monks and mechanics" (III, 237). Now he doubts that there can be a discrepancy between the achievements and the handling.

For worthy deeds are not often destitute of worthy relaters, as by a certain fate great acts and great eloquence have most commonly gone hand in hand, equalling and honoring each other in the same ages. 'Tis true that in obscurest times by shallow and unskillful writers the indistinct noise of many battles and devastations, of many kingdoms overrun and lost, hath come to our ears. . . . But he whose just and true valor uses the necessity of war and dominion not to destroy but to prevent destruction, to bring in liberty against tyrants, law and civility among barbarous nations, knowing that when he conquers all things else he cannot conquer time or detraction, wisely conscious of this his want as well as of his worth not to be forgotten or concealed, honors and hath recourse to the aid of eloquence, his friend-liest and best ally; by whose immortal record his noble deeds, which else were transitory, becoming fixed and durable against the force of years and generations, he fails not to continue through all posterity over envy, death, and time also victorious. Therefore when the esteem of science and liberal study waxes low in the commonwealth we may presume that also there all civil virtue and worthy action is grown as low to a decline; and then eloquence, as it were consorted in the same destiny, with the decrease and fall of virtue corrupts also and fades, at least resigns her office of re-lating to illiterate and frivolous historians such as the persons themselves both deserve and are best pleased with, whilst they want either the under-standing to choose better or the innocence to dare invite the examining and searching style of an intelligent and faithful writer to the survey of their unsound exploits, better befriended by obscurity than fame.   (X, 32–33)

A civilization gets the historians it deserves. All its aspects are so interrelated that the deeds probably had no more nobility, no more meaningful idea in them, than the words in which they have been chronicled. Thus where the historians are "illiterate and frivolous" we may draw the inference that what they have recorded would scarcely have interested "an intelligent and faithful writer"—if indeed the times could have produced any.

He recurs to the thesis when he writes of the fall of Rome:

And with the Empire fell also what before in this Western World was chiefly Roman: Learning, Valour, Eloquence, History, Civility, and even Language itself, all these together, as it were, with equal pace diminishing, and decaying.   (*History of Britain*, X, 101)

Thus Milton arrives at a principle of historiography wholly different from his casual acceptance as an undergraduate of rhetorical common-places about the writing of history. Out of his large knowledge of ancient historians he evolved his own standard. Then out of larger knowledge, won from the task of historical composition, he moved from agreement with a favorite historian's view of the role a writer can play in dignifying his country's achievements to emphatic denial. Things are as they are, and the historian cannot give factitious importance to what was not itself noble.[13] An era capable of truly glorious deeds will produce men adequate to their narration. Obviously what has happened is that Milton has given searching examination to deeds supposedly glorious—and found them merely so many battles, so many devastations, so many kingdoms overrun and lost. It is the poet of *Paradise Lost* speaking his comment on what the world calls great, "not that which justly gives heroic name to person"—or to nation. The standards by which he had come to judge all the varied phenomena of the scene about him became the standards too for judging mankind's long story. Poet, historian, and man agree in Milton. In a letter dated December 20, 1659, he comments to Henry Oldenburgh:

Of any such work as compiling the history of our political troubles, which you seem to advise, I have no thought whatever: they are worthier of silence than of commemoration. What is needed is not one to compile a good history of our troubles, but one who can happily end the troubles themselves.   (XII, 109)

And in *Paradise Lost* Raphael, instead of commemorating the rebel angels, declares of them:

> In might though wondrous and in acts of war,
> Nor of renown less eager, yet by doom
> Cancell'd from Heaven and sacred memory,
> Nameless in dark oblivion let them dwell.
> For strength from truth divided and from just,
> Illaudable, naught merits but dispraise
> And ignominy.   (VI, 377–83)

Men and events, feigned and actual, must meet the same Miltonic test: *Paradise Lost* proceeds to commemorate not the troubles of the war in Heaven, but the Son, who happily brings them to an end.

Hunter College

NOTES

1. Cf. George Parks, "The Occasion of Milton's *Moscovia*," *SP*, XL (1943), 399–404, and J. A. Bryant, Jr., "Milton and the Art of History: A Study of Two Influences on *A Brief History of Moscovia*," *PQ*, XXIX (1950), 15–30, on Milton's purposes in that work. And cf. Mark Pattison, *Milton* (New York, 1879), p. 158; J. H. Hanford, *A Milton Handbook*, 4th ed. (New York, 1946), pp. 115–16; J. M.

French, "Milton as a Historian," *PMLA*, L (1935), 469–79; Sir Charles Firth, "Milton as an Historian," *Essays Historical and Literary* (Oxford, 1938), pp. 61–102; and French R. Fogle, "Milton as Historian," in Fogle and H. R. Trevor-Roper, *Milton and Clarendon* (Los Angeles, 1965), pp. 1–20, on Milton's purposes in his *History of Britain*.

2. Fogle surely exaggerates in suggesting that Milton was more concerned with the art than with the content of history (p. 11); Firth deals better with Milton's sense of how to weigh evidence and reach independent conclusions (p. 83). Both, I think, distort Milton's way of thinking, Fogle when he concludes that the intention of the *History of Britain* is to "establish a meaningful relationship between time and eternity" (p. 18), Firth when he observes, "Poet or historian, Milton was ever a preacher" (p. 100).

3. *The Early Lives of Milton*, ed. Helen Darbishire (London, 1932), p. 61.

4. See, e.g., Cicero, *Orator* xi, 37–xii, 39, and the *Rhetorica ad Herennium* I, ix, 14–16 for typical discussions.

5. *The War with Catiline* VIII, 2–5, tr. J. C. Rolfe (Loeb). Sallust's position is the opposite of what Plutarch says: "if you take away the men of action you will have no men of letters" and "if it be unworthy to compare painters with generals, let us not compare historians either" ("On the Fame of the Athenians," *Moralia*, tr. F. C. Babbitt, Loeb IV, pp. 493, 503). As Babbitt suggests in his introduction, p. 491, Plutarch may not be serious in the work.

6. Cf. Cicero on Cato in *Brutus* xvi, 63–xviii, 69, and note the praise of Caesar's *Commentaries* on like ground, lxxv, 262.

7. Firth notes the contradiction of Milton's practice in his *History of Britain* (p. 87 ff).

8. Cf. *Orator* ix, 30–32 and *Brutus* lxxxiii, 287 on Thucydides' style as excellent for a historian, but not—even in the speeches he introduces—for an orator.

9. Here I agree with Fogle, p. 6, rather than Bryant, pp. 22–23.

10. The recent study of the question by F. W. Walbank, *Speeches in Greek Historians* (Oxford, 1967), concludes that Polybius himself does not invent speeches for the persons in his history, but uses the convention that goes back to Thucydides of shaping material, keeping essentially what was in fact said but improving its form. Walbank notes that the convention remained in favor with historians into the seventeenth century. The classic statement in Thucydides 1, 22, 1 is discussed by K. J. Dover in the introduction to his translation (Oxford, 1965), p. xi.

11. The first edition has "antiquit*ie*"; the Columbia edition gives the plural "antiquities." I have in using the Columbia edition checked the passages I quote against the first edition, normalized spellings and punctuation, but given references to the Columbia edition for the reader's convenience in locating passages.

12. From a note written in April 1967, to which I am also indebted for the references to Dover's comment and the passages in Plutarch cited above and below.

13. Milton's position here differs also from Plutarch's:

And indeed the compilers of histories are, as it were, reporters of great exploits who are gifted with the faculty of felicitous speech, and achieve success in their writing through the beauty and force of their narration; and to them those who first encountered and recorded the events are indebted for a pleasing retelling of them. We may be sure that such writers are lauded also merely through being remembered and read because of the men who won success; for the words do not create the deeds, but because of the deeds they are also deemed worthy of being read. ("On the Fame of the Athenians," *Moralia,* tr. F. C. Babbitt, Loeb, IV, 505)

In Milton's view the same spirit creates deeds and words.

VOCATION AND SPIRITUAL RENOVATION IN *SAMSON AGONISTES*

John S. Hill

Samson Agonistes deals with the spiritual education of a Christian "hero" and his development from a self-motivated agent operating on what he presumes to be the will of God to a humbled instrument of that divine will. The real meaning of Samson's regeneration is seen in his resolution of the tension between prophecy (he is God's chosen champion) and fact (he is a blind Philistian bondslave). As the poem opens, Samson is guilty of three sins—pride, presumption, doubt—which obscure his divinely ordained vocation. In the course of the poem, Samson learns that humility, patience, and faith are necessary to his divine mission. These three virtues are the spiritual antidotes to the three sins of which he has been guilty, and enable Samson to be readmitted to the active service of his God. "True experience" and an understanding of God's ways to men are achieved by Samson in the first four movements of the poem (lines 1–1440); the fifth and final movement (lines 1441–1758) educates Manoa, the Chorus, and the reader in these same virtues.

THE MOST remarkable aspect of Milton's *Samson Agonistes* is its internalization of the action. Samson's movement back to God, his recovery of his own lost paradise, is recorded, not in terms of his external actions, but rather in terms of his progressively more acute spiritual awareness. It is in the spiritual movement of the poem that the Aristotelian "middle," which Dr. Johnson found wanting in *Samson Agonistes,* is to be found.[1] Indeed, as A. E. Barker has somewhat facetiously noted (in a reversal of Dr. Johnson's charge): "Samson's experience is so far from having no middle that it is in effect all middle."[2]

Almost without exception, recent commentators have read *Samson Agonistes* as a study in regeneration. But this sort of reading must be seen as an aspect of a larger whole: Samson's fulfilment of his divinely predicted vocation. It is in the resolution of the tension between prophecy and fact, between Samson's promised vocation as God's champion and Israel's deliverer and his actual position as a Philistian bondslave, that the true meaning of Samson's inward and spiritual growth, his regeneration, must ultimately be seen. I would not deny the importance of the "despair" and "patience" motifs, nor of the "reason-passion" dichotomy,[3] but would stress the fact that these themes are included in a larger thematic whole: the spiritual education of a Christian "hero" and his development from a self-motivated agent operating on what he presumes to be the will of God to a humbled instrument of that divine will.

Samson and the Chorus: Lines 1–325

At the beginning of *Samson Agonistes*, the reader learns from Samson's own mouth of his current situation and his initial state of mind. Led from the confines of the Philistian prison, he bemoans the fact that, although the cessation of labor afforded by the feast in Dagon's honor may grant some ease and rest to his body, it allows none to his mind, which is the more assailed by "restless thoughts" that

> like a deadly swarm
> Of Hornets arm'd, no sooner found alone,
> But rush upon me thronging, and present
> Times past, what once I was, and what am now.
> O wherefore was my birth from Heaven foretold
> Twice by an Angel, who at last in sight
> Of both my Parents all in flames ascended
> From off the Altar, where an Off'ring burn'd,
> As in a fiery column charioting
> His Godlike presence, and from some great act
> Or benefit reveal'd to *Abraham's* race?
> Why was my breeding order'd and prescrib'd
> As of a person separate to God,
> Design'd for great exploits; if I must dye
> Betray'd, Captiv'd, and both my Eyes put out,
> Made of my Enemies the scorn and gaze;
> To grind in Brazen Fetters under task
> With this Heav'n-gifted strength? O glorious strength

> Put to the labour of a Beast, debas't
> Lower then bondslave! Promise was that I
> Should *Israel* from *Philistian* yoke deliver;
> Ask for this great Deliverer now, and find him
> Eyeless in *Gaza* at the Mill with slaves,
> Himself in bonds under *Philistian* yoke.   (19–42)[4]

I have quoted this passage at length since it contains the initial formulation of Samson's problem, a problem which will be resolved only after he has undergone the necessary educative and regenerative process. The Samson whom the reader encounters in this opening speech is indeed a tragic figure: he is blind, worn by the "servile toil" which the Philistines exact from him, and mocked by his enemies. Yet, it is with moving words that he bewails his loss of sight and speaks of "all the miseries of life, / Life in captivity / Among inhuman foes." And it is with a noble sort of self-pity that he bemoans the fact that his "glorious strength" is "put to the labour of a Beast, debas't / Lower then bondslave." If *Samson Agonistes* were a "classical" tragedy, if it were capable of being judged solely on the tragic principles laid down by Aristotle in the *Poetics,* then one would say that Milton has successfully excited the reader's "pity" and "fear" in presenting a man who is neither unusually good nor unusually evil, a man of eminence who, through wilfulness or some error of judgment, suffers disproportionately for his sin. However, *Samson Agonistes* is not a "classical" tragedy.

It is true that Samson is guilty of an error of judgment: in a moment of weakness he "gave up [his] fort of silence to a Woman" and so, almost unconsciously, betrayed his God. In Aristotelian terms, it is certainly true to say that Samson—blind, imprisoned, and scorned by his captors—suffers disproportionately for having broken the arbitrary command that he guard in secrecy the source of his strength. However, it is not the act itself which is important; it is the state of mind which permitted Samson to break this arbitrary command with which Milton is concerned. It is, as Gossman has observed, "not the act itself, but the agent's state of mind" which "marks the act as sinful."[5] In yielding to his carnal desires and (consequently) in betraying the secret of his strength, Samson has unwittingly "set God behind," which action, as he later realizes, "shall never, unrepented, find forgiveness." In spite of the noble self-pity that he manifests in the face of adversity,

Samson suffers proportionately for his sin; and his anguish, like his sin, is more significant because it is prompted by essentially internal rather than external considerations: he finds some ease from his physical afflictions, but none from the "restless thoughts" that continually rush upon him "and present / Times past, what once I was, and what am now."

Milton's Samson is more than a fallen Hercules or Prometheus, more than a tragic image of despoiled strength; he is spiritually dead. This form of death, as Milton explains in the *De Doctrina Christiana*, is characterized by "the loss of divine grace, and that of innate righteousness, wherein man in the beginning lived unto God."[6] Not only is Samson spiritually dead, but he realizes that he is, that spiritually as well as physically he has fallen from his former preeminent height. This awareness of his spiritual degeneration is capable of producing in the protagonist effects which are diametrically opposed.

Samson knows only too well that he alone is responsible for his loss of "innate goodness" and for the present evils—blindness and imprisonment—by which he is beset. Prompted by this sense of personal responsibility and guilt, he bewails the lack of wisdom which caused him to betray the secret of his God and resulted in the loss of divine favor:

> O impotence of mind, in body strong!
> But what is strength without a double share
> Of wisdom, vast, unwieldy, burdensom,
> Proudly secure, yet liable to fall
> By weakest suttleties, not made to rule,
> But to subserve where wisdom bears command.   (52–57)

The significance of Samson's conviction of his own responsibility is readily apparent when it is seen in connection with Milton's discussion of renovation and regeneration in the *De Doctrina Christiana*. In this work, Milton notes that those who are, by the work of God, delivered from a state of spiritual death are said to be regenerated or created anew. The effects of regeneration are repentance and faith; and, he continues,

we may distinguish certain progressive steps in repentance; namely, conviction of sin, contrition, departure from evil, conversion to good.[7]

Samson's recognition of error, his "conviction of sin," is the first of these "progressive steps" toward repentance. Nevertheless, in this first movement of the poem, one must avoid confusing remorse with repentance. At this point, although it is a step in the right direction, Samson's sense of guilt is too self-oriented to be true repentance; while he freely acknowledges his error, he gauges its effect more in physical—blindness and imprisonment—than in spiritual terms. In any case, Samson's "conviction of sin" provides the starting point of his gradual return to God.

If Samson's sense of guilt is the first step on his road to recovery, then, conversely, his sense of alienation from divine favor, nurtured by doubts concerning his divinely ordained vocation as Israel's deliverer, leads him to the very brink of the chasm of despair. It is as "one past hope," as one wallowing hopelessly in the Slough of Despond, that the Chorus first describes the fallen Nazarite:

> See how he lies at random, carelessly diffus'd,
> With languish't head unpropt,
> As one past hope, abandon'd,
> And by himself given over.   (117–21)

Despair, it will be remembered, is a sin for which no forgiveness is possible. The mortal sin of *tristitia*, when man succumbs to it, puts him at the furthest remove from God, and is, as Milton notes, a sin which "takes place only in the reprobate."[8] If Samson despairs—and at the beginning of the poem he is tempted to do just that—he nullifies that first step toward repentance which he had made in recognizing his guilt and, what is worse, effectively extinguishes any chance of spiritual renovation.

"The principal purpose of this mainly expository first Act is, then," writes A. S. P. Woodhouse, "to underline Samson's remorse (not yet repentance) and his religious despair: to give us the starting point of the movement back to God—and on to the catastrophe."[9] Is this, however, all that Milton achieves in the first movement of the poem? I would agree with Woodhouse (and a number of other critics) that Samson's remorse and his temptation to despair are, indeed, important elements in the first section of the poem. Nevertheless, as I suggested earlier, these aspects of Samson's initial state of mind must ultimately be referred to, and judged in terms of, a greater whole: Samson's fulfilment of his divinely ordained vocation which finds expression in the unresolved tension between prophecy and fact.

The first step toward the solution of this problem is, of course, Samson's realization that he has, through sin, failed in his role as deliverer; this is his "conviction of sin." However, this sin is far more complex than critics have generally assumed; and, in this connection, there is an almost universally ignored passage in *Samson Agonistes* which merits examination. The passage in question occurs as Samson is relating to the Chorus the tale of his two unions with Philistian women:

> The first I saw at *Timna,* and she pleas'd
> Mee, not my Parents, that I sought to wed,
> The daughter of an Infidel: they knew not
> That what I motion'd was of God; I knew
> From intimate impulse, and therefore urg'd
> The Marriage on; that by occasion hence
> I might begin *Israel's* Deliverance,
> The work to which I was divinely call'd;
> She proving false, the next I took to Wife
> (O that I never had! fond wish too late)
> Was in the Vale of *Sorec, Dalila,*
> That specious Monster, my accomplisht snare.
> *I thought it lawful from my former act,*
> *And the same end: still watching to oppress*
> *Israel's oppressours:* of what now I suffer
> She was not the prime cause, but I my self,
> Who vanquisht with a peal of words (O weakness!)
> Gave up my fort of silence to a Woman.
>
> (219–36; emphasis mine)

Critics of the poem have, for the most part, taken it for granted that Samson's *hamartia* was pride, or *hubris.* Pride, they have maintained, accounts for Samson's fall from grace and, to illustrate their point, they have invariably cited Samson's words to this effect in the second movement of the poem.[10] However, in the passage cited above, Milton suggests that there is another sin of which Samson is guilty—the sin of presumption.

Samson tells us that his marriage to the woman of Timnath, although it necessitated his transgressing ceremonial and Nazaritic law, was prompted by God. For this reason, Samson "urg'd / The Marriage on," in order that he "might begin *Israel's* Deliverance, / The Work to which [he] was divinely call'd." However, the marriage to Dalila, through which he sought to continue his harassment of the Philistines and to further the work of his promised vocation, was *not* "motion'd" by God; it was an action undertaken by Samson alone ("I thought it lawful from my former act, / And the same end"), an action not sanctioned by God. In marrying the woman of Timnath, Samson had transgressed the law out of respect to the will of the Lawgiver, for God, although He made the law, is not bound by it and, consequently, His servants must be prepared, through that absolute submission which they owe to God, to obey His commands—even when doing so requires breaking His law. The supreme value is, after all, not the law but the Lawgiver. In marrying Dalila, on the other hand, Samson was guilty of presumption. Although his intentions were good, he presumed, without that certainty provided by divine inspiration or impulsion, to carry forward what *he* felt to be God's plan for the liberation of Israel.

At this point it should be made clear that Samson's act of presumption was not *merely* an intellectual error—that is, an error in judgment. Samson's presumption, motivated by a sincere desire to carry forward God's work, is in one sense his most human failing. Throughout *Samson Agonistes,* Milton emphasizes the fact that Providence works in mysterious ways and that God's will is not always easily to be discerned, even by a chosen servant like Samson. Thus, on a purely human level, it would be difficult to fault Samson for his decision to marry Dalila in pursuance of his divinely ordained vocation. Samson was not aware that such an act was presumptuous; he simply responded emotionally, as anyone in his position might have, to an ambiguous situation, for, while God had not commanded Samson to marry Dalila, neither had He forbidden it. Indeed, since God had earlier commanded His champion to marry the woman of Timnath, since his marriage to Dalila, an infidel, had in his own experience a precedent sanctioned by God, Samson's action seems the less reproachable. His response was a fully human response. On the other hand, it must be remembered that Samson's action was fostered by spiritual blindness and feebleness, and that as such it was blameworthy.

Samson had always assumed that, as God's chosen champion, he must be at all times *actively* engaged in the service of his God. What he had not realized was that the divine scheme for Israel's deliverance must be carried out in God's time and as God wills, not in Samson's time and at Samson's will. Man does not know God's plans or the manner in which those plans will be fulfilled; all he can do is await

God's commands and obey them. Samson's desire for action, and his belief in the necessity of action for the purpose of Israel's deliverance, led him to presume and, in presuming, to fall from grace.

Samson's act of presumption, although it may perhaps seem innocent enough, is connected with a number of other sins which accentuate its gravity. It is, for instance, associated with the loss of humility and the deadly sin of pride. As God's chosen servant, Samson owes absolute humility to Him, and he must realize that the feats of strength against the Philistines were effected not by his own strength but by God, who *is* his strength, operating through him. The credit for the glorious victories over the Uncircumcised must go to God and not to Samson. However, Samson began to take personal pride in, and personal credit for, these victories; he began to glory in his strength and, forgetting the source of that strength, attempted to elevate himself to the position of a god: "like a petty God / I walk'd about admir'd of all." As his self-esteem grew, his humility before God, quite naturally, disappeared; and, as pride and self-reliance replaced humility, Samson was led irrevocably toward the sin of presumption.

When the poem opens, all of this is past. Samson has presumed and has fallen from grace. Nevertheless, even as a sightless Philistian bondslave, he continues to sin: he doubts the promise of his vocation as Israel's deliverer and, as these doubts (aggravated by a sense of alienation from God) become more intense, he is tempted to indulge himself in the worst of sins: despair. In short, not only has Samson lost his humility before God, he has lost his faith.

Before Samson can be reinstated as an instrument of the divine will, before he can realize his vocation as Israel's deliverer, he will have to learn the three lessons that will bring about the process of his spiritual renovation. First, he must learn the lesson of *humility;* he must learn that instead of self-sufficient arrogance before God he must manifest absolute submission. Second, he must learn the lesson of *patience;* he must learn that, as God's servant, his role will not always be an active one and that he must patiently await God's commands, for "they also serve who only stand and wait." Third, he must learn the lesson of *faith;* in spite of his sins and in spite of his present deplorable situation, he must believe in the power and mercy of God, and he must have faith in the promise concerning his vocation. In sum, then, humility, patience, and faith are the spiritual antidotes to the three sins—pride, presumption, doubt—of which Samson is guilty as the poem begins. These three virtues can provide Samson with a means of release from that state of spiritual death in which he finds himself.

As Samson cannot know God's plan for him or for the deliverance of Israel, humility, patience, and faith—standing and waiting, active inactivity—must be his lot; but, he must be ready to act when called upon by God. "Every hero," as Joseph H. Summers has noted, "is a hero of patience. The question whether the patiently crowned heroism shall proceed to active public deliverance depends upon the will of God."[11]

It is through suffering and through the series of temptations presented to him by Manoa, Dalila, Harapha, and the Philistian Officer that Samson, having learned the lessons of humility, patience, and faith, is spiritually created anew and made the fit instrument of the divine wrath against the worshippers of Dagon: "the inward man is regenerated by God after his own image, in all the faculties of his mind, insomuch that he becomes as it were a new creature, and the whole man is sanctified both in body and soul, for the service of God, and the performance of good works."[12] In short, by means of suffering and temptation, Samson undergoes a process of supernatural renovation whereby he is enabled to overcome spiritual death and fulfil his divinely ordained vocation as Israel's deliverer.

If suffering sets Samson on the path back to God by bringing him to a "conviction of sin," it is by overcoming temptation that he is led toward union with God and the fulfilment of the promise of his nativity. And Milton, it is important to notice, regards temptation as a part of God's providence:

Temptation is either for evil or for good. . . . A good temptation is that whereby God tempts even the righteous for the purpose of proving them, not as though he were ignorant of the dispositions of their hearts, but for the purpose of exercising or manifesting their faith or patience, as in the case of Abraham and Job; or of lessening their self-confidence, and reproving their weakness, that both they themselves may become wiser by experience, and others may profit by their example.[13]

Temptation, then, is a means of causing Samson to manifest patience, to exercise or assert his faith, and to realize the necessity of humility ("lessening their self-confidence"). That both Samson and "others" (Manoa, the Chorus, the reader) should profit from the experiences of the protagonist is clearly evident in the last lines of *Samson Agonistes*:

> His servants he with new acquist
> Of true experience from this great event
> With peace and consolation hath dismist,
> And calm of mind all passion spent.   (1755–58)

SAMSON AND MANOA: LINES 326–709

In the second movement of the poem, Samson is confronted by Manoa who, like the Chorus (115–74), laments his son's change of fortune. As Samson had done earlier, Manoa questions the motive of this "divine justice" which raised his son to such eminence and then, after he had made but one mistake, abandoned him:

> Why are his gifts desirable, to tempt
> Our earnest Prayers, then giv'n with solemn hand
> As Graces, draw a Scorpions tail behind?
> For this did the Angel twice descend? for this
> Ordain'd thy nurture holy, as of a Plant;
> Select, and Sacred, Glorious for a while,
> The miracle of men: then in an hour
> Ensnar'd, assaulted, overcome, led bound,
> Thy Foes derision, Captive, Poor, and Blind
> Into a Dungeon thrust, to work with Slaves?
> Alas methinks whom God hath chosen once
> To worthiest deeds, if he through frailty err,
> He should not so o'rewhelm, and as a thrall
> Subject him to so foul indignities,
> Be it but for honours sake of former deeds.   (358–72)

Manoa's bitterness here indicates both a lack of spiritual insight and a lack of faith; however, the important thing to notice is that, beneath this questioning of divine justice, lie the implicit questions, "How can Samson now be of service to God? What is his role now in the work of Israel's deliverance, or is he no longer of use?"

Although Samson reproves his father for his presumptuous questioning of God's ways, although he accepts the responsibility for his present deplorable situation, it is obvious that Samson is affected by his father's words. Manoa has indeed touched a sore spot, for (we remember) these were precisely the questions which Samson had been asking himself in his first speech. Having acknowledged that "I this honour, I this pomp have brought / To Dagon," Samson reveals the extent to which he is affected by the subject of his father's queries:

> This only hope relieves me, that the strife
> With me hath end; all the contest is now
> 'Twixt God and *Dagon; Dagon* hath presum'd
> Me overthrown, to enter lists with God,
> His Deity comparing and preferring
> Before the God of *Abraham*. He, be sure,
> Will not connive, or linger, thus provok'd,
> But will arise and his great name assert.   (460–67)

Here again, Samson voices his sense of heaven's desertion. Earlier, he had lifted himself above pride and self-confidence enough to realize that his marriage to Dalila was an act of presumption; but here, when Manoa complains that "bitterly has thou paid, and still art paying / That rigid score," when Manoa calls into question God's "injustice" toward His former champion, Samson is plunged into despair. This despair leads him to another act of presumption: he presumes in assuming that God has finished with him. His only "hope" is hopelessness, for there is no possibility (he feels) that he can now fulfil his promised mission: "All the contest is now / 'Twixt God and *Dagon*." It always has been. And this is the crux of the matter. Samson accuses Dagon of presumption; however, because he despairs, Samson fails to realize that presumption is his fault as well. In saying that the battle for Israel's freedom is *now* between God and Dagon, he is assuming that before his fall the battle was between Dagon and himself. "Swoll'n with pride," he had acted as a free agent prosecuting justice in God's name, but without His consent; instead of a humble instrument submissive to the divine will, he had acted as an independent agent, assuming that his actions were sanctioned by God. Confronted by his father's doubts (which reflect his own), Samson again falls prey to this same sin. He assumes that God no longer intends to use him, and this is a form of presumption.

It is at this point that we have the explicit wording of the first temptation. Manoa, who has been trying to ransom his son, advises:

> Be penitent and for thy fault contrite,
> But act not in thy own affliction, Son,
> Repent the sin, but if the punishment
> Thou canst avoid, self-preservation bids;

Or th' execution leave to high disposal,
And let another hand, not thine, exact
Thy penal forfeit from thy self; perhaps
God will relent, and quit thee all his debt.
. . . .
Reject not then what offerd means, who knows
But God hath set before us, to return thee
Home to thy countrey and his sacred house,
Where thou mayst bring thy off'rings, to avert
His further ire, with praiers and vows renew'd.   (502–20)

Manoa counsels liberty, ease, peace in retirement from active service, and the expiation of error through "praiers and vows renew'd." On the human level, this advice to one who has suffered much seems reasonable enough; however, as Milton makes clear in the *De Doctrina Christiana*, "chastisement is often the instrumental cause of repentance."[14] Samson, therefore, must not attempt to avoid punishment. Nevertheless, the main point of Manoa's temptation hinges once again on the sin of presumption. Manoa presumes that Samson's mission is over and that God has no further need of his services; and he asks his son to *act* on this assumption. This is the essence of the temptation presented by Manoa.

Samson admits that his father is probably right, that his days as God's servant against the Philistines are over:

Now blind, disheartn'd, sham'd, dishonour'd, quell'd,
To what can I be useful, wherein serve
My Nation, and the work from Heav'n impos'd,
But to sit idle on the houshold hearth,
A burdenous drone; to visitants a gaze,
Or pitied object, these redundant locks
Robustious to no purpose clustring down,
Vain monument of strength; till length of years
And sedentary numness craze my limbs
To a contemptible old age obscure.
Here rather let me drudge and earn my bread,
Till vermin or the draff of servil food
Consume me, and oft-invocated death
Hast'n the welcom end of all my pains.   (563–76)

Given Samson's lack of physical, moral, and spiritual strength, and his skepticism (aggravated to some degree by self-pity) concerning his usefulness to God, one would think that he would succumb inevitably to Manoa's temptation. However, he rejects it, and one need not look far afield for the reason: pride. Samson's pride, the memory of his former self, will not permit him to become a "gaze" to curious visitors or a "pitied object"; after the glories of his past life, he refuses to face the prospect of senility and "a contemptible old age obscure." Similarly, his desire for, and belief in, the necessity of action find the notions of "sedentary numness" and sitting "idle on the houshold hearth, / A burdenous drone" repulsive. Thus, Samson rejects Manoa's temptation, but he does not *overcome* it. He does the right thing for the wrong reason.

Manoa's temptation only succeeds in bringing Samson's present situation squarely before him; and the reassertion of what he *is* only serves to lead Samson further into the Slough of Despond:

> So much I feel my genial spirits droop,
> My hopes all flat, nature within me seems
> In all her functions weary of herself;
> My race of glory run, and race of shame,
> And I shall shortly be with them that rest.   (594–98)

Since he has no hope and no mission, why, he asks, does death delay?

SAMSON AND DALILA: LINES 710–1060

In the third movement of the poem, Samson is confronted by Dalila, who "like a stately Ship" comes sailing in,

> With all her bravery on, and tackle trim,
> Sails fill'd, and streamers waving,
> Courted by all the winds that hold them sway.   (717–19)

The imagery here suggests that the confrontation between Samson and Dalila will take on the character of a naval engagement, a battle between a merchantman whose armament is cleverly hidden from view and a broken warship wandering rudderless on the sea of doubt. In support of this reading, one remembers that Samson had earlier likened himself to a derelict, had lamented that he was one who

> like a foolish Pilot have shipwrack't,
> My Vessel trusted to me from above,
> Gloriously rigg'd.   (198–200)

The encounter here, however, is to be fought not with cannon but with rhetoric. Dalila's temptation is that of *concupiscentia oculorum* (temptation by fraud or persuasion), and, as F. M. Krouse observes, "it is she, more than either Manoa or Harapha, who tries to persuade Samson."[15]

Merely the arrival of Dalila, his "accomplisht snare," is enough to lift Samson from the Slough of Despond. When the Chorus tells him of her approach, he cries, "My Wife, my Traytress, let her not come near me." This cry, although it is motivated by wounded pride and the memory of how he had been "effeminatly vanquish't," lifts Samson enough above the apathy and despair into which Manoa's visit had thrown him that he is psychologically capable of meeting her challenge. In spite of her seeming penitence, Dalila is still a fraudulent temptress. She has, it would appear, taken to heart Lady Macbeth's advice to "looke like th' innocent flower, / But be the Serpent under 't" (*Macbeth*, I, v, 74–75). She is a "specious Monster," and Samson reproves her for her "wonted arts" and "circling wiles."

The most important point, however, is that Samson does not merely reject Dalila's temptation (as he had Manoa's); he overcomes it. His point by point refutation of Dalila's specious arguments forces him to manifest *recta ratio* (right reason).[16] The effectual working of Samson's *recta ratio* has been obscured by sin; however, in order to see through Dalila's specious reasoning and refute her arguments, he is forced to employ this faculty and, as a result, he achieves a measure of self-knowledge.

With feigned penitence, and "still dreading thy displeasure, Samson," Dalila has come, moved by "conjugal affection," to seek pardon for her "rash but more unfortunate misdeed." Samson immediately sees through her:

> Out, out *Hyaena;* these are thy wonted arts,
> And arts of every woman false like thee.   (748–49)

He accuses her of "feign'd remorse," the object of which is to regain his faith and trust, and then to lead him to transgress once more.

Having failed in her first attempt, Dalila tries a different approach. She admits that she was at fault for publishing the secret of his strength; but weakness, she maintains, should serve to expiate in part at least that crime. She further contends that, as she betrayed Samson's secret, so he betrayed God's. They differ, therefore, not in kind but only in degree. Not content to rest here in her "circling wiles,"

Dalila says that she wanted the secret of his strength so that he would not desert her as he had his Timnite wife, and that she had given this secret to the Philistines since she did not want him to hazard his life on the field of battle. She admits that "love hath oft, well meaning, wrought much wo," but contends that she was motivated by love and did not foresee the evil consequences of her action. Still seeking Samson's pardon, she ends with the petition:

> If thou in strength all mortals dost exceed,
> In uncompassionate anger do not so.   (817–18)

Samson, however, is not deceived by her polished rhetoric, her "wonted arts." Once again he acknowledges that he is alone responsible for his present evils. Nevertheless, neither for himself nor for Dalila will weakness serve as an excuse:

> All wickedness is weakness: that plea therefore
> With God or Man will gain thee no remission.   (834–35)

Failing yet once more to reassert her sway over her former husband, Dalila again shifts the grounds of her argument. Her sense of public duty and religion, augmented by the importunities of the Philistian magistrates and priests, "took full possession of me and prevail'd." Samson remains undeceived.

In one final attempt, Dalila suggests that she intercede on his behalf with the Philistian lords:

> that I may fetch thee
> From forth this loathsom prison-house, to abide
> With me, where my redoubl'd love and care
> With nursing diligence, to me glad office,
> May ever tend about thee to old age
> With all things grateful chear'd, and so suppli'd,
> That what by me thou hast lost thou least shalt miss. (921–27)

The temptation here is to sloth and physical ease and, except that Dalila adds the note of carnal indulgence, is precisely the temptation which Manoa had earlier offered his son. His *recta ratio* more fully restored as a result of the preceding debate, Samson has no difficulty in overcoming this temptation:

> Thy fair enchanted cup, and warbling charms
> No more on me have power, their force is null'd,

So much of Adders wisdom I have learn't
To fence my ear against thy sorceries.   (934–37)

As soon as Dalila realizes that Samson will not again be duped,
that she can no more deceive him, she begins to show her true colors
and stalks off in a fit of *hubris:* "a manifest Serpent by her sting /
Discover'd in the end, till now conceal'd." The important point, however, is that Samson has refuted her specious arguments and, with the
aid of right reason, has overcome—not merely rejected—her subtle
temptations to draw him again "into the snare / Where once I have
been caught."

The encounter with Dalila does not teach Samson humility, patience, or faith, but it does succeed in raising him out of the apathy,
hopelessness, and despair into which Manoa's visit had thrown him.
The function of the series of temptations presented by Dalila is to prepare Samson spiritually for the encounters which follow. Samson's
reactions to Dalila's temptations are too self-motivated (his pride is
piqued), but he will learn the value of selfless service in the
following visits of Harapha and the Philistian Officer to which the trial
by Dalila is the necessary prelude.

Samson, Harapha, and the Philistian Officer: Lines 1061–1440

In the fourth movement of the poem, Samson is confronted by
two instruments of force: Harapha, the giant of Gath, and the Philistian
Officer. The taunts of Harapha and the demands of the Officer are, in
terms of his spiritual renovation, the most significant of Samson's trials.

Harapha, the first to arrive, says that he has heard much of Samson's martial feats and now is come "to see of whom such noise /
Hath walk'd about." He laments that he and Samson had not met on
the battlefield so that he, Harapha, might have vindicated Philistian
glory; but now, alas,

> that honour,
> Certain to have been won by mortal duel from thee,
> I lose, prevented by thy eyes put out.   (1101–03)

Samson's immediate reaction to Harapha's cowardly taunt is to challenge the Philistian giant to a trial by single combat. Harapha, who has
come only to scoff in safety at the fallen Hebrew, is obviously rather
shaken by Samson's spirited challenge, and he attempts to take refuge

in the charge that Samson's strength is the product of "spells / And black enchantments," of "some Magicians Art" which "arm'd thee or charm'd thee strong." Almost without realizing what he is saying, Samson replies:

> I know no Spells, use no forbidden Arts;
> My trust is in the living God who gave me
> At my nativity this strength, diffus'd
> No less through all my sinews, joints and bones,
> Then thine, while I preserv'd these locks unshorn,
> The pledge of my unviolated vow.   (1139–44)

Harapha's taunts have drawn from Samson, almost unawares, an expression of hope—the first in the poem. During the visit of Manoa, Samson had given over all hope of his divine mission: "all the contest is now / 'Twixt God and *Dagon*." Here, however, forgetting his present lamentable situation, Samson has almost unconsciously assumed once more his role as God's instrument and Israel's deliverer.

Harapha's suggestion that Samson, as a Philistian prisoner, is neglected by God draws from the Hebrew champion a positive assertion of faith:

> All these indignities, for such they are
> From thine, these evils I deserve and more,
> Acknowledge them from God inflicted on me
> Justly, yet despair not of his final pardon
> Whose ear is ever open; and his eye
> Gracious to re-admit the suppliant;
> In confidence whereof I once again
> Defie thee to the trial of mortal fight,
> By combat to decide whose God is god,
> Thine or whom I with Israel's Sons adore.   (1168–77)

The conversation with Dalila succeeded in lifting Samson from despair; and his despair, as the Manoa episode illustrated, was born of his self-centered remorse. Once the protagonist's attention is focused on the spiritual rather than on the temporal or physical aspects of his situation, the door is opened to returning humility and faith. Harapha's taunts have called forth the Hebrew's latent belief in God's mercy, his hope of "final pardon." Samson has always believed in God's justice, and from the beginning has realized that he has only himself to blame; however, because his thoughts have centered too much on his own lamentable case, he began to doubt, and finally to despair, that God tempers justice with mercy. Here, on the other hand, guided more by right reason and piqued more by Harapha's suggestion that Heaven has deserted him than by the slight to his own pride, Samson asserts that he has no cause to despair of God's pardon for His "ear is ever open; and his eye / Gracious to re-admit the suppliant." The important word here is "suppliant." Samson is become a humble petitioner imploring God's mercy, and his returning faith leads him to hope for final pardon.

If the verbal encounter with the giant of Gath causes Samson to reassert his faith and humility before God, it does not teach him patience. Without God's sanction, he challenges Harapha to "the trial of mortal fight, / By combat to decide whose God is god." As was the case in his marrying Dalila, Samson's motive here is, in itself, good. However, his defiant and almost selfless challenge to Harapha puts him on the verge of committing another act of presumption, of sacrificing all the spiritual headway he has made through one negligent, though well-meaning, act. It is, ironically, a sudden burst of pride which prevents his carrying this presumptuous threat into execution. He disdains to fight with a "vain boaster" who uses every excuse to avoid combat (he cannot fight a blind man; he cannot lower himself to duel with a slave). Samson contemptuously dismisses Harapha with the words:

> Go baffl'd coward, lest I run upon thee,
> Though in these chains, bulk without spirit vast,
> And with one buffet lay thy structure low,
> Or swing thee in the Air, then dash thee down
> To the hazard of thy brains and shatter'd sides.   (1237–41)

His spiritual renovation is not yet complete. He must still learn that, as God's champion, patience is a necessary virtue.

Few critics have regarded the summons given by the Philistian Officer as a significant trial, and yet, in many ways, it is the most significant. Samson must learn that as an instrument of the divine will he must act only when God commands. It is the function of the temptation presented by the Philistian Officer to teach him the necessity of patience, of standing and waiting. After the Chorus has ironically observed that Samson's lack of sight "May chance to number [him] with those / Whom Patience finally must crown," the Officer enters and commands that Samson follow him to the temple of Gaza, where there is a festival being held in Dagon's honor. Although Samson advances his fidelity to Hebrew law as his reason for refusing to go with the Officer, it is apparent that this refusal is prompted more by wounded pride:

> Have they not Sword-players, and ev'ry sort
> Of Gymnic Artists, Wrestlers, Riders, Runners,
> Juglers and Dancers, Antics, Mummers, Mimics,
> But they must pick me out with shackles tir'd,
> And over-labour'd at thir publick Mill,
> To make them sport with blind activity?   (1323–28)

Once again, he is on the verge of doing the right thing for the wrong reason. However, when the Officer reminds him that he should obey for his own safety's sake, Samson remembers that *his* safety is not important, that his strength is the gift of God and must not, especially now that he has hope of pardon, be profaned in "feats and play before thir gods."

Ultimately, Samson refuses to accompany the Officer because he realizes that in doing so he would be breaking God's law and prostituting his "Heav'n-gifted" strength to the amusement of idol-worshippers. He must obey God's law or Philistian commands and, since he has free will, the choice is his:

> the *Philistian* Lords command.
> Commands are no constraints. If I obey them,
> I do it freely; venturing to displease
> God for the fear of Man, and Man prefer,
> Set God behind: which in his jealousie
> Shall never, unrepented, find forgiveness.   (1371–76)

It is a confirmation of Samson's faith and absolute humility that, in the end, he gives credence to the supreme value: he determines to obey God's law, whatever the consequences to himself. But he goes still further, for he notes that God

> may dispense with me or thee
> Present in Temples at Idolatrous Rites
> For some important cause.   (1377–79)

He will not obey the Philistines' command, but if, he says, *God* were to command his presence at the temple, he would obey without hesitation. However, since God has not directed him to accompany the Officer, he has no alternative but to wait for His command. He has finally learned the lesson of patience: "they also serve who only stand and wait."

Entirely baffled by Samson's decision to disobey the Officer's command, the Chorus can only observe with uncomprehending astonishment, "how thou wilt here come off surmounts my reach." No one in the poem understands fully the reasons for Samson's decision and, at this point, he is completely isolated from everyone—except God. Until God commands otherwise, Samson is prepared to pass the remainder of his days in patient waiting; at last he has become a true hero, a hero of patience, and one who exemplifies that "better fortitude / Of Patience and Heroic Martyrdom" (*Paradise Lost*, IX, 31–32). His spiritual renovation is now complete. Having learned humility, faith, and patience, Samson has been sanctified "both in body and soul, for the service of God, and the performance of good works."

It is at this point that Samson begins to feel those "rouzing motions in me which dispose / To something extraordinary my thoughts" (1382–83). Directed by the spirit of God, Samson determines to go with the Officer. Although he tells the Chorus that he will do nothing to dishonor "our" law, he does not know the purpose for which God, through the Officer, has summoned him:

> Happ'n what may, of me expect to hear
> Nothing dishonourable, impure, unworthy
> Our God, our Law, my Nation, or my self,
> The last of me or no I cannot warrant.   (1422–25)

He goes to the temple not knowing the particulars of the events to follow, but fully aware of the significance of the "rouzing motions": he has been re-admitted to God's service, and his prophesied mission will find expression in some glorious action—perhaps his last.

In going to the pagan festival, Samson transgresses the law out of respect for the will of the Lawgiver. (His decision here is, of course, paralleled by his earlier decision to marry the woman of Timnath at God's command.)[17] He has been re-admitted to the *active* service of his God, and it is as God's chosen champion that Samson, humbled and trusting, follows the Philistian Officer to Dagon's festival and to the fulfilment of the promise of his nativity.

MANOA AND THE CHORUS: LINES 1441–1758

If "true experience" and an understanding of God's ways to men are achieved by Samson in the first four movements of the poem, then it is the function of the fifth and final movement to educate Manoa and the Chorus in these same virtues. At the beginning of the fifth movement, Manoa comes in with the news that there is hope that he can ransom his son from the Philistines:

> that which mov'd my coming now, was chiefly
> To give ye part with me what hope I have
> With good success to work his liberty.   (1452–54)

Manoa operates on a lower level of awareness than does Samson. He judges everything in human terms. Indeed, as Allen notes, the characterization of Manoa is perhaps Milton's broadest irony for, wanting a true conception of God's mysterious ways, Manoa unwittingly substitutes himself for God.[18] It is only the true experience that he gains as a result of Samson's death that will put things into their proper perspective for Manoa.

For the present, Manoa is concerned with his son's redemption, and the irony here arises because the reader realizes that this is also God's concern. However, whereas Manoa (characteristically) thinks of redemption in physical and monetary terms,

> For his redemption all my Patrimony,
> If need be, I am ready to forgo
> And quit,   (1482–84)

it is obvious that God's concern is solely spiritual. Manoa, writes R. B. Wilkenfeld, "would just change Samson's physical location—from a prison house to a domestic house—without transforming the inner man."[19] Samson's spiritual transformation is complete before he leaves with the Officer. Ironically, while Manoa has been treating with the Philistian lords about his son's physical redemption, Samson has, with God's aid, achieved that victory over doubt and despair, and has learned the importance of humility, patience, and faith, thus completing the process of his spiritual redemption. Furthermore, as Manoa and the Chorus speak of the former's attempts to procure his son's freedom, Samson is simultaneously performing that one final act which will at once secure his physical release from Philistian bondage and mark the resolution, in action, of his spiritual metamorphosis.

In the distance, Manoa and the Chorus hear the sounds of destruction as Samson pulls the temple down upon himself and the gathered Philistines. Manoa remarks:

> Of ruin indeed methought I heard the noise,
> Oh it continues, they have slain my Son.   (1515–17)

This is precisely the reaction one would expect of Manoa. It is prompted by the consideration of events on the human level alone. It is the reaction of a human father. Similarly, when Manoa is informed by the Messenger that Samson is indeed dead, his immediate reaction is again confined to the purely human level:

> O all my hope's defeated
> To free him hence! but death who sets all free
> Hath paid his ransom now and full discharge.
> What windy joy this day I had conceiv'd
> Hopeful of his Delivery, which now proves
> Abortive as the first-born bloom of spring
> Nipt with the lagging rear of winters frost.   (1571–77)

Manoa thinks only of the physical results of Samson's act, and the fact that his own attempts to liberate his son from bondage have been frustrated.

Awareness on a lower level, however, is not confined to Manoa alone, for the Chorus has not recognized the significant spiritual pattern of Samson's responses to his visitors in the earlier movements of the poem. Nor, it will be remembered, has the Chorus understood Samson's decision to disobey the Officer's command, or his ultimate resolution, as a result of the "rouzing motions," to accompany the Officer to Dagon's festival. "The Chorus," writes Joseph H. Summers,

is often wrong in typically unheroic ways, and . . . only as a result of the action does it acquire "true experience" and understanding. Those Danites, friends and contemporaries of Samson, represent the "conventional wisdom" of the drama; but the premise of the poem is that conventional wisdom is inadequate for tragic experience.[20]

Space does not permit a full examination of the role of the Chorus; it is enough to note here that the Chorus, like Manoa, needs to be educated in the spiritual significance of Samson's actions and responses.

At lines 1596–1659, the Messenger describes in detail the circumstances of Samson's death. He relates that, in spite of the scorn and derision which rang out at his appearance, Samson was "patient but undaunted," and that he stood before destroying the temple,

> with head a while enclin'd,
> And eyes fast fixt . . . as one who pray'd,
> Or some great matter in his mind revolv'd.   (1636–38)

This is not the picture of a toil-worn slave or the tale of an ignoble death. Except that now he is fully aware of the spiritual significance of his vocation, Samson dies as he had lived before his imprisonment: the noble and glorious champion of his God.

Finally, for the Chorus and for Manoa the spiritual pattern of Samson's victory begins to take form. The Chorus remarks that "living or dying" Samson has fulfilled his mission. He has died, they realize, not ignobly or unheroically, not as a slave and without cause, but as the servant of his God and guided by His "uncontroulable intent":

> But he though blind of sight,
> Despis'd and thought extinguish't quite,
> With inward eyes illuminated
> His fierie vertue rouz'd
> From under ashes into sudden flame.   (1687–91)

Even old Manoa now sees that there is nothing to lament in Samson's death:

> Nothing is here for tears, nothing to wail
> Or knock the breast, no weakness, no contempt
> Dispraise, or blame, nothing but well and fair,
> And what may quiet us in a death so noble.   (1721–24)

To these bystanders, it is now apparent that Samson's recovery of lost "vertue" has restored him to his rightful place as God's "faithful Champion." Samson's victory, they realize, is more spiritual than physical; his victory over himself is more significant than that over the flower of Philistia. It is with new understanding and a new sense of religious purpose gleaned from Samson's experience that the Hebrew Chorus takes its leave at the end of the poem:

> His servants he with new acquist
> Of true experience from this great event
> With peace and consolation hath dismist,
> And calm of mind all passion spent.   (1755–58)

And, lest we miss the point of this *nunc dimittis*, it is worth observing that the reader too is expected to lay down *Samson Agonistes* with new insight into the mysterious workings of Providence: "For mine eyes have seen thy salvation, Which thou hast prepared before the face of all people; A light to lighten the Gentiles, and the glory of thy people Israel" (Luke ii, 30–32).

Royal Military College of Canada

NOTES

1. Although I have called Milton's internalization of the action the most remarkable aspect of *Samson Agonistes,* one must avoid the temptation either to underrate Milton's artistic achievement in the psychological characterization of his protagonist or to take that achievement for granted. There is little in the pre-Miltonic treatments of the story to suggest that Samson was a figure noted for his strength of mind. He emerges from the biblical account in Judges xiii–xvi as an arrogant and boisterous Israelite *shôphet* revelling in his physical prowess, a conceited ruffian of vast and primitive energy. Although Flavius Josephus attempts to ennoble this rather uncouth figure of Hebrew legend, to make him more appealing and acceptable to Roman readers, Samson nevertheless appears in the *Jewish Antiquities,* Book V, chap. viii, as a hero of strength, a hero of action. In the medieval analogues of Peter Abelard, Geoffrey Chaucer, John Lydgate, and John Gower, and in the anonymous fourteenth-century *Cursor Mundi,* he is still noted for his strength of body rather than for his strength of mind. Indeed, it is not until one comes to the Renaissance Samson dramas of Marcus Andreas Wunstius and Joost van den Vondel that one finds a conscious attempt—rudimentary at that—to depict the spiritual growth of the protagonist. In both of these plays the hero's spiritual development is stressed solely in order to reinforce the dramatic verisimilitude: to preserve, that is to say, the Aristotelian notions of *probability* and *necessity* by explaining Samson's final action in the Philistian temple in terms of his developing spiritual awareness. Yet neither Wunstius nor Vondel explores the potential inherent in a dramatic examination of Samson's inward and spiritual growth *per se.* This, however, is precisely what Milton does accomplish in *Samson Agonistes.* See Peter Abelard, "Planctus Israel Super Samson," in J.-P. Migne, ed., *Patrologia Latina* (Paris, 1880), CLXXVIII, 1820 et seq.; Geoffrey Chaucer, "The Monkes Tale," Part III; John Lydgate, *Fall of Princes,* I, 6336–6510; John Gower, *Confessio Amantis,* VI, 94 and VIII, 2703–04; *Cursor Mundi,* 7083–7262. See also Marcus Andreas Wunstius, *Simson, Tragœdia Sacra,* and Joost van den Vondel, *Samson, of Heilige Wraeck, Treurspel;* English translations of both of these works are available in Watson Kirkconnell, *That Invincible Samson* (Toronto, 1964). I have examined in detail the relationship between *Samson Agonistes* and the pre-Miltonic Samson analogues in my "Sophistication of Samson: Milton's *Samson Agonistes* and the Literary Samson Tradition from Judges to 1670" (unpub. Master's thesis, Queen's University, Kingston, Ontario, 1968).

2. A. E. Barker, "Structural and Doctrinal Pattern in Milton's Later Poems," in *Essays in English Literature from the Renaissance to the Victorian Age,* ed. M. MacLure and F. W. Watt (Toronto, 1964), p. 176.

3. See, for example, D. C. Allen, "The Idea as Pattern: Despair and *Samson*

Agonistes," The Harmonious Vision: Studies in Milton's Poetry (Baltimore, 1954); A. Gossman, "Milton's Samson as a Tragic Hero Purified by Trial," *Journal of English and Germanic Philology,* LXI (1962), 528–41; W. O. Harris, "Despair and 'Patience as the Truest Fortitude' in *Samson Agonistes," Journal of English Literary History,* XXX (1963), 107–20.

4. All quotations from *Samson Agonistes* are reproduced from *The Student's Milton,* rev. edition, ed. F. A. Patterson (New York, 1957).

5. "Milton's Samson as a Tragic Hero Purified by Trial," p. 532.

6. Milton, *De Doctrina Christiana,* I, xii, as printed in *The Works of John Milton,* 18 vols., ed. F. A. Patterson et al. (New York, 1931–38), XV, 205. Cited hereafter as Milton, *De Doct.* and Columbia *Works.*

7. Ibid., I, xix; Columbia *Works,* XV, 385.

8. Ibid., I, xii; Columbia *Works,* XV, 209.

9. A. S. P. Woodhouse, "Tragic Effect in *Samson Agonistes," University of Toronto Quarterly,* XXVIII (1958–59), 208.

10.   Fearless of danger, like a petty God
I walk'd about admir'd of all and dreaded
On hostile ground, none daring my affront.
Then swoll'n with pride into the snare I fell
Of fair fallacious looks, venereal trains,
Softn'd with pleasure and voluptuous life;
At length to lay my head and hallow'd pledge
Of all my strength in the lascivious lap
Of a deceitful Concubine who shore me
Like a tame Weather, all my precious fleece,
Then turn'd me out ridiculous, despoil'd,
Shav'n, and disarm'd among my enemies.   (529–40)

11. Joseph H. Summers, "The Movements of the Drama," in *The Lyric and Dramatic Milton,* ed. Joseph H. Summers (New York, 1965), p. 169.

12. Milton, *De Doct.,* I, xviii; Columbia *Works,* XV, 367.

13. Ibid., I, viii; Columbia *Works,* XV, 87–89.

14. Ibid., I, xix; Columbia *Works,* XV, 387.

15. F. M. Krouse, *Milton's Samson and the Christian Tradition* (Princeton, 1949), p. 127.

16. *Recta ratio,* writes Douglas Bush, "is not merely reason in our sense of the word; it is not a dry light, a nonmoral instrument of inquiry. Neither is it simply the religious conscience. It is a kind of rational and philosophic conscience which distinguishes man from the beasts and which links man with man and with God. . . . Though its effectual workings may be obscured by sin, it makes man, in his degree, like God; it enables him, within limits, to understand the purposes of a God who is perfect reason as well as perfect justice, goodness, and love." *"Paradise Lost" in Our Time* (Ithaca, N. Y., 1945), p. 37.

17. Samson's willingness to break ceremonial law because he recognizes the existence of a higher authority which contradicts (in his case) the tenets of that written law might well be compared with the case of Abraham as recorded in Genesis xxii, 1–19. In a flagrant breach of Mosaic Law, Abraham is prepared to sacrifice his only son, Isaac, because God orders him to do so. Genesis xxii, 1 explicitly refers to God's command as a trial designed to "tempt" Abraham. As

Abraham is on the point of carrying out this command, the Lord appears and commends him for his willingness to place God's will above the authority of His law: "for now I know that thou fearest God, seeing thou hast not withheld thy son, thine only son from me." The implications of Abraham's "teleological suspension of the ethical" are fully discussed by Kierkegaard in his *Fear and Trembling*. It is also worth mentioning that Milton, in the *Trinity MS*, had contemplated writing a drama on the Abraham and Isaac theme.

18. D. C. Allen, *The Harmonious Vision*, pp. 85–87.

19. R. B. Wilkenfeld, "Act and Emblem: The Conclusion of *Samson Agonistes*," *Journal of English Literary History*, XXXII (1965), 165.

20. *The Lyric and Dramatic Milton*, pp. 161–62.

LANGUAGE AND THE SEAL OF SILENCE IN *SAMSON AGONISTES*

Marcia Landy

Milton's preoccupation with the nature of language in *Samson Agonistes* becomes itself a major vehicle for describing psychic processes. He examines language nondiscursively through metaphors relating to words, hearing, seeing, sounds, and silence. By means of these metaphors, he portrays the nature of psychic disintegration and reintegration. He dramatizes this recovery of self in an internalized landscape rather than in the externalized metaphors of time and space found in *Paradise Lost.* In the various verbal encounters between the characters, who are themselves preoccupied with words, the different levels of discourse symbolize different levels of reality. In the transformation of Samson, the metaphor of hearing rises to prime importance, antecedent even to the ever-important Miltonic metaphor of light. Only after Samson works through the problem of self-definition on a verbal level does he attain insight. When he finally listens with his inner ear, there is no more language, but there is illumination. Paradoxically Milton shows the limitations and the creative possibilities of language for conveying the nature of nonverbal experiences.

ALTHOUGH MILTON places his poem in the Christian tradition, and although one can carefully map out the traditional stages of conversion which the work dramatizes, most modern readers find it very difficult to identify with the work on this level. The Judaeo-Christian view of history and the traditional heroic modes of expression are interesting as archaeological relics. In the twentieth century our views of history, our expectations of individuals and of society, are far different from the medieval and Renaissance periods, and to imply that this is so much the worse for us is to ignore both the kind of reader who now approaches Milton and to assume that there is nothing of value in our world and nothing in Milton beyond the iteration of traditionally formalized truths.

A modern reader can respond quite passionately to the crucial exploration in *Samson Agonistes* of the nature of language, meaning, and reality, because Milton conveys these ideas nondiscursively through imagery relating to words, hearing, seeing, sounds and silence. The haunting act of Samson's breaking of the "seal of silence," and then of returning to silence again after the deadening sounds and numerous words which assault him, is part of the central question of how Milton conveys "ideas of feeling" in *Samson Agonistes*. Milton forces the reader to face and to feel the frightening possibilities of psychic disintegration and to work through to a psychic reintegration which for the Christian reader has specific ideological implications, but for the non-Christian appeals more fundamentally to the modern problem of modes of psychic reorganization. Milton's primary technique for embodying his situation is his exploration of the nature of language, the tool whereby man attempts to apprehend and fix reality. Milton also conveys in *Samson* the limitations of language, the fact that the actual contemplation and experience of a transcendent reality can only be dimly approximated in words.

In Book III of *Paradise Lost* Milton confronted the problem of trying to verbalize the nonverbal, and many critics have complained that silence would have been preferable to Milton's presentation of God. Whatever arguments one can put forward about Milton's success in Book III, there seems to be general agreement that he does not recreate "the heart of the rose of fire." It is in *Samson* that Milton seems to focus centrally on the opposition between verbal and nonverbal dimensions of experience. Words seem to signify the temporal world inhabited by the suffering Samson and by Manoa, Dalila, and Harapha. Samson passes through and then beyond the limits of speech into the final noise and then into silence. It is tempting to speculate that if *Samson* is indeed one of Milton's last works, then he too had crossed over into silence, where "language simply ceases, and the motion of spirit gives no further outward manifestation of its being. The poet enters into silence. Here the word borders not on radiance or music, but on night."[1]

Although the symbol of light has been examined as a radical

archetypal symbol for Milton, more recent studies like Madsen's have indicated how the sense of hearing has important symbolic significance, because "for Milton, Christianity is a religion not of the eye but of the ear. . . . For Milton and for Puritans in general the flesh remains only in the word. . . . It is Christ alone who gives significance to the shadowy types of the Old Testament, just as words alone give significance to physical objects."[2] Madsen describes how in *Paradise Lost* both the eye and the ear are assaulted by Satan. Eve's temptations are involved with the ear, whereas Adam's are involved with the eye. However, Adam's regeneration is accomplished through the ear.

In *Samson*, however, the temptations which caused him to give up his "fort of silence" seem to have been both visual and auditory; that is, it was both the beauty of Dalila and her "tongue-batteries" which led to his fall. But the circumstances of his transformation are basically auditory. This is not to say that the light and dark metaphors are not significant in *Samson*, but it is important to recognize that the light which symbolizes varying levels of reality for Samson is not primarily embodied through either the outward or the inward eye but through the organ of the ear. Milton equates light with sound and then with silence. Madsen claims that Milton did not believe in the inner eye, but I believe that by means of synesthesia the process of hearing becomes equivalent to the process of inward illumination. It is important, of course, to recognize that Milton's technique of fusing the senses of vision and hearing may be the inevitable physical act of a blind man who is compensating through the other senses for the loss of sight. Nonetheless, he is able to make effective aesthetic use of his physical limitations in *Samson*, as he had in *Paradise Lost*.

From the outset of the poem, when Samson seeks a place of withdrawal, he equates his despair over the fragmented physical and psychic world he inhabits with the sounds which assault and torment him:

> Retiring from the popular noise, I seek
> This unfrequented place to find some ease,
> Ease to the body some, none to the mind
> From restless thoughts, that like a deadly swarm
> Of Hornets arm'd, no sooner found alone,
> But rush upon me thronging, and present
> Times past, what once I was, and what am now.   (16–22)[3]

It is significant that the pain from the noise without and from his thoughts within causes him to review in linear fashion both past and present, as if the sounds he hears, like the linear discursive mode of perception, are further reminders of the lost totality of union with God and of the whole being that he once was. He translates his loss specifically in terms of his loss of vision: "O loss of sight, of thee I most complain . . . / dark, dark, dark amid the blaze of noon." It seems too as if the painful sounds are antecedent reminders of the loss of light.

Coupled throughout these early speeches are double references to both sight and hearing. For example, Samson laments, "The Sun to me is dark / And silent as the Moon" (86–87). Also, when Samson hears approaching footsteps, he assumes that these are "My enemies who come to stare / At my affliction, and perhaps to insult" (112–13). The affliction is both visual and auditory, just as his darkness is double— the "real darkness of the body" and the lack of a "visual beam . . . For inward light" (161–62). This focus on the conjunction of seeing and hearing draws the reader further into the circumscribed world of Samson's psychic condition, and therefore defines more clearly the close interconnection between intrinsic and extrinsic reality. Since, as Jackson Cope asserts, "words are significative of 'things' in an almost mystical sense," Milton's involvement with sight and sound in *Samson* becomes his metaphor for working out the nature of language and its limitations.[4] Thus language or sound becomes the means for both defining and transcending the temporal world. The final transformation is conveyed in terms of the metaphor of light. In his discussion of Ramistic logic and *Paradise Lost*, Cope states:

What has been developing is clearly a terrible paradox. It begins with the assumption that words should correspond to things. . . . As one moves from Fox's projection of himself into this state echoed in the related cries from Quakerism, one can perceive the poetic function of language asserting itself over the significative, the word itself becoming the thing. The paradox lies precisely in the origin of the iconoclastic and anticommunicative use of language, in a strenuous and dedicated effort to repair the havoc worked by empty words, sounding rhetoric.[5]

Also, significantly, Cope finds that "metaphors of light and darkness, blindness and vision, falling and rising are only the visible counters of private insight in theology, even for a Milton. Yet, released from meaning into being, from the paths of argument into the patterns of poetry, these *topoi* become in Milton's verse that great metaphor which we have found the writers of our own age seeking as an ideal culmination of the poet's challenge to the limits of language."[6] To Cope's list one should add, too, the combined metaphors of seeing and hearing as further "counters" of private insight.

One can also apply Cope's perceptive discussion of Milton's use of time and space in *Paradise Regained* to *Samson Agonistes*. For, in *Samson*, as in *Paradise Regained*, Milton has chosen not "to exploit space and dimension."[7] Milton's "real stage" is not the external but the internal world, and for this reason the conjoining of the senses of hearing and seeing focuses the reader on the nature of meaning, on inner reality in terms of the process of psychic disintegration and reintegration. In order to convey the impact of these internal processes, Milton uses as his points of identification the organs of perception, since they come the closest to embodying the states of feeling which Samson experiences and with which the reader, in his own groping to find a vocabulary for the conditions of despair, rage, and hope, can make personal identification. *Samson*, like *Paradise Regained*, utilizes the dialectical method, but unlike *Paradise Regained*, in which one witnesses the situations "only as flat encounters for ideas without sensuous dimension,"[8] *Samson* translates the ideational into sensuous and affective terms by means of heavy emphasis on sense metaphors. The difference between the two works, aside from their generic and formal differences, lies obviously in the nature of the two central characters, Christ and Samson. In *Samson*, as A. S. P. Woodhouse says, Milton works with a human hero: "It is of the first importance to observe that Samson's tragedy is considered, and the effect summed up, on the purely human level before the Chorus is permitted to raise its eyes to the larger issue of the place of his sacrifice in God's providential plan." Samson "does not cease to be an individual, fallible, though corrigible, heroic—and by his own action doomed."[9] Although Woodhouse's statements are directed toward the larger problem of defining the nature of the tragedy in *Samson*, they are also relevant for discussing where and how Milton incarnates the "ideas of feeling" which are so crucial for our understanding of our levels of response to Milton's work.

Milton has taken the human world of Book X of *Paradise Lost* and used it as the total context for *Samson*. It is significant that in both Book X and *Samson*, the dialectical method, the mode of self-preoccupation and self-definition, the problem of defining the self in relation to others, the profound working through of the sickness of despair, the very obvious indebtedness to the Book of Job—all focus the reader on the purely human problem of trying to come to terms with the pain of loss and of living in a valid and creative manner. And in all three works—*Paradise Lost*, the Book of Job, and *Samson Agonistes*—this process is antecedent to the reunion with God. In modern psychological terms, Adam and Eve, like Samson, are trying to acquire "ego integrity":

the ego's accrued assurance of its proclivity for order and meaning. It is a post-narcissistic love of the human ego—not of the self—as an experience which conveys some sense of order and spiritual sense, no matter how dearly paid for. It is the acceptance of one's one and only life cycle as something that had to be and that, by necessity, permitted of no substitutions: it thus means a new different love of one's parents. It is a comradeship with the ordering images of distant times and different pursuits.[10]

Erikson's description of the processes of ego identification is also helpful for explaining the frequency of sense metaphors in *Samson:*

In describing the growth and crises of the human person as a series of alternative attitudes such as trust versus mistrust, we take recourse to the term "a sense of" although, like a "sense of health," or a "sense of being unwell," such senses pervade surface and depth, consciousness and unconsciousness. They are, then, at the same time, ways of experiencing *accessible* to introspection; ways of *behaving*, observable by others; and unconscious inner states determinable by test and analysis.[11]

Because Milton was only secondarily concerned in *Samson* with dramatizing personality in relation to the external world, especially the cosmos, and because in Book X of *Paradise Lost* his scope had moved from the cosmic to the personal, he strove for different methods of incorporating the particular ways of feeling which constitute the individual human life style. One way of describing more particularly how this works is to show, again by contrast with *Paradise Lost*, two different methods of poetic representation. For example, in Books VII and VIII Milton presents the creation of the cosmos and of life, both animal and human. In his description of the creation, as both MacCaffrey and Cope have shown, Milton exploits the combined metaphors of time and space in order to give the reader the sense of the large cosmic background against which the drama of Adam, Eve, Satan, and the Son is played. In this way he also portrays God's abundance, the plenitude of life, and the inherent ordering possibilities of life in contrast to the demonic, destructive forces set in motion by Satan, which work toward fragmentation, un-creation, or subversion of life. The world of the fallen angels, in contrast to Heaven and prelapsarian Eden, is filled with noise, false light, stench, turbulent winds, and images of intimidating size. After the fall, in Book X, the magnificent design of God seems flawed and temporarily in danger of resembling Chaos. For a while, the reader is constantly reminded of the world of Hell, for the internal psychic conditions of Adam and Eve seem to resemble the outer landscape of Hell. The possibilities of internal order are in danger of extinction, and for a while a kind of un-creation is part of the inner landscape of Adam and Eve. In *Samson,* Milton does not use the direct epic analogy with the external cosmos. A condition similar to the unformed Chaos of *Paradise Lost* and to the Hell of the fallen angels is expressed by the disjointed sounds, the total darkness of the hero, the temporary failure of his capacity to utilize his physical strength appropriately, the turbulent tempests within (signifying the lack of inward meaning), the "ship-wrecked" hero's feeling of estrangement from God and life, the metaphors of physical sores which "Rankle, and fester, and gangrene," and the lack of correspondence between sound and meaning, object and sight. But, because Milton removes *Samson* from the larger spatial context of *Paradise Lost,* the inner world of man becomes the scene of the drama and the physical senses have the same function as the space metaphors in *Paradise Lost.* Similarly, the process of re-creation, of reorganization, of transforming psychic ambivalence into paradox, of going beyond sound to another dimension of meaning, and of going beyond the world of physical sight to spiritual illumination becomes Milton's analogous metaphor for the creation of form out of chaos.[12]

When the reader first meets Samson, he is a "Prisoner chain'd," seeking an "unfrequented place" away from the confusion and humiliation of his present environment. Throughout his early descriptions one sees the spiritual and psychic chains which bind both him and his people, and which reinforce all of the images of curtailment, imprisonment, and impairment. Israel is described as being under "Philistian yoke," from which it must be liberated. When Samson describes the vivid contrast between the blaze of noon and the darkness of his own eclipse, the reference to the eclipse seems to suggest an image of the sun as captive. Carrying through this picture of the physically and spiritually fettered Samson is his description of himself as a "Sepulchre, a moving Grave, / Buried" in this "Life in captivity." The Chorus, too, corroborates Samson's self-image when it describes him as living in a "Prison within a prison."

The Chorus' reference to a double prison is typical of the double references in *Samson Agonistes:* double vision, physical and psychic imprisonment, strength without a "double share of wisdom," seeing and hearing, and the double meanings in the crucial words, speeches, and actions in the poem. By contrasting the levels of perception, Milton does not create a sense of antagonism between physical and psychic experience, but rather reinforces the sense of complete loss which Samson experiences. Furthermore, since Samson's problem arose out of his inability to coordinate physical experience with spiritual wisdom, the references to sensual and spiritual reality remind the reader of Samson's past and also point forward to the harmonizing of the initial schism. Finally, by means of the double references throughout, Milton accentuates the fact that, as Samson himself so often articulates, the real loss is both physical and spiritual, although the spiritual loss causes the greater suffering: "Thou art become / (O worst imprisonment!) / The Dungeon of thyself; thy Soul . . . / Imprison'd now indeed, / In real darkness of the body dwells" (155–59). The double confines of the prison become the topography of *Samson Agonistes,* and the reader becomes sensitized to the future liberation which will occur on both the physical and psychic levels. Thus, the metaphors become the expressive modes for describing both Samson's limitations and the transcendence of those limitations.

When the Chorus comes to Samson for the first time, it tells him that

> Counsel or Consolation we may bring,
> Salve to thy Sores, apt words have power to swage
> The tumors of a troubl'd mind,
> And are as Balm to fester'd wounds.   (183–86)

The Chorus translates Samson's psychic condition into physical terms, but what is equally significant about its speech is its reference to "apt words," something which Samson immediately picks up and carries further:

> Your coming, Friends, revives me, for I learn
> Now of my own experience, not by talk,
> How counterfeit a coin they are who friends
> Bear in their Superscription.   (187–90)

Already the distinction emerges between talk and gesture. The Chorus, unlike those others who crowded around Samson in more prosperous days, seems more important to him for its coming, its presence, than for the words of counsel and comfort which it brings. Again, later in the same speech, Samson reiterates his preoccupation with words: "tell me, Friends, / Am I not sung and proverb'd for a Fool, / In every street" (202–04). Samson indicates in this speech that he is by no means liberated from the bondage of words. They still have power to hurt, when they remind him of what he was and what he has become, and when his vulnerability to worldly standards, to being "proverb'd for a Fool," especially assails his ears. Not only is he not freed in a spiritual sense, but the prospect of his physical humiliation in contrast to his past deeds still torments and immobilizes him. As Stein says: "The presence of others returns the hero to the larger aspect of his failure, not merely to the promise ruined, but beyond that to the trust betrayed."[13] By means of Samson's preoccupation with words one can glimpse the specific factors of both his past actions and his present need to face the particular ingredients of his failure. In his next response—to the Chorus' question about his marriages to Philistine women (215–18)—Samson again returns obsessively to the problem of words:

> She [Dalila] was not the prime cause, but I myself,
> Who vanquisht with a peal of words (O weakness!)
> Gave up my fort of silence to a Woman.   (234–36)

Samson's role as *agonistes*—both ruined hero and liberator—is treated much more selectively by Milton than in the Bible. The major psychological and spiritual factor which Milton emphasizes is Samson's relinquishing his vow of silence concerning the sources of his strength. Since the silence was symbolic of his unique relationship with God, the breaking of it is symbolic both of the betraying of the trust and, more significantly, of his lack of awareness of the nature of words and of the way they can be debased by uttering certain things to those who would both misunderstand and misuse them. Furthermore, Samson's actions indicated that he was totally unaware of the function of words on a temporal as opposed to a spiritual level. Samson, in breaking his seal of silence and then in recognizing that this is first the key to his ruin and later to his salvation, is finally able to assess with a "double share of wisdom" the nature of worldly wisdom in contrast to divine.

Another aspect of Samson's being "vanquisht with a peal of words" has to do with Judaic ritual. The powerful tetragram which was not merely the name of God but seemed to contain magic efficacy could only be uttered by God's selected under circumstances favorable to God. The name seems to have been synonymous with God's power— again we return to the idea that words contain the reality of things. One of the themes brought out in the Harapha episode is the nature of divinely inspired power: Samson's strength, as he tells the giant, does not come from magic arts, but from the direct trust that he has in God. By debasing this trust, by breaking silence and revealing what is between him and God to Dalila and thus to the Philistines, Samson has not given away a mere secret of magic. He has betrayed the one great truth which gives his existence meaning. Apparently, then, just as there are levels of seeing and hearing in the poem, there are levels of discourse, and Samson was indiscriminate in not recognizing that silence is as great an obligation as speech.

The references to coinage, counterfeiting, and legalisms in the poem, and Samson's reference to his friends as counterfeit coins, all point to Samson's awakening to the appearances of things. Milton seems to be working with a favorite Spenserian and Shakespearian distinction, the distinction between words and deeds, and Samson's painful preoccupation with words is therefore also a painful reminder of misdirected actions. For all three writers, reality is conceived of as efficacious action rather than verbalization dissociated from gesture. Samson's "The deeds themselves, though mute, spoke loud the doer" (248) corroborates the fact that it is the actions that speak and not the words alone. This statement causes Samson and the Chorus to examine other cases of failure involving the nature of words—for example, that of Jephtha, who was "adjudg'd to death, / For want of well pronouncing Shibboleth,"

When Manoa comes and Samson is led deeper into himself to relive the past and to articulate further the sources of pain, he recalls —again in terms of "words"—how "With blandisht parleys, feminine assaults, / Tongue batteries, she [Dalila] surceas'd not day or night / To storm me over-watcht, and wearied out" (403–05). The presentation of Dalila's words in the context of martial and militant behavior— "parleys," "assaults," "tongue-batteries," "storm," "over-watcht"—indicates that Milton here conceives of language as a form of aggression. This dramatizes a reversal of masculine and feminine roles which betokens here, as it did after the Fall in *Paradise Lost,* an inversion of the proper nature of things. Samson is the passive tower or fortress who allows himself to be taken and victimized by Dalila, the active battering ram. The situation further reveals, because it is couched in the terms of heroic struggle, that Dalila's role, which she later corroborates herself, is that of a militant liberator of the Philistine people and that this role takes precedence over her conjugal responsibilities to her husband. Finally, the speech intensifies the idea of language as a hostile force both in the past and in the present, the agent of Samson's fall and the paradoxical agent of his liberation. When Samson confronts Dalila, the reader will have the opportunity to see reenacted what Samson has here described in his speech to his father. But, again, Milton engages our attention in the foreground on the basic tension between sounds and silence, words and deeds—a conflict described by Arnold Stein as the conflict between conventional and heroic commitment. Language for Dalila, in her commitment to Dagon and the Philistines, is reality, because her god is a temporal, historical entity; Samson's God, however, is all-inclusive and gives meaning to history and beyond history.

As has often been noted, Manoa's concern with ransoming Samson has a double meaning, since Samson will be ransomed not by his earthly father but by his heavenly one. Furthermore, Manoa's suggestion that Samson return "Home to thy country and his sacred house, / Where thou mayst bring thy offrings, to avert / His further ire, with prayers and vows renew'd" (518–20) implies that the verbalization of penitence—"prayers" and "vows"—is sufficient to restore Samson to God, without the inevitable pain, suffering, and sense of estrangement and humiliation which Samson knows are inseparable from true recognition. Again, as with the description of Dalila's behavior, the reader is given another embodiment of the literal, logical, verbal approach to experience, and again it seems inadequate to the complexities of human existence. Samson has here been able to talk about the past without the need for self-deception. He "tells everything, all the intimate details of the bedroom folly, and he does this frankly and cleanly, to an embarrassing father, without suppression or excess."[14] The contrast between Manoa's mode of expression, which is legalistic, literal, and inclusive, and Samson's, which suffers from the great strain of trying to embody in language the agonies which he suffers and which admit of no easy solution, dramatizes the differing levels of communication and behavior operating within the work. Manoa's parting words to Samson are consistent with his conventional outlook, and it is significant that they contain at their heart another reference to "words": "meanwhile be calm, / And healing words from these thy friends admit" (605–06). Since Samson is waiting for a different kind of sign, a different mode of communication, a different form of release, Manoa's well-meant suggestion can only increase the psychological and spiritual distance between father and son.

By the time Dalila appears on the scene, the audience is sufficiently aware that Samson has passed the crisis in facing up to the full implication of his guilt. Therefore, the scene with her does not present any danger of Samson's regressing; but it reveals more fully the specific motives for Samson's suffering, and it also allows Samson to see again and thus to validate what had happened in the past. Most significantly, this confrontation allows Samson to test his returning inward strength. And, of course, the Dalila–Samson scene demonstrates, as did the earlier one with Manoa, the conflicting views of reality which are at the heart of the work and which contributed to the original cleavage between Dalila and Samson. Samson reacts to her immediately by accusing her of verbalizing sorrow and penitence without feeling the emotions. And yet his accusations sound more valid than the inevitable complaint of an outraged husband, coming as they do after other significant citations of spuriously uttered sentiments.

Dalila, intent upon mitigating her revelation of Samson's "secret," ascribes her "publishing" of it to a "common female fault." And she attempts to minimize her error by comparing it to Samson's error of breaking the seal of silence. Both acts are equivalent to her, since she does not distinguish between Samson's obligation to his God and her obligation to her husband. If Samson forgives and pardons her, he will acknowledge that his sin is also pardonable by men; but of course this spurious logic is dependent on Samson's acceptance of the equality of the two acts. The scene demonstrates that Dalila's view of the world, like Manoa's, is dictated by legalistic considerations.[15] Her emphasis on the idea of forgiveness indicates a belief that actions of any magnitude are easily mitigated by the expression of contrition. And her notion that words can be taken as a sign of the appropriate inner condition is in direct contradiction to Samson's desire truthfully to articulate and work out his impaired communication with God.

There is something painfully ironic in Dalila's "Yet hear me Samson," since this immediately recalls Samson's earlier description of her "tongue-batteries." More significantly, this reminds us that Samson is waiting to hear something else, something far different from Dalila's rhetoric, which seeks to convince not only by "cunning" but also by the sheer weight of verbiage and sound which assault Samson and the reader. Dalila's decision to reveal Samson's secret was not completely without inner conflict, and it is significant that her conflict also is described in terms of language and silence: "Only my love of thee held long debate, / And combated in silence all these reasons / With hard contest" (863–65). But the debate is resolved by Dalila's acknowledgment that "to the public good / Private respects must yield" (867–68). Here language becomes synonymous with external reality and takes precedence over the demands of the personal. Similarly, Dalila's description of the priest "ever at my ear, / Preaching how meritorious with the gods / It would be to ensnare an irreligious / Dishonourer of Dagon" (857–61) contrasts ironically with the silent affirmation Samson receives from his God before his final act. Her parting boast to Samson recalls again her distinctions between public and private allegiances: "I shall be nam'd among the famousest / Of Women, sung at solemn festivals, / Living and dead recorded" (982–84). Fame for her resides in the record of her deeds, in their being circulated in song; words have taken the place of genuine experience or love. She is truly seen at last as a shipwrecked "vessel," who has foundered in her linguistic conception of things. Throughout *Samson Agonistes* a tension exists between adequate and inadequate definitions of the self in relation to the "public good," in relation to public rituals and ceremonies, and especially in relation to the varying conceptions of "fame" and "glory" which had always preoccupied Milton. It seems appropriate, therefore, that the characters' varying responses to these problems should be conveyed by different responses to language.

Samson carries further the image of hearing when he reminds Dalila that he was "worried with thy peals," as she was worried by those of the priest. The hearing motif is picked up again by Dalila: "I to the Lords will intercede, not doubting / Thir favorable ear, that I may fetch thee / From forth this loathsome prison-house" (920–22). Every word of Dalila's reverberates with double meaning. Her words recall the Son's offer in *Paradise Lost* to intercede for man and Manoa's offers to ransom Samson. But they take on larger significance later when Samson describes his Lord "Whose ear is ever open; and his eye / Gracious to re-admit the suppliant" (1172–73). Samson's words are therefore directed at God's ear and the final validation of his supplications will be "seen"—that is, acknowledged—by God, as opposed to the Philistine lords. The double motif of hearing and sight operates in the Dalila–Samson episode to indicate the total lack of communication between the two characters.

Samson's determination not to succumb to Dalila is again couched in terms of listening: "So much of Adder's wisdom have I learn't / To fence my ear against thy sorceries" (936–37). Samson, like the deaf adder, has travelled beyond Dalila's deceptive language of persuasion and intimidation. The adder image reinforces Stein's account of this confrontation: "The effort exacted from the hero was less than before; his own feelings were less complicated; he has come through the trial more clearly the master of himself and his condition."[16] And Dalila corroborates this picture of Samson's implacability in terms of the same image of deafness: "I see thou art implacable, more deaf / To prayers, than winds and seas, yet winds to seas / Are reconcil'd at length, and Sea to Shore" (960–62). Dalila's reference to winds and seas reminds us that she approached Samson like a tempest, that her assaults on Samson were tempestuous in nature, and that Samson's thoughts were described as tempests earlier in the play.[17] The emphasis on this image and its relationship to sound is a further reminder of the chaos against which Samson steels himself, especially the chaos of language and meaningless gestures.

The conjunction of the images of tempests and words is carried over from the Dalila episode into the Samson–Harapha encounter when Samson is this time worried with the "peals" of the "tongue-doughty Giant." The Chorus warns Samson that "another kind of tempest" approaches, and to "Look now for no enchanting voice, nor fear / The bait of honied words; a rougher tongue / Draws hitherward" (1065–67). Harapha, who has come to gloat and voyeuristically humiliate the once-great Samson, tells him, "Much have I heard / Of thy prodigious might," and asserts that he has "come to see of whom such noise / Hath walk'd about" (1082–83, 1088–89). His words invoke the earlier conjunction between seeing and hearing which occurred when Samson lamented the "stares" and "insults" of the multitude, reminders to him of his humiliation, and Harapha's use of these images takes on a different connotation for Samson and the reader since he has worked through some of his pain in the confrontations with Manoa and Dalila. Harapha's statements also echo Dalila's references to public gestures, historical records, and words without intent.

It is especially appropriate that Samson, the glorious hero of the past, the Israelite strong man who was concerned about the possibility of being recorded as a fool, should see mirrored in Harapha what he once was and what he did. And the fact that his earlier fears have been surmounted is indicated in his famous passage: "I know no spells, use no forbidden arts; / My trust is in the living God, who gave me / At my Nativity this strength" (1139–41). And, what is most significant, he is aware of the possibility of restored communication with God when he states, fully aware of his previous failures:

> All these indignities, for such they are
> From thine, these evils I deserve and more,
> Acknowledge them from God inflicted on me
> Justly, yet despair not of his final pardon
> Whose ear is ever open; and his eye
> Gracious to re-admit the suppliant.   (1168–73)

The conjunction of this speech with Harapha's taunts is the clearest indication thus far of the widening gap between Samson and the world which was once so important to him. No words of Harapha can convince Samson that his God has deserted him. In a sense Samson is no longer really listening to Harapha, but to the inner voice which gives him the strength to respond to the giant without being intimidated by his threats. It is also significant that in this confrontation with Harapha there should be the most important conjunction thus far of seeing and hearing, since it is at this crucial turning point that we now become more completely aware of Samson's returning psychic and spiritual integrity. The ear—the mode of communication— and the eye—the validation of the communication—are expressed in Samson's speech about his God. The former sources of Samson's suffering in the bondage of sense distortion, in his inner prison of double darkness and tempestuous sound, are slowly being transformed into an affirmation.

At this point it is relevant to examine the Chorus' speeches on patience (1287–97), since they bear crucially on the nature of intrinsic as opposed to extrinsic reality. Patience, as defined by the Chorus, is the capacity to wait for the appropriate time of deliverance. It is not a mere passive suffering but an active inner process which leads paradoxically to a higher form of action:

For the greater part of the drama, his [Samson's] "labours" (as the Chorus rightly points out) are those of the mind. Until the final, valiant denouement of the tragedy, he conforms essentially to the type of the suffering hero. Though the play culminates in a "tryal" of physical strength and a physical victory over the Philistines, it primarily portrays a psychological ordeal—the trial of the hero's spiritual fortitude, patience, and faith—and his moral victory over the enemy within. The internal conflict precedes the external.[18]

The real crux, therefore, of Samson's confrontation with Harapha has been for him to stay alert to the real implication of Harapha's visit—the temptation to construe the real as residing in the efficacy of one's external self-image, in this case especially the image of the heroic champion whose own physical power is the key to his deliverance. But Samson recognizes that antecedent to effective action is the awareness of public, verbalized conceptions of the self and the world. Samson's patience resides in his capacity to withstand this view, to which he himself had formerly adhered. By means of his truthful confrontation of his condition, his rejection of temporal modes of mitigating his discomfort, and his acquisition of trust, he is able to avoid a repetition of his former attitudes and actions.

With the arrival of the Officer, Samson has the opportunity to *act* on his verbalizations of trust and faith. He has acknowledged God's presence; he has rejected the images of himself and of his God presented by Dalila and Harapha. It yet remains to be seen how efficacious his statements are when put to the test. When the Chorus urges Samson to reconsider his refusal to appear before the Philistines, he says, "Commands are no constraints. If I obey them, / I do it freely; venturing to displease / God for the fear of Man, and Man prefer, / Set God behind" (1372–75). The dual appearance of the Officer and the dual decision of Samson, first not to go and then to go, seem to be consistent with the heavy emphasis throughout the poem on the double perception of things. In this scene, as Samson finally makes his decisive choice, it is highly appropriate that the Chorus, Samson, and the reader should review the alternatives of behavior and thinking open to Samson, since so much of the work has been preoccupied with gestures that look and sound alike but are really crucially different. It is not the well-meaning words of the Chorus, nor any words, which trigger Samson's decision to go, but rather that corroboration of his sentiments which comes from within in the form of "Some rousing motions" (1382). This, of course, absolves Samson of being browbeaten and intimidated by the threats of the Philistines; and it indicates that Samson is "listening" and responding to a form of communication other than the constraints and limitations of worldly demands.

The imagery of sound and silence does not cease after Samson has been led out of prison. The reader is offered a striking contrast between the people's shouts when Samson is led out into the arena and the picture of Samson, "patient but undaunted where they led him" (1623), a contrast which reinforces the constant antithesis between noise and silence, words and action. And in the midst of this great din, with "eyes fast fixt he stood, as one who pray'd, / Or some great matter in his mind revolv'd" (1637–38). Then, in a devastating series of sounds, the pillars come down over Samson and the Philistines. In this scene, by the physical act which symbolizes the psychic one, Samson is liberated from the deadening and chaotic sounds and thus from the inappropriate and destructive conceptions of the self. The sound of the crowd is drowned out by the "burst of thunder." The noisy crumbling of the Philistine pillars can be likened to the destruction of the debased verbal currency which symbolized the debased life style which for a time had held Samson in bondage.

In the last segment of the play one is impressed by the acceleration and intensification of the noises. Manoa exclaims, "O what noise! / Mercy of Heav'n! what hideous noise was that?" (1508–10). The Chorus describes the noise as a "universal groan . . . Blood, death, and doubtful deeds are in that noise" (1511, 1513). The Messenger describes also how "the people with a shout / Rifted the Air clamouring thir god with praise" (1620–21). And then we have the actual description of the falling pillars, like the trembling of mountains and thunder. These sounds are related to other references throughout the work—the hornets, the tempests, the winds, the seas, the storms, the tongue-batteries. By means of sound, the destruction of the pillars, Samson has passed beyond sound, just as in the confrontations with his antagonists he had passed through and beyond language. He who had broken the "seal of silence" had now returned to silence, and the Chorus feels the effect of this translation when they describe the strange peace which descends after the previous discords as "peace and consolation," and "calm of mind, all passion spent." Samson's gesture not only brings peace to him but also leaves behind a subdued calm.

According to Northrop Frye "the central myth of mankind is the myth of lost identity. The recovery of identity is not the feeling that I am myself and not another, but the realization that there is only one man, one mind, one world, and that all walls of participation have been broken down forever."[19] The Philistine world which Samson has destroyed, the world of "institutionalized morality," was the Babel of sound without sense, listening without really hearing, blindness in a world of light. It becomes the symbol for the fragmentation which Samson experiences both internally and externally. It is what keeps him imprisoned in language removed from meaning, and the bursting of his chains thus represents both physical and spiritual liberation, especially the liberation from decadent and moribund modes of self-expression. The hero's preoccupation with the sound and meaning of words and the significance of silence has allowed the reader to witness at closer hand the complex and intricate problems of self-mastery, of recovered identity. In order to portray this inner reconstruction, Milton needed to create through words a condition which transcends words.

Samson had spoken both of the ear and the eye of God. The references to both blindness and deafness are intricately interwoven in the work. Samson is not only liberated at the end from the world of sound; he is freed also from his double darkness. The eclipse which created the darkness at noon is balanced against the final vision of the bursting radiance of the Phoenix long encased in darkness.[20] Antecedent to the illumination must be the receptiveness. The sound metaphors thus represent the refinements and limits of communication. Without Samson's first working through on a verbal level the problems of self-definition, it would have been impossible for him to experience the rebirth which is conveyed by means of the phoenix-emblem:

> Like that self-begott'n bird
> In the *Arabian* woods embost,
> That no second knows nor third,
> And lay erewhile a Holocaust,
> From out her ashy tomb now teem'd
> Revives, reflourishes, then vigorous most
> When most unactive deem'd.   (1699–1705)

The causes of the revival, of Samson's reflourishing like the bird, are thus intimately connected with the painful and discordant sounds which both anguish him and finally lead to his renewal.

Through the complex interplay of the sense metaphors, Milton draws the reader more intimately into the process of Samson's suffering and inward transformation. Both his technique and the problems he dramatizes allow the reader to get beyond the theological issues within the work and to identify on an affective level with personal and cultural problems which have relevance for the modern reader—the questioning of the "performance principle" through Milton's treatment of fame and public commitment; the nature of creative psychic insight; the possibilities and limitations of language; and the nature of that silence which transcends the inadequate verbalizations of experience.

University of Pittsburgh

NOTES

1. George Steiner, *Language and Silence* (New York, 1967), p. 46.

2. William G. Madsen, *From Shadowy Types to Truth* (New Haven, 1968), pp. 144, 163–65, 178. See also A. B. Chambers, "Wisdom at One Entrance Quite Shut Out: *Paradise Lost*, III, 11–55," in *Milton: Modern Essays in Criticism,* ed. Arthur E. Barker (New York, 1965), pp. 218–24.

3. Quotations are from *John Milton: Complete Poems and Major Prose,* ed. Merritt Y. Hughes (New York, 1957), cited throughout by line numbers in the text.

4. Jackson I. Cope, *The Metaphoric Structure of "Paradise Lost"* (Baltimore, 1962), p. 37.

5. Ibid., p. 46.

6. Ibid., p. 49.

7. Ibid., p. 68.

8. Ibid., p. 69.

9. A. S. P. Woodhouse, "Tragic Effect in *Samson Agonistes,*" in *Milton: Modern Essays in Criticism,* ed. Arthur E. Barker (New York, 1965), p. 456.

10. Erik H. Erikson, *Childhood and Society* (New York, 1963), p. 268.

11. Ibid., p. 251.

12. The anti-creation imagery is a principal means of conveying the feeling of Samson's despair discussed by D. C. Allen, *The Harmonious Vision* (Baltimore, 1954). See also Arnold Stein's perceptive analyses, in *Heroic Knowledge* (Hamden, Conn., 1965), of "the grim tension within the self, the angry feeling and the terrible separation" (p. 142).

13. Stein, op. cit., p. 144.

14. Ibid., p. 151.

15. Thomas Kranidas, in "Dalila's Role in *Samson Agonistes,*" *SEL,* VI (Winter 1966), 124–37, discusses the legalistic nature of Dalila's rhetoric (128).

16. *Heroic Knowledge,* p. 178.

17. See Barbara Kiefer Lewalski, "The Ship–Tempest Imagery in *Samson Agonistes,*" *N & Q,* CCIV (1959), 372–73.

18. John M. Steadman, *Milton and the Renaissance Hero* (Oxford, 1967), p. 34.

19. *The Return of Eden: Five Essays on Milton's Epics* (Toronto, 1965), p. 143.

20. Roger Wilkenfeld says that the phoenix-emblem "is to elaborately establish, for the last time in the poem, the basic themes of freedom and transformation. For most of the poem, the emblem standing for Samson has been the blind man without motion in chains. But with the sudden turn of events, with the reconstitution of the heroic fortitude and animal vitality of Samson, a new emblem must replace the old" ("Act and Emblem: The Conclusion of *Samson Agonistes,*" *ELH,* XXXII [1965], 166). See also Albert R. Cirillo's comments on *Samson* in "Noon-Midnight and the Temporal Structure of *Paradise Lost,*" *ELH,* XXIX (1962), 372–95.

SAMSON'S OTHER FATHER:
THE CHARACTER OF MANOA IN
SAMSON AGONISTES

Nancy Y. Hoffman

While not the protagonist of Milton's drama, Manoa, nevertheless, is the character who ties the action together through
beginning, well-known "middle," and ending. Milton's expansion
of Manoa's role and limitations as earthly father deepens the
ironies of Samson's search for some sign from his heavenly
father and thus heightens the dramatic tension. The differing
and developing responses of Manoa and Samson, as father
and son, to the same experience intersect and interact, defining
each other by contrast. Samson is the son larger than life,
caught in life and reaching beyond it and beyond his physical
and spiritual blindness; Manoa is the too-human father,
trapped by the limitations of his own vision and by his relationship to his son. The ambiguity of the drama—whether it
be tragedy or triumph or both—perhaps derives from the
polarities of father and son.

A LTHOUGH SAMSON undeniably is the protagonist of Milton's *Samson
Agonistes*, it is Samson's father, Manoa, with whom the modern reader can sympathize most readily. Manoa is the human parallel,
at times the human antithesis, always the human continuum, of the
more distant, mythic Samson. The oppositions between spiritual and
physical, between ways of seeing and not seeing, ways of being bound
and being freed, ways of ransom and deliverance, are set up in the
interactions between Manoa and Samson. Manoa is the human connection to the episodic drama that transcends the human. Not
merely a participant in one of three interior incidents in the "middle,"[1]
Manoa ties the action together from the beginning (that period of

long ago depicted in Judges before the play began *in media res*),
the middle (the interview with Samson), and the ending (we witness not Samson's tragic triumph, but Manoa's anticipation of something far different, and his reaction to Samson's vengeance upon
the Philistines). Further, because the antitheses work both consciously
and unconsciously between Manoa and Samson, Manoa is both instrument and victim of a deep tragic irony. And because these antitheses
work between father and son, the interactions suggest the workings
between the Eternal Father and His Son, albeit obliquely, and between Adam, as first father, and all mankind as his posterity. Milton
has, then, expanded the character of Manoa from its limited role in
Judges to that of the bewildered human father of a superhuman, yet
all-too-human, son. Manoa is the father who is the connection between
his son and everyday life, and who cannot understand his son's withdrawal from and transcendence of existential reality.

Manoa's actions in the Biblical story reveal that he has always
had trouble coming to terms with the "ways of God" (293)[2] even
when they seem beneficent. After the "angel of the Lord appear[s]"[3]
for the second time and then "ascend[s] in the flame of the altar,"
Manoa is fearful of the consequences and predicts, "We shall surely
die, because we have seen God."[5] His wife calms him, but that sense
of awestruck terror at the intersection of his life with eternity remains in Milton's Manoa. Throughout the play it is as though Manoa
has received far more than he bargained for in Samson, and is never
quite sure how to act with him. He prayed for a human son; God gave
him a son larger than life, and his human frailties limit his dealings
with his strange child.

For the angel of God prophesied Samson never would be quite
the son Manoa wanted: "the child shall be a Nazarite to God from
the womb to the day of his death."[6] Samson will be apart from other
men because of his religious mission, because he is ordained to deliver Israel from the Philistines. But Samson is no Christ figure, nor
does Milton depict Manoa as a Mary who can submit to Christ's
long absence in the wilderness with

> this is my favor'd lot,
> My exaltation to Afflictions high;
> Afflicted I may be, it seems, and blest,
> I will not argue that, nor will repine.　　(*PR* II, 91–94)

It is the frailty of the human relationship that Milton stresses in the character of Manoa.

And yet Manoa has a sense of mission for his son, of guarding "that one Talent which is death to hide,"[7] and this sense will inform all his actions with Samson, as it motivates Samson himself.[8] Milton depends upon his audience to remember that the angel comes twice for a reason: Manoa calls him back to learn the best way to raise this special child, this deliverer of Israel, as he pleads, "O my Lord . . . teach us what we shall do unto the child that shall be born."[9] His audience would recall that the angel comes again, but comes only to the woman; it is she who calls her husband. And the angel apparently does not answer Manoa's question, for he only repeats his injunctions about eating and drinking to Manoa's wife. And before he leaves "in the flame of the altar," the angel must rebuff Manoa for his close questioning of the angel's name.

Thus, before Manoa ever comes on stage his figure suggests the faith that is not quite enough, the fear of God greater than the love, the father who would fulfill the mission of raising this special child, yet, because of his lack of sufficient faith, cannot quite make contact with the angel of annunciation. Significantly then, Manoa enters the scene just after the Chorus' speech beginning

> Just are the ways of God,
> And justifiable to Men;
> Unless there be who think not God at all.   (293–95)

While the choral utterances usually function to intensify the emotion preceding them, their heavy irony also adumbrates characters and actions to come. In this instance, the concern is with the relationship between God and man, and with the undercutting human need to ask questions when silence and submission are required. The Chorus thus implicitly delineates the finite quality of Manoa's mind, which is forever reaching, never apprehending, forever stating truths not understood. As in the similar lines in *Paradise Lost*—

> to the highth of this great Argument
> I may assert Eternal Providence,
> And justify the ways of God to men   (I, 24–26)

—Milton is here not concerned with explaining the unexplainable; he wishes to make God's justice *apparent*. And it is Manoa's tragedy that he cannot see this justice until his son is dead.

The abyss between the generations is apparent from the first moment Manoa appears. Describing his "careful step" (327), symptomatic of his age and the cautious common sense of partial truths characterizing him, the Chorus tells Samson that his father is coming. Again anticipating, the Chorus advises Samson to consider carefully "how thou ought'st to receive him" (329). This is then no warm spontaneous relationship between father and son, as Samson attests with a groan at the news:

> Ay me, another inward grief awak't
> With mention of that name renews th'assault.　　　(330–31)

While Samson's initial rejection of his father (as he is later to reject his father's offers) may be a measure of his isolating despair, it is also a measure of the gap between father and son, a gap so great that Samson expects to derive no comfort from his father's visit. Indeed, Samson's expectations are not disappointed. Yet in the total failure of communication between father and son, the onus should not all be on the father.[10] For while Manoa serves an ironic function, while he is the human foil for his son, he is also a psychological study of all fathers who cannot understand their children, who try to help their children, find themselves doing all the wrong things, and keep on doing them in spite of themselves. Manoa appears inferior to his son[11] because of his finite limitations, because his is the older generation, fearing change while guarding a way of life that must be changed. It is a mark of Milton's psychological penetration that this figure of antithesis, serving to illuminate the bondage, the blindness, and the redemption of the protagonist, is in himself a searching psychological study of the demands and limitations of parental love.

Manoa's first wound, as he greets the Chorus, is that he does not know his son. They must point him out to his father, "behold him where he lies" (339). The shock of mutability is Manoa's as he laments, "O miserable change!" (340). Just as the Chorus has compared Samson's past glories with his present bondage and physical blindness, so, too, does Manoa. But the Chorus is distanced. It is only friends paying "old respect" (333), friends whom Manoa does not know, as though emphasizing the distance between father and son when the son was strong. The father who asked the angel, "How shall we order the child, and how shall we do unto him?" sees the blow to his son as a blow to himself. To see a son brought low, particularly a son born to greatness, implies that the father did not properly "nurture" (362) the precious talent entrusted to his care, and that the son suffers as inheritor of the father's tainted environment. Manoa indulges in self-pity, but, in so doing, he tries to take Samson's sin upon his shoulders and finds they are not sufficiently broad. Samson asks, "Why was I born?" in a series of "why" questions that probe and doubt the nature of the universe:

> Why was my breeding order'd and prescrib'd
> As of a person separate to God,
> Design'd for great exploits, if I must die
> Betray'd, Captiv'd, and both my Eyes put out.   (30–33)

Manoa asks the same question, but he puts the responsibility on himself as a father praying for his son, and then, childishly, on God's way of answering his prayers:

> Nay, what thing good
> Pray'd for, but often proves our woe, our bane?
> I pray'd for Children, and thought barrenness
> In wedlock a reproach; I gain'd a Son,
> And such a Son as all Men hail'd me happy;
> Who would be now a Father in my stead?   (350–55)

He berates God for giving him a son beyond his parental possibilities, a son "with such pomp adorn'd" (357). With Milton's peculiarly modern relevance, Manoa asks the eternal parental question, that explicitly asks why we raise our children so carefully if they must end like this, the question that implicitly wonders, "What did we do wrong?":

> For this did th'Angel twice descend, for this
> Ordain'd thy nurture holy, as of a Plant?
> Select, and Sacred, Glorious for a while,
> The miracle of men; then in an hour
> Ensnar'd, assaulted, overcome, led bound,
> Thy foes derision, Captive, Poor, and Blind,
> Into a Dungeon thrust, to work with Slaves?   (361–67)

But Manoa cannot bear this burden of responsibility. He blames God. He questions the cosmic hierarchy, as he questions the punishment of sin. He pities Samson as he pities himself, and reveals the danger of mercy without justice. This is the moment of Manoa's nadir. "The ways of God" are not "justifiable." Just as he questioned the angel too closely, he now examines God's justice too closely. Yet he never denies God, he never is one "who think[s] not God at all." As the father echoes the series of rhetorical questions asked by the son,[12] Samson sees his own self-pity objectified in his father. He reverses roles with his father as he does repeatedly throughout the drama: Samson becomes father-teacher, while Manoa is the recalcitrant, unbelieving child, when Samson *appears* to assume his own guilt:

> Appoint not heavenly disposition, Father,
> Nothing of all these evils hath befall'n me
> But justly; I myself have brought them on.　　　(373–75)

In defending God to his father, Samson blames Dalila as he, too, compares his former state with his present, and finds marriage with her a more "base . . . servitude" (413–16). As Samson deals with his father's spiritual blindness, the comparison with Samson's earlier life sharpens the sense of contrast between physical and spiritual loss of vision. Manoa reacts like a father, dropping down sharply from an investigation of cosmic causation to the human folly of pinpointing a single reason for grief, when he says:

> I cannot praise thy marriage choices, Son,
> Rather approv'd them not; but thou didst plead
> Divine impulsion prompting how thou might'st
> Find some occasion to infest our Foes.　　　(420–23)

Although Manoa is voicing the parentally self-poisonous "I told you so," he nevertheless has reason to doubt God's inspiration of the affair with the Woman of Timna.[13] From Manoa's point of view, if Samson's ill-fated marriages were God-inspired, then a vengeful God is implied, a God who would pervert that special talent sent to and with Samson. And Manoa cannot sink so deep into despair as to think there is no God, or that his God would deliberately lead his son astray. For Manoa, like Samson, murmurs—and submits.

Manoa comes close to the truth and then skirts it, when he tells Samson, "A worse thing yet remains" (433), since this holiday is in honor of the Philistine triumph over Samson, of the elevation of the Philistine god Dagon, so that:

                              God,
Besides whom is no God, compar'd with Idols,
Disglorified, blasphem'd, and had in scorn,
By the Idolatrous rout amidst thir wine;
Which to have come to pass by means of thee. . . .   (440–44)

Manoa's spiritual blindness, foil for Samson's physical blindness, under-
cuts the false vision of God as supplanted by bringing the vision
down to the "shame" brought to "thy Father's house" (447). Repeatedly, Milton makes the earthly father an ambivalent figure, and
repeatedly he uses the word "Father" ambiguously. Whether Milton
means Manoa's house or the heavenly mansions is left open, for
Manoa is the character fated to say more than he means or understands.

Samson agrees he is responsible, that he has "to God . . . brought /
Dishonor, obloquy" (451–52), but neither he nor his father realizes
they are placing a false value on Samson's "shame." For Samson,
while chiding his father, does assume responsibility for his downfall,
but it becomes an hubristic assumption of accountability, for no one
is "Sole Author . . . sole cause" (376) of his destiny, and no one's
default can cause the true God to be "Disglorified, blasphem'd" by
an "Idolatrous rout." Samson answers his father by saying "the strife /
With mee hath end; all the contest is now / 'Twixt God and Dagon"
(460–62), but he does not see that the strife always was between God
and Dagon. Samson is merely God's agent—as are all men.

Grasping at straws, Manoa receives Samson's evidence of faith
in God's ultimate assertion of supremacy "as a Prophecy" (473). But
just as Manoa could not grasp the full meaning of the angel's prophecy,
so does he doubt God's willingness to take care of Samson (a doubt
Samson also voices, but never to his father, who stands as objectifi-
cation of all Samson would suppress). Manoa juxtaposes God's
vindication of "the glory of his name / Against all competition"
(475–76) with the question, "But for thee what shall be done?" (478).
For Manoa, as earthly father, wishes to compete with God, the
Heavenly Father, for his son. And Samson's dependence is too great
a temptation for Manoa, as he turns around and offers dependence
as a temptation to Samson. Perhaps never really able to be a human
father to his Nazarite son, and yielding to the human tendency to
play God in any human relationship, to substitute the self for God,

Manoa says in essence, "God will neglect you, but I, your father, will never neglect you." And he proposes the ransom that is, paradoxically, the antithetical parallel of Samson's final redemption. The ransom is another Miltonic addition to the Samson story, an addition stressing the importance of individual choice, of human will in determining human fate.

Using the same monetary imagery as his father, Samson rejects his father's proposal. He is an adult and his father cannot assume his responsibility. Samson would pay his own spiritual and physical debts, "pay on my punishment / And expiate, if possible, my crime" (489–90). He is rejecting the image of his father as *pater familias,* rejecting the dependent position that his father would perpetuate. Father and son seem deliberately to hurt each other, deliberately to increase the suffering of each other, when Samson replies to Manoa's lament of the injustice of his punishment by remarking that there may be further suffering to come. Manoa responds with truths that become partial because of his own motivation; he speaks the common-sense morality of parents, as the voice of experience, the voice of Polonius in *Hamlet,* the voice of balanced precepts on "getting along":

> Be penitent and for thy fault contrite,
> But act not in thy own affliction, Son;
> Repent the sin, but if the punishment
> Thou canst avoid, self-preservation bids;
> Or th'execution leave to high disposal,
> And let another hand, not thine, exact
> Thy penal forfeit from thyself; perhaps
> God will relent, and quit thee all his debts;
> Who evermore approves and more accepts
> (Best pleas'd with humble and filial submission)
> Him who imploring mercy sues for life,
> Than who self-rigorous chooses death as due;
> Which argues over-just and self-displeas'd
> For self-offence, more than God offended.   (502–15)

The dramatic embodiment of the truth to love life, the injunction against a self-judgment hubristic in considering the self worthy to judge, Manoa's speech clearly defines Samson's nature and his final tragic actions, and yet it is Belial's counsel of accommodation. And Belial, too, is a speaker of truths that are beyond him. By warning against suicide as a sin of both pride and despair, Manoa suggests suicide as a possibility to the audience, and perhaps to Samson.[14]

So Manoa offers life on his terms, and this is not to condemn him, for these are the only terms he knows. He is calling Samson to come home, to the place where his birth was predicted, where his nurture was "holy, as of a Plant." It is the most a parent can offer a child in despair. It is all Manoa has to offer—but it is not enough. For Manoa, seeing only the suffering of his son and suffering vicariously with and for him, would have Samson entreat God "to avert / His further ire" (519–20). But Samson, aware that he has only revealed part of his guilt, the sin of speech, would expiate his sin with more suffering. Manoa is offering life, as we force life upon our children, unconscious though they be of the gift. Samson is rejecting life, for "as for life / To what end should I seek it?" (521–22), as he apparently yields to the sin of despair. Fighting his rebellious heart, he finds life too hard, too grim; by denying life, he is denying God at the very moment he reproves his father for condeming "heavenly disposition." Both father and son are seeking God and denying Him, advising submission and telling God what to do; and each is criticizing the other for his lack of faith. Each talks to himself and *at* the other, rather than *to* the other. Samson, seeking connection with God, desires no contact with his father; Manoa, seeking contact with his son, forgets to seek the connection with God.

When Samson rebuffs his father's desire to take him home and care for him, to revive the parent-child relationship, Manoa recalls the divine sense of mission linking father and son by asking:

> Wilt thou then serve the Philistines with that gift
> Which was expressly given thee to annoy them?   (577–78)

Offering the martyrdom of everyday living to an apocalyptic figure lost in an existential world, Manoa seems to realize the emptiness of his overture, and shifts to a faith in God's omnipotence, a faith that because "God . . . *can*" (581–83, italics mine) restore vision, he *will*. God has sent His angel not once, but twice. And, confusing God's power with God's will, God's justice, Manoa becomes the child, looking to the Heavenly Father to send the angel again to restore order in his chaotic world. Manoa, the Jewish patriarch, invokes

a Christian image of baptism and renewal, of the Second Coming
and the second chance, as he recalls the power of

> God who caus'd a fountain at thy prayer
> From the dry ground to spring, thy thirst to allay
> After the brunt of battle.   (581–83)

Manoa's is a facile optimism, but it is all he can present to Samson.
From the moaning and groaning at God's injustice, a moaning rebuked
by Samson, Manoa has moved to the other extreme of hope that God
will restore his son. In neither instance can Manoa see that the
suffering is merited, for such recognition would involve condemnation
of his son and of himself as father-guide, and what parent can bear
such painful self-knowledge?

From the proleptic and apocalyptic vision of God's restoration,
Manoa plummets to earthly concerns, for his faith is never quite firm
enough. Not listening to Samson, and succumbing to the parental
desire to play God to his son, Manoa says:

> I however
> Must not omit a Father's timely care
> To prosecute the means of thy deliverance
> By ransom or how else.   (601–04)

The danger of the dictum, "God helps those who help themselves,"
is the inherent danger of not trusting God's help and of trying to
assume God's role. And, in a way, Manoa is God's surrogate for Samson. He cannot repudiate God; and when he does, he quickly checks
himself with "Yet stay, let me not rashly call in doubt / Divine
Prediction" (43–44). It is difficult to admit in his heart the guilt Samson accepts on the surface. Thus, in this first interview, when Samson
is just beginning to probe his heart and strength, it is easy to reject
his human father. God is invisible (and this is the root of much of
Samson's searching); but his earthly father is visible. Questioning
the familial order, refusing the comfort of returning home, is a way
of probing the cosmic order. Further, rejecting dependency is the
only way Samson has of asserting his will as an individual, of retaining
his identity, of leaving open the possibility of finding again the
contact with God.

Manoa's offer is in essence Dalila's offer. Both would care for
Samson, both would offer the illusion of a changeless security, both

find a new human attraction in Samson because he is dependent. It is as though Samson, the strong Nazarite, always has been too separate to those who love him. For the first time they see the possibility that this strong man might need them, and human beings need to be needed. But Samson remains apart, rejecting human love, and accusing heavenly love of having "cast me off as never known" (641). As we noted with Manoa, Samson never considers the possibility that there is no God—only the possibility that God has forsaken him, the "sense of Heav'n's desertion" (632). From this nadir, this point of contrasting the earthly father who wants him and whom he does not want, with the heavenly father he seeks and feels has deserted him, Samson slowly and tortuously moves upward while Manoa runs around in earthly circles. The interaction between the two kinds of movement is basic to the drama.

When Manoa returns to the stage (1441), the audience has seen Samson in the process of rediscovering the reason for his being in the eternal design, discovering possibilities within himself through exchanges with others, but Manoa has seen none of this, has only witnessed—without seeing—the beginnings of Samson's revelation. In the Judges story, Manoa is long since dead at this point, for Samson is to be "buried . . . between Zorah and Eshtaol in the buryingplace of Manoah his father."[15] By keeping Manoa very much alive, by having him partake as a human father in the suprahuman feats and regeneration of his son, Milton ties the drama together and relates the eternal visionary experience to the humdrum world of everyday living.

Manoa's "youthful steps . . . much livelier than erewhile" (1442) are deliberately and ironically contrasted with the lagging steps of the first scene, as he comes to enact his own personal tragedy within the greater drama. Samson has moved from despair to the glimmerings of faith, while his father has moved from wanhope to a new hope. But Manoa's new hope is based on ignorance; it is unearned. He has willingly humiliated himself with the Philistines, in a gesture not without its own nobility, but it is for "some convenient ransom" (1471). Manoa still does not realize that redemption never can be "convenient," that it must be the painful paying of the debt—and that without the pain, there is no payment. To be sure, Manoa will sacrifice "my whole inheritance . . . all my Patrimony" (1476, 1482), which is a sacrifice from someone involved in the world of getting and spending.

But when Manoa says, "No, I am fixt not to part hence without him" (1481), only the audience—and God—are aware how meagre is his offering, compared with the suffering to be exacted from him. "Not wanting him, I shall want nothing" (1484), he adds in the poignant tones of a father who loves his son too much. Samson's tragedy—or his triumph—occurs offstage; it is Manoa's tragedy that the audience witnesses, Manoa's purgation by the fires of awareness.

And between the two shouts, from the first that prophetically "tore the Sky" (1472) and tore Manoa's world apart (for his world remains somehow intact so long as Samson lives, and for this Samson cannot forgive him), to the second, that "universal groan" (1511), Manoa and the Chorus discuss the problem closest to Manoa's heart, the bond between fathers and sons. The Chorus contrasts other fathers with this father, and comments that this father is "bent to lay out all" (1486), little knowing how much more there is to "lay out" in grief to come. The Chorus proleptically remarks the father-son reversal: sons usually care for fathers in their old age; this father must care for his son "Made older than thy age through eyesight lost" (1489). Sons usually mourn their fathers; the Jewish son traditionally says "Kaddish" for his dead father, yet the audience knows this father must mourn his dead son in but a few moments.

Not knowing the burden to be placed upon him, not knowing that Samson is at this moment seeking his destiny, Manoa assumes his son's care, again welcoming the possibility of his son's dependence. As Manoa states his faith that God will "use him further yet in some great service" (1499), his faith in Samson's mission as deliverer of Israel, his faith in his own mission as caretaker of the deliverer, the "hideous noise" (1509) rends the air. The reader knows Manoa is right; the deliverer has been delivered, Samson is performing "some great service" at the very moment Manoa speaks. The unspoken question is, had Manoa known of Samson's fate, what then would he have said or done? Would the parents of Medal of Honor winners exchange the honored deed for the lost son?

At the fearful sound, the law of self-preservation, recommended by Manoa to Samson, goes into operation. The Chorus and Manoa decide discretion is the better part of valor.[16] While they wait trem-blingly, the Manoa who believed in God as a medicine man, as a capricious magician who will restore what he has taken away, suddenly begins to see the light, to penetrate to the vision his son will find in death. For when the Chorus suggests that God may have renewed Samson's eyesight and his strength, that Samson will "over heaps of slaughter'd walk his way" (1530), Manoa replies, "That were a joy presumptuous to be thought" (1531). And when the Chorus pushes further, "Yet God hath wrought things as incredible / For his people of old; what hinders now?" (1532–33), Manoa sees for the first time the distinction between divine power and divine will, and replies, "He can, I know, but doubt to think he will" (1534).

The Messenger's arrival, characteristic of Greek tragedy, dispels speculation and increases tension. The dramatic interplay between the grievously worried father and the messenger delineates Manoa's purgative movement toward the light of all-encompassing truth. For the Messenger's answers to Manoa's agitated questions are all in the half-truths so characteristic of Manoa himself. Manoa learns of his son's death and finally yields his fatherly claims to Samson's greater Father, finally realizes he cannot play God to his son, when he says:

> O all my hope's defeated
> To free him hence! but death who sets all free
> Hath paid his ransom now and full discharge.   (1571–73)[17]

By yielding, he achieves a new dignity, while asking:

> Yet ere I give the reins to grief, say first,
> How died he? Death to life is crown or shame.   (1578–79)

The realization that death can be "crown or shame" would not have come to the man who berated God for His injustice to his son. When Manoa learns the cause of Samson's death, that "Inevitable cause / At once both to destroy and be destroy'd" (1586–87), he realizes the meaning of the truths spoken without understanding in the first scene. The "ever failing trust / In mortal strength!" (348–49) has become

> O lastly over-strong against thyself!
> A dreadful way thou took'st to thy revenge.   (1590–91)

For Samson's physical strength is only a loan from God to be returned within the human context. Thus, his strength is both triumph and tragedy, the human triumph and tragedy that "to destroy" evil he must "be destroy'd"; that to deliver his people he must destroy another people; that even the angel Abdiel had to go to war to defend his convictions. Samson and Death have ransomed Samson. Ironically, he kills more Philistines in death than in life, just as the image of the Phoenix is linked with the fire of the Annunciatory Angel in the oxymoron of life and death that Manoa and the Chorus enunciate.

Samson's triumph and his death are not an unmixed blessing, and Manoa, the grieving father with the limited but expanding vision, realizes this. He comforts the Chorus and takes comfort himself that "Samson hath quit himself / Like Samson, and heroicly hath finish'd / A life Heroic" (1709–11), but it is a comfort born of revenge, of the knowledge that he mourns not alone, that the Philistines (or what remains of them) have "years of mourning" (1712). Samson has given "Honor . . . and freedom" to Israel, but it is a contingent freedom: "let but them / Find courage to lay hold on this occasion" (1715–16). Manoa, who earlier believed he could ransom his son, now raises the question of what constitutes deliverance in a fallen world. But Manoa's joy that Samson has brought "To himself and Father's house eternal fame" (1717) is a reminder of his reproaching Samson "with shame that ever / Could have befall'n thee and thy Father's house" (467–68). Thus, despite the ennobling catharsis of grief, human beings remain self-centered, concerned with the ephemeral dream of earthly repute.

For, always human, Manoa in this final speech moves back and forth between the life force and the vision of the transcendence of life. With the greater part of himself, he rejoices that Samson has reached the God who he feared had deserted him, and with whom Manoa had thought to compete:

> And which is best and happiest yet, all this
> With God not parted from him, as was fear'd,
> But favoring and assisting to the end.   (1718–20)

He will solace himself with the ritual dignities of death. As Manoa vows to "build him / A Monument" (1733–34), he assumes a bardic role, and emerges as a poet-priest-prophet immortalizing his son:

> with shade,
> Of Laurel ever green, and branching Palm,
> With all his Trophies hung, and Acts enroll'd
> In copious Legend, or sweet Lyric song.   (1734–37)

Samson's life is to be inspiration to all youth, when his father affirms the continuity of life in the ritualistic aspects of memorial. In these youths, Manoa will see the son his Nazarite never could be; in them will be the perpetuation of the generations that Samson never can give to Manoa. From the possibility of chaos, for all grief and loss is chaotic, Manoa orders his world though the power of the poetic imagination.

But human beings cannot sustain the vision of life writ large for long. If Samson has come to eternal stasis, Manoa still is caught in the motion of life when he laments Samson's "lot unfortunate in nuptial choice, / From whence captivity and loss of eyes" (1742–43). He has seen Samson's triumph, his moral victory, his recovery of dignity at the moment of yielding it—but he also sees that he is a lonely father mourning the loss of his only son. The public hero doing public deeds is gone. The private father is left to grieve, still seeing cause and effect, flaw and punishment operating in their inexorable course, even though he has learned through his son to overcome despair and uncertainty. Thus, while Samson's life may be a glory and an inspiration to "valiant youth" (1738)—an inspiration, ironically, to more destruction—his life and his death remain tragic to his father. For, like Adam, Manoa has learned the meaning of death from his son. And like Adam, Manoa does not have sufficient faith in eternal life, but he does have faith in the ongoing processes of life. Indeed, whether Samson's drama be tragedy or triumph—or both—Manoa's story *is* Adam's tragedy of the fallen father. It is from Adam that Manoa has inherited the noble potential for tragedy, but it is from his son, Samson *agonistes*, that Manoa has learned to exercise that potential. And it is through the spiritual athletics of both father and son that the audience achieves tragic catharsis, for the human father leads the way to the mythic son.

St. John Fisher College

NOTES

1. All literary criticism concerning *Samson Agonistes* in the past two hundred years appears to be fighting Dr. Johnson's dictum that "the intermediate parts have neither cause nor consequence, neither hasten nor retard the catastrophe,"

and this paper probably is no exception, although I have tried to avoid direct argument.

2. The text of Milton's poetry cited throughout is that in *John Milton, Complete Poems and Major Prose*, ed. Merritt Y. Hughes (New York, 1957), 551–93. Lines will be indicated in parenthesis following the quotation.

3. Judges xiii, 3.

4. Ibid., xiii, 20.

5. Ibid., xiii, 22.

6. Ibid., xiii, 7. See also Numbers vi, 1–21, especially 7–8: "He shall not make himself unclean for his father, or for his mother, for his brother, or for his sister, when they die: because the consecration of his God is upon his head. All the days of his separation he *is* holy unto the Lord."

7. Sonnet XIX, "When I Consider . . . ," line 3.

8. For an excellent discussion of this interpretation as it animates the drama, see G. A. Wilkes, "The Interpretation of *Samson Agonistes*," *HLQ*, XXVI (1962), 363–79.

9. Judges xiii, 8.

10. Critical interpretation has not been kind to Manoa. It is apparently easier to sympathize with a luscious creature like Dalila than with an old man like Manoa. My major objection to most discussions of Manoa is the one-dimensional aspect attributed to this exceedingly complex character, the fulcrum of the drama.

11. See Marcia Landy, "Character Portrayal in *Samson Agonistes*," *TSLL*, VII (1965), 249.

12. Compare lines 30–97 with lines 355–67.

13. William R. Parker, *Milton's Debt to Greek Tragedy in Samson Agonistes* (Baltimore, 1937), p. 36, cites Sheppard, *Aeschylus and Sophocles*, 161: "Manoah doubts—and so, of course, does Milton—whether God really prompted the affair with the woman of Timna."

14. This speech is also a dramatic prolepsis of the controversy over whether Samson's death was suicide or necessity. In the Messenger's speech, Milton apparently opts for necessity, but one is not sure whether certain of Manoa's speeches represent blindness or Milton casting doubts—most likely, the latter.

15. Judges xvi, 31.

16. This waiting period serves a definite dramatic purpose, heightening suspense, allowing for the Messenger's traditional arrival to tell the news, and permitting the audience to witness Manoa's development.

17. I am aware that my reading of this speech departs from the usual critical reading, and this may be part of my vision as *advocatus Manoæ* (with apologies to Don Cameron Allen, the *"advocatus Delilæ"* in his *Harmonious Vision*). For a discussion of the Christian implications of the concept of ransom in the poetry of Milton's contemporary, George Herbert, see Bernard Knieger, "The Purchase-Sale: Patterns of Business Imagery in the Poetry of George Herbert," *SEL*, VI (1966), 111–24.

SAMSON'S CATHARSIS

Sherman H. Hawkins

In *Paradise Lost*, Michael shows Adam future history in a series
of dramatic scenes, recalling Milton's view of Revelation as a
tragic drama. Adam, the audience, undergoes a catharsis which
turns his "terrour" and "compassion" to joy and wonder as
the sin deriving from Adam himself yields to the redemption
effected by Christ. In *Samson* this redemptive catharsis centers
on the hero. Epigraph and epistle include both possible meanings of catharsis: purgation and *lustratio* (sacrifice and ablution). Both Donne and Bunyan make purgation the symbol
of repentance. So Milton describes Samson's sin and punishment in dietary and medical terms. His cure uses like against
like, passion to purge passion. Samson's grief, pity, and fear
are raised only to be tempered and reduced in the three central
acts by Manoa (grief), Dalila (pity), Harapha and the
Officer (fear). But the efficacy of this purgation depends on a
lustratio, the sacrifice of Christ, of which Samson's death is a
dramatic and ritual mimesis. Samson's fall thus conforms him to
the image of the first Adam; his sacrificial self-offering renews
him in the image of the second, completing the pattern of
human history and of Milton's three great poems.

L ET ME begin where everything begins: with Adam in the garden.
The notion that in *Paradise Lost* God intends to deny Adam and
Eve the knowledge of good and evil is a heresy invented by the
Enemy: "It is impious to believe that God is grudging of truth or does
not wish it to be shared with men as freely as possible."[1] Indeed it is
precisely to instruct man in the nature of good and evil that God sends
Raphael and Michael to the garden. Before the fall, Adam knows good
directly and immediately, in himself and in his world; he must learn
about evil by the example of Satan. After the fall, he finds the con-

flict of good and evil in himself, but evil is now natural to him and the motions of grace within him come from above; the innate goodness which once was his he can now know only in another, by the example of Christ. This heavy change is reflected in the contrast between the poem's middle and its end: Raphael's remembrance of things past, Michael's vision of things to come. The contrast amounts almost to a difference of genre, with Raphael's narrative as epic and Michael's as tragedy. The action of Raphael's epic is cosmic and mythical, a war between superhuman forces of good and evil. In this direct confrontation, evil is defeated and good triumphant; the destruction of Book VI and the creation of Book VII are separate and sequential actions. The world of epic affirms the good: Abdiel, the exemplar of solitary virtue, the epic hero proposed for Adam's imitation, is finally with the majority, the side that wins. In contrast, the action of Michael's prophecy is historic and human: the conflict of God and Satan takes place in this world and in the heart of man. Creation and destruction are strangely interwoven throughout human history, in the tragic paradox that good is produced from evil. For the world of tragedy is "To good malignant, to bad men benigne" (XII, 538) and Christ, the one just man alive, the tragic hero proposed to Adam's faith, is on the side that loses—at least in this world and in time. The story of man since the fall, if it be epic, is tragic epic, that mixed kind to which *Paradise Lost* itself belongs.

It is significant, then, that Raphael's method is narrative, while Michael's is—at least initially—dramatic. Future history is presented in a series of "solemn Scenes and Acts" with Michael as chorus commenting between. This visionary drama recalls that "majestick image of a high and stately Tragedy" which Milton—following the "grave autority [*sic*] of *Pareus*"—found in the Apocalypse of St. John.[2] "For as in humane Tragedies, diverse persons one after another come upon the Theater to represent things done, and so again depart," writes Pareus, so "in this Heavenly Interlude, by diverse *shewes* and *apparitions* are represented . . . things touching the Church, not past, but to come." Like musicians in a theater, the choirs of elders, angels, and beasts serve to "distinguish the diversity of the *Acts*," but their purpose is "not so much to lessen the wearisomnesse of the Spectators, as to infuse holy meditations into the mindes of the Readers, and to lift them up to Heavenly matters."[3] The form of this

"Propheticall Drama" is "truely Tragicall. For it representeth Tragicall motions and tumults of the adversaries against the Church of Christ, and at length the Tragicall end also of the wicked themselves" (pp. 20, 26). But though the general argument of Revelation forewarns the church of sorrows to come, at the same time it arms her with comfort against them: Pareus' idea of tragedy includes consolation as well as grief. Thus both in Revelation and in *Paradise Lost* the future is revealed to man by an angel in visions of tragical motions and tumults, with these prophetic acts and scenes divided and distinguished by choral passages which "propound Morall Doctrine . . . celebrating the workes of God, and his Judgements unto the Church" (p. 26).

Michael's tragic drama serves likewise both to warn and console, in accordance with its double argument:

> good with bad
> Expect to hear, supernal Grace contending
> With sinfulness of Men; thereby to learn
> True patience, and to temper joy with fear
> And pious sorrow, equally enur'd
> By moderation either state to beare,
> Prosperous or adverse. (XI, 358–64)

The actions that follow illustrate the tragic and ambiguous intermingling of "good with bad": the flood ends in a rainbow of promise; Christ's resurrection is followed by the corruption of his church. Nevertheless, as with Raphael's narrative in Books VI and VII, the action moves from destruction to creation, from a world lost to a world restored. Book XI—despite Enoch and Noah—is mainly concerned with the "sinfulness of Men," Book XII—despite Nimrod and Pharaoh—with "supernal Grace." The first three episodes in Book XI—the murder of Abel, the diseases due to gluttony, the sciences and lusts of the children of Cain—dramatize the perennial themes of tragedy: death, suffering, and evil. They also repeat, in precise sequence, the crimes of Satan, Eve, and Adam. The end of playing, we are told on good authority, is to hold the mirror up to Nature, the nature of its audience. In this tragic glass, Adam can see himself, can know the evil he has chosen. The two following episodes of war and license, aggression and appetite, show the fall as a perennial and continuous event, the tragic act of which all history is the mimesis. But the mirror is an emblem of the ideal as well as the real, what we may be as well as what we are. So in Book XII Michael shows Adam, whom he is about to lead out of Eden, the figures of Abraham and Moses, men who became pilgrims and strangers, leaving their country for the better country of God's promise (Hebrews xi, 8–16, 24 ff.). But the knowledge of good after the fall is the recognition of divine grace, not human heroism. All seven visions in the Apocalypse, according to Pareus, show the same events in different but ever clearer forms. So the motif of the one just man, first seen in Enoch, looks forward to the revelation and recognition of the Son of God. The redemptive movement of history from evil to good is thus in essence the movement from the first Adam to the second.

Adam's reactions to this prophetical drama are presumably those Milton thought tragedy should produce, and from them we can infer his concept of catharsis. It is suggestive that Michael's mission is described as a purgation: man is to be expelled from the garden like corrupted matter from the body:

> Those pure immortal Elements that know
> No gross, no unharmoneous mixture foule,
> Eject him tainted now, and purge him off
> As a distemper, gross to aire as gross.   (XI, 50–53)

Ignorant of the judgment upon them, Adam and Eve believe the worst is past and try to reconcile themselves to their lot: "Here let us live, though in fall'n state, content" (XI, 180). But this is not true contentment: it is the pre-tragic condition, the condition of any audience before the drama begins. This state of mind resists the advent of tragic awareness: Adam views Michael's approach with eyes dimmed by "doubt / And carnal fear" (XI, 211–12). This "Filme," like Samson's blindness, is bred by sin; the angel removes it, purging Adam's eyes with "Euphrasie and Rue" together with water from the "Well of Life." The healing power of grace works through both pleasure and pain, producing joy through grief.[4] So Adam, his "mental sight" purged by the angel, closes his eyes and sinks down "intranst" until Michael raises him to show things invisible to mortal sight (XI, 412–22). This fall and rise is the redemptive pattern that informs the drama of human history; it also suggests the working of catharsis.

Here the pattern is cognitive, as blindness leads to vision; its emotional complement is Adam's reaction to the flood:

> How didst thou grieve then, *Adam*, to behold
> The end of all thy Ofspring, end so sad,
> Depopulation; thee another Floud,
> Of tears and sorrow a Floud thee also drown'd,
> And sunk thee as thy Sons; till gently reard
> By th'Angel, on thy feet thou stoodst at last,
> Though comfortless.   (XI, 754–60)

Yet this intolerable knowledge of evil—"O Visions ill foreseen!"— leads to the knowledge of good, of "peace from God, and Cov'nant new," whereat "the heart of *Adam* erst so sad / Greatly rejoyc'd" (XI, 763, 867–69). So Michael's prophetical drama as a whole excites first the emotions proper to tragedy—"terrour" at the sight of death, tearful "compassion" at the sight of suffering (XI, 464, 496)—and then joy and wonder as the sinfulness of men is gradually overcome by supernal grace. What makes this process tragic is the necessity of suffering: joy and wonder are attained only through pity and fear. So in the action of the poem, Adam must leave Eden in order to attain the paradise within. Doom becomes promise, but only after it is experienced as doom. This, then, is the difference between Michael's instruction and Raphael's. The understanding of good and evil which Raphael gives the unfallen Adam is a form of nourishment, that food of knowledge by which man is growing up to godhead. Such knowledge is delight, and brings with its sweetness no satiety. But knowledge too requires temperance over appetite, and Adam has surfeited, turning wisdom to folly as nourishment to wind. So Michael's instruction is not nourishment but cure, the purgation of tragedy that works knowledge of good through the experience of suffering, evil, and death. Adam's final mood is that "True patience" which, knowing both good and evil, tempers "joy with fear / And pious sorrow" (XI, 361–62). We are here close, even in wording, to Milton's famous definition of catharsis in the epistle to *Samson Agonistes* as the power of tragedy "by raising pity and fear, or terror, to purge the mind of those and such like passions, that is to temper and reduce them to just measure with a kind of delight, stirr'd up by reading or seeing those passions well imitated." So Adam's passions have been raised; so they have been reduced and

tempered with delight.[5] His final speech is very like the closing
lines of *Samson*, in which God's servants are dismissed with peace
and calm of mind and "new acquist / Of true experience" (1755–56).

> Greatly instructed I shall hence depart,
> Greatly in peace of thought, and have my fill
> Of knowledge, what this Vessel can containe. (XII, 557–59)

The prophetical drama of Books XI and XII illustrates Milton's
conception of tragedy as the "gravest, moralest, and most profitable
of all other Poems" (*SA*, epistle). The catharsis which teaches Adam
and Eve to "love with fear the onely God" and so dismisses them, as
he commanded, "sorrowing, yet in peace" (XII, 562; XI, 117)—this
catharsis is not merely aesthetic or even didactic; it is redemptive.
In *Paradise Lost*, this redemptive process is shown acting upon the
audience; in *Samson Agonistes*, it acts upon the hero. That Samson
himself undergoes the catharsis described in Milton's prefatory
epistle has been recently—and very ably—argued by Martin Mueller.[6] But I think the purgation of the hero is central in all redemptive
tragedy. Scholarship has done its wonderful work; we can no longer
say with confidence what Aristotle meant by catharsis, or indeed
any major term in the *Poetics*. But if we turn from Aristotle to the
poets, from tragic theory to tragic practice, then I think we must
conceive of catharsis as a central and inclusive process which affects
all the parts of tragedy—action, characters, language, thought—but
centers in the hero. Think of Hamlet; think of Lear. Through sharing
in their passion we achieve catharsis; it is their more consummate and
immediate encounter with suffering and transcendence that gives to
ours its sense of "true experience." This is simply the way tragedy—
at least redemptive tragedy—works. But in Milton, tragic practice
characteristically becomes conscious principle, and the form it takes
is typically moral and religious. It is Samson's sin which must be
purged: catharsis is the tragic or dramatic counterpart of what theology calls repentance and regeneration.[7]

Milton's translation of καθαρσις as *lustratio* in his epigraph permits
him to include both the religious and medical meanings of the word:[8]
purification from sin and guilt by rituals of sacrifice and ablution; the
purging of excessive or corrupted matter from the body and (by extension or analogy) the mind. But if both senses are intended, the em-

phasis of the prefatory epistle makes purgation the primary meaning, and at first glance it may seem odd that Milton should have preferred a medical explanation to a religious one. In fact, the antithesis is misleading: the two senses are complementary in Milton's poem and in the tradition that lies behind it.

Seventeenth-century medicine is radically psychosomatic. I suppose the four humors provide the most familiar instance of the interaction of mind and body: choler is a bodily fluid, a passion of the mind, and a moral vice. The passions are, in fact, one of the six "non-natural" factors that determine health, along with diet, evacuation, air, sleep, and exercise. "Religious melancholy" can originate in soul or body, a guilty conscience or a peccant humor, and its cure— as Burton observes and Macbeth discovers—may require the divine or the physician, or both at once. Thus the science of medicine borders on ethics and theology. And when we turn to the gospels, we find the analogy between sin and disease enforced by that physician whose power to heal the body signifies his mission to redeem the soul (e.g., Luke v, 22–25). It is hardly surprising, therefore, that disease and cure form one of the most common tropes in seventeenth-century religious writing. Such "figures of speech" are grounded upon the double truth of science and religion, on the tradition of philosophical medicine anatomized by Burton, and a tradition of theological symbolism authorized by Christ himself.

The most famous and elaborate example of this religio-medical analogy is Donne's *Devotions Upon Emergent Occasions*. Here, as so often elsewhere in Donne, wit consists less in creating new conceits than in recreating old ones, so that the traditional and commonplace are brought alive by an unexpected application, a fresh extension, an extravagant proliferation of association or detail. Thereby Donne's sickness and recovery is made an emblem of regeneration, the dying and renewal of the Christian soul. In this spiritual physic, purging has its necessary place and function: "I am come by thy goodnesse, to the use of thine ordinary meanes for my *body*, to wash away those *peccant humors,* that endangered it." And Donne prays that by observing God's "mercifull proceedings towards [his] *bodily restitution*," he may "goe the same way to a *spirituall*."⁹ The spiritual equivalent of purgation is the "free and entire evacuation of my *soule* by *confession*." The scriptural "*cup of Salvation*" here becomes the bitter *"Cup* of *compunction"*: "The working of *purgative physicke,* is *violent* and contrary to *Nature.* O Lord, I decline not this *potion* of *confession,* however it may bee contrary to a *naturall man"* (p. 124). Given Donne's metaphor of the sea of sin, *purgatio* evolves towards *lustratio,* a washing of the soul in the sinner's tears and the blood of Christ. The river of humors in Donne's body is paralleled by the deluge of sin in his soul. But "there is a *red Sea,* greater than this *Ocean;* and there is a little *Spring,* through which this *Ocean* may powre itselfe into that *red Sea.* Let the *Spirit* of true *contrition,* and *sorrow* passe all my *sinnes,* through these *eies,* into the *wounds* of thy *Sonne,* and I shall be cleane, and my *soule* so much better purged than my *body,* as it is ordained for a *better,* and a *longer* life" (p. 126).

For a contrasting use of the symbolism of purgation, we may turn to the second part of *Pilgrim's Progress.* In the spectrum of seventeenth-century prose, Donne and Bunyan are nearly polar opposites. Donne's wit exalts the undignified facts of illness into metaphysical conceits; Bunyan's homely allegory reduces transcendental truths to almost naturalistic fictions. Thus Christiana's son Matthew falls sick of the gripes, "for he was much pained in his Bowels, so that he was with it, at times, pulled as 'twere both ends together." Mr. Skill, the Physician, recognizes that *"This Boy has been tampering with something which lies in his Maw undigested. . . .* he must be purged or else he will dye."[10]

So he made him a Purge; but it was too weak. 'Twas said, it was made of the Blood of a Goat, the Ashes of an Heifer, and with some of the Juice of Hyssop,&. When Mr. *Skill* had seen that that Purge was too weak, he made him one to the purpose. 'Twas made *ex Carne & Sanguine Christi.* (You know Physicians give strange Medicines to their Patients) and it was made up into Pills with a Promise or two, and a proportionable quantity of Salt.

Poor Matthew is loth to take this stronger medicine, but it "wrought kindly with him. It caused him to Purge, it caused him to sleep, and rest quietly, it put him into a fine heat and breathing sweat, and did quite rid him of his Gripes" (p. 328). Bunyan, like Donne, emphasizes that this spiritual physic is contrary to the natural man. Matthew asks Prudence why medicine is so bitter to our palates. Prudence—one of those allegorical ladies who exist to ask and answer questions—replies that this shows "how unwelcome the word of God and the Effects thereof are to a Carnal Heart." And when Matthew asks, "*Why does Physick, if it does good, Purge, and cause that we Vomit?*" Prudence tells him, "the Word when it works effectually, cleanseth the Heart and Mind. For look what the one doth to the Body, the other doth to the Soul" (p. 329).

Both Donne and Bunyan make purgation the symbol of repentance, though to the Anglican dean this connotes the ritual of confession, while the Puritan preacher stresses the effectual working of God's word within the heart. There is a ritual element in Matthew's purgation, but it is biblical and not ecclesiastic. The marginal notes on Mr. Skill's "strange Medicines" refer the reader to Hebrews x and ix, the contrast between the unavailing sacrifice of goats and bulls and the blood of Christ. Donne and Bunyan stress the necessity of both purgation and *lustratio,* contrition and sacrifice: the "*Spring*" from the sinner's eyes flows into the "*red Sea*" of Christ's blood; the pill compounded "*ex Carne & Sanguine Christi*" must be taken with a glass of the "Tears of Repentance" (p. 328). So in *De Doctrina* we find that the external cause of regeneration is Christ's death and resurrection, while its internal effects are repentance and faith (XV, 377, 379). I suggest, then, that the *lustratio* of the epigraph to *Samson* and the purgation described in the epistle are not opposed "religious" and "medical" interpretations of catharsis. Rather, they represent complementary aspects of the same tragic and redemptive process.

Matthew's sickness in *Pilgrim's Progress* results from eating fruit from "Belzebubs *Orchard*" and the first thing the pilgrims are shown after his recovery is "one of the *Apples* that *Eve* did eat of" (pp. 327, 331). The relation of Matthew's "*Green Plums*" (p. 329) to Eve's apple is that of all subsequent human sinning to the primal and archetypal sin. So the fall of Samson, far from being "Since man on earth unparallel'd" (165), repeats the fall of Adam; and its peculiar circumstances—divine favor betrayed out of uxorious love—only make the universal parallel precise and vivid. The vision in which Adam sees the "sober Race of Men, whose lives / Religious titl'd them the Sons of God" yield up all their virtue, caught in the "amorous Net" of the daughters of Cain (XI, 621–22, 586), is a mimesis and mirror of his own sin, but it also sets the stage for the tragedy of Samson.

The later story likewise turns on a sudden and total fall from innocence. So when Adam and Eve wake from lust and sleep, naked and
shamed, Milton recalls how *"Herculean Samson"* rose from the
"Harlot-lap / Of *Philistean Dalilah,* and wak'd / Shorn of his strength"
(IX, 1060–62). There is the same sense of dramatic reversal, of
absolute and irremediable loss. In generic terms, the Samson story re-
capitulates the movement from epic to tragedy. The exploits of the
youthful hero belong to the irrational and naive epics of the folk.
"Full of divine instinct" (526), Samson moves in a violent Eden
where strength brings forth sweetness, where the desires of the flesh
provide occasions to serve God, where infidels fall by thousands and
bonds are threads touched by the flame. That early rapture Samson
still partly remembers:

> Where ever fountain or fresh current flow'd
> Against the Eastern ray, translucent, pure,
> With touch ætherial of Heav'ns fiery rod
> I drank, from the clear milkie juice allaying
> Thirst, and refresht; nor envy'd them the grape
> Whose head that turbulent liquor fills with fumes.   (547–52)

For Samson in his morning, all nature was translucent to the touch
of grace, and abstinence was joy. But his innocence, like that of Adam,
depended on this abstinence, and now his paradise is lost. Entangled
with a bosom serpent, Samson finds in desire a bondage that he cannot break. No longer is he God's "nursling" (633), fed with clear
milky juice. He has tasted Dalila's "fair enchanted cup" (934), a
liquor more turbulent than any wine, and now he must drain the
tragic cup of suffering, that medicine so contrary to the natural man.

This dietary imagery has its source in the Book of Judges, where
the angel tells Samson's mother, "drink not wine, nor strong drink,
and eat not any unclean thing . . . for the child shall be a Nazarite
unto God from the womb" (xiii, 4–5). The Nazarite's vow to "separate
himselfe from wine and strong drink" (Numbers vi, 3) signifies—
according to seventeenth-century commentators—the "renouncing
of all sensuall pleasures and worldly delights."[11] So Milton understood it: in *The Reason of Church-Government,* he describes the
ideal king as a Samson "disciplin'd from his birth in the precepts
and the practice of Temperance and Sobriety, without the strong
drink of injurious and excessive desires" (I, 858–59). In the traditional

triad of gluttony, vainglory, and avarice, gluttony stands by synecdoche for all fleshly appetites. So, on the other hand, Milton in *De Doctrina* defines temperance, the opposite of drunkenness and gluttony, in equally general terms as "the virtue which prescribes bounds to the desire of bodily gratification"; it includes chastity as well as "abstinence from immoderate eating and drinking" (XVII, 213). Samson as Nazarite is bound by a general "vow of strictest purity" (319), from which he must be specially dispensed to wed the woman of Timna. Lest his reader miss the analogy between the "injurious and excessive desires" of gluttony or drunkenness, and lust, Milton makes the Chorus praise Samson's abstinence from "wine and all delicious drinks" and has Samson reply:

> But what avail'd this temperance, not compleat
> Against another object more enticing?   (541, 558–59)

The symbolism of the Samson story thus invites the interpretation of catharsis as purgation. For it is what Richard Rogers, commenting on Judges, calls "a distemper and spirituall drunkennesse" that must be purged: "*Samson* was deeply drunken, and therefore his vomit was the stronger."[12]

As James Holly Hanford noticed long ago, Samson's diagnosis of his own condition echoes and amplifies the medical imagery of the epistle.[13] All the "non-naturals" on which health depends contribute to his "lingring disease" (618). Sleep has deserted him; for diet he has the "draff of servil food" (574); for exercise his drudgery at the mill, for air the "Unwholsom draught" of "air imprison'd also, close and damp" (8–9); and the passions of the mind afflict him worst of all, "Exasperate, exulcerate, and raise / Dire inflammation" (625–26). He thinks of his cure in terms of opposites: the cooling herb or breath of vernal air that might assuage his inflammation, the opium of death to give him rest. But in fact healing comes by the sixth of the non-naturals, evacuation; and this purgation works homeopathically, employing "like against like."

Scholars continue to find precedents for Milton's homeopathic definition of catharsis. Thus Lorenzo Giacomini, a sixteenth-century commentator on the *Poetics*, observes that tragic catharsis, like medical purgation, works "*non come contrario, & inimico, ma come simile & amico al humore.*"[14] What deserves emphasis is not Milton's originality but his clear understanding of the paradox of using "things of melancholic hue and quality . . . against melancholy, sowr against sowr, salt to remove salt humours" (epistle). Samson's tragic situation at the beginning of the drama is not an arbitrary punishment of his sin, but its logical consequence and symbolic likeness. "All wickedness is weakness" (834), so Samson becomes weak. Desire is blind and servile, so Samson is blinded and enslaved. He is not cured of sin by opposites, by being freed from prison and regaining sight, as Manoa hopes. Here the logic—or paralogic—of tragedy and theology are at one. Samson's suffering becomes his cure, blindness the means to inner vision, prison the "house of Liberty" (949). Thus what seems punishment is in fact "a saving med'cin ordaine'd of God."[15] In *The Reason of Church-Government*, Milton explains how God through the ministers of his church goes about to purge and clean the inmost soul. For when a "Christian patient by feeding otherwhere on meats not allowable, but of evill juice, hath disorder'd his diet, and spread an ill humour through his vains immediatly disposing to a sicknese," the minister begins with a "gentle potion of admonishment." He then proceeds to reproof and exhortation, and then to "such engines of terror" as God has given his minister to "search the tenderest angles of the heart: one while he shakes his stubbornnesse with racking convulsions nigh dispaire, other whiles with deadly corrosives he gripes the very roots of his faulty liver to bring him to life through the entry of death." The most extreme measure is excommunication. "Yet even this terrible denouncement is left to the Church for no other cause but to be as a rough and vehement cleansing medcin, where the malady is obdurat; a mortifying to life, a kind of saving by undoing. And it may be truly said, that as the mercies of wicked men are cruelties, so the cruelties of the Church are mercies" (I, 846–47). The mercy of God, like the mercies of the church, is a cruel mercy; and it is this paradox of healing and pain that makes Milton's Christian tragedy both tragic and Christian.

More specifically, catharsis is the cure of passion. Milton mentions "pity and fear, or terror," but his translation of Aristotle's τοιούτων παθημάτων as "those and *such like* passions" implies that there may be others as well (epistle; italics mine). And we notice that Milton's analogy from Nature lists three parallel examples: melancholy, sour, and salt. Milton is not usually careless in such matters; in the present instance he has combined the rival humoral and chemical physiologies of his day to produce a triad. This should be enough to send us to the play in search of a third tragic passion. We find it, I think, in Samson's "affliction," "sorrow," and "anguish" (457–58) at the beginning of the drama. This is grief, an emotion that includes both self-pity and fear but is more basic and elementary than either, is indeed the ground of both. As Samson explores and articulates his pain, he finds its source and essence in his sorrow for his sin and in the consequent sense of God's desertion. By the cruel paradox we have observed, his successful diagnosis intensifies his agony, racking him with convulsions "nigh dispaire." This passion is indeed of "melancholic hue": it proceeds, says Manoa, from "anguish of the mind and humours black" (600).

Catharsis thus emerges as a principle of structure in the drama. Each of the three central episodes in *Samson* treats one of the tragic passions. Manoa seeks to comfort Samson but in fact increases his grief. Dalila, appealing to sexual passion masked as compassion, asks his pity. Finally Harapha and the Philistine Officer try to excite his fear. But in Samson all these passions are reduced to just measure. He does not fear death; he shows Dalila no more pity than he shows himself; and true grief for sin makes him blame himself rather than God, determining him to "pay on my punishment; / And expiate, if possible, my crime" (489–90). The resolution of the temptation by fear is especially instructive. Samson defies the threats of the Philistine Officer because what he now dreads most is the loss of "Favour renew'd" by "venturing to displease / God for the fear of Man" (1357, 1373–74). Purgation does not eliminate passion but reduces it to "just measure": the brave man, says Aristotle, fears what ought to be feared.[16] So Samson fears God. And by this fear, which is the beginning of wisdom, he is delivered from the fear of men or anything that they can do to him. But the homeopathic formula of like against like does not always work this neatly. A more general idea of passion is at work in this strange therapy.

For the Renaissance, as we all know, the moral life turns on the control of passion by reason. And it is significant that all Samson's temptations—even the sensual lure proffered by Dalila—take the form of debates. This is equally true of *Comus, Paradise Lost,* and *Paradise Regained:* a temptation that does not threaten to seduce reason did not seem to Milton fit subject for a tragedy, an epic, or even a masque. Samson's victory over temptation is shown in the fact that he wins all his arguments. What he replies to his tempters is, if not truth, certainly closer to truth than what they say to him. Yet compared to the unmoved hero of *Paradise Regained*—and surely this comparison is intended—Samson does not strike us as a very reasonable man. He is full of turbulent passions: grief, shame, resentment, scorn. When Christ shows anger against Satan, we feel that it is wrath inspired by reason, by clear perception and just abhorrence of the blasphemy in Satan's demand for worship. But when Samson argues with Dalila, we feel that his reason is inspired by wrath. He speaks of best men "principl'd" to forgive the penitent (760); and as a matter of principle, he brings himself to say that he forgives Dalila—"At distance" (954). But this forgiveness is not much more convincing than her penitence: it is far easier to believe in the "fierce remembrance" and "sudden rage" that threaten to tear her joint by joint (952–53). Not so did Christ forgive—nor even, in a similar case, John Milton. But precisely this burning resentment makes Samson invulnerable to Dalila's charms: passion, not reason, arms him against temptation. So too in the other episodes, in the proud combativeness that spurs him on against Harapha, the shame and grief that prompt him to resist Manoa's busy plans. Throughout, Samson's arguments and reasonings only confirm and justify resolutions reached by passionate instinct. Yet even as we watch, these passions—so powerfully raised—are purified, reduced, and tempered. Self-pitying remorse becomes a true repentance, wrath turns to righteous indignation, contentious pride to zeal for Israel's God. And seeing this, the Chorus feel their grief and pity change to joy and wonder:

> Oh how comely it is and how reviving
> To the Spirits of just men long opprest!   (1268–69)

This, then, is the paradox of the divine physic that uses passion to cure passion, unreason against irrationality. It is indeed a kind of saving by undoing. "What is the present necessary *action?*" writes Donne, "purging: A *withdrawing*, a violating of *Nature, a farther weakening:* O *deare price,* and O *strange* way of *addition,* to doe it by *subtraction;* of *restoring* Nature, to *violate* Nature; of *providing strength, by increasing weaknesse.*"[17] But by weakness Samson is made strong.[18]

Manoa, Dalila, and Harapha represent aspects of Samson as he is or was: his grief, his lust, his pride. In them he sees his own passions well imitated, if not with delight, then with those "rouzing motions" of the spirit (1382) that are its heroic counterparts. Summarizing the effects of Samson's visitors upon the hero, Una Ellis-Fermor writes, "The quality and kind of stimuli that Milton applies to Samson's mind are like a highly skilled course of psychotherapy: each comes at its due moment, before which it would have been overpowering and after which inadequate. We are in the hands of a man who knows this experience intimately and of an artist who can assemble the raw material of life into form."[19] The true medical analogy is not "psychotherapy," nor did Milton mean us to think of him as that physician in whose hands both we and Samson are. But Ellis-Fermor is right in seeing that it is the process of Samson's cure that determines the course of the action. There is no logical connection between the episodes: Samson's visitors simply appear, promptly and without explanation, when they are needed. Milton omits the natural causation which Aristotle demands and a little ingenuity could supply to hint a cause that is above nature. Samson himself glimpses it: "So let her go," he says of Dalila; "God sent her to debase me" (999). He has the wrong motive, but the right agent. Manoa, Dalila, and Harapha come because—all unknowingly—they are sent. Friend and foe alike, they become the antagonists of Samson *agonistes*. In defeating them, he conquers himself, until he stands alone in the arena, "None daring to appear Antagonist" (1628). In a sense, the ultimate antagonist with whom Samson wrestles throughout is one who never appears. As Samson's tempters grow more hostile, God's love becomes more evident. But it is a love which must give pain in order to heal, which works through blindness and captivity to give freedom and light, which must destroy in order to create, confirming Samson's bitter paradox:

> But come what will, my deadliest foe will prove
> My speediest friend, by death to rid me hence,
> The worst that he can give, to me the best.   (1262–64)

The action of Milton's drama is the purgation of the hero. But this psychological and moral purgation is made possible and valid by the lustration of a sacrifice which is its external cause. The ritual for cleansing a Nazarite of accidental pollution is prescribed in the Book of Numbers. The Nazarite shall shave his head, and bring the priest doves and a lamb for a sin offering and a burnt offering, and the priest shall make atonement for him (vi, 9–12). But Samson's sin is no casual pollution; it cannot be cleansed by "those shadowie expiations weak, / The bloud of Bulls and Goats" (*PL* XII, 291–92). The necessary sacrifice, as the Epistle to the Hebrews tells us, is that of Christ, the true high priest who offers up himself, whose blood replaces those earlier ceremonies, the "meats and drinks, and divers washings" of the law (ix, 10). By this sacrifice, we are made clean: "Having therefore, brethren, boldness to enter into the holiest by the blood of Jesus . . . Let us draw near with a true heart in full assurance of faith, having our hearts sprinkled from an evil con- science, and our bodies washed with pure water" (x, 19, 22).[20] In *De Doctrina* Milton explains that though men who lived before Christ are saved by faith in God alone, it is still through the sole merits of Christ, "inasmuch as he was given and slain from the beginning of the world, even for those to whom he was not known" (XV, 405). In *Samson*, as befits an Old Testament tragedy, this true *lustratio* is glimpsed through veils and shadows, types and figures: ransom, circumcision, ablution, change of garments.[21] But in Samson's death, symbol becomes fact. Drama merges with ritual in a "Theatre" (1605) which is also a "Temple" (1370), where feasts and games are accompanied by sacrifice. Or rather, the Philistine sacrifice *is* a feast, a eucharist of praise and thanksgiving to Dagon. His worshippers are "Drunk with Idolatry, drunk with Wine, / And fat regorg'd of Bulls and Goats" (1670–71). There is no need to labor the contrast of this gluttony and drunkenness to Samson's final act of self-emptying, or the idolatrous offering of bulls and goats to the true sacrifice Samson now performs, offering himself in the likeness of one who is both priest and victim. And by this atoning sacrifice, his Nazariteship is renewed. To the Nazarite, contact with the dead is pollution, even "for his father, or for his mother, for his brother, or for his sister when they die" (Numbers vi, 7). But Samson lies at last among the Philistines he has slain. From this final pollution, Manoa seeks to cleanse his son, as before he sought to ransom him:

> Let us go find the body where it lies
> Sok't in his enemies blood, and from the stream
> With lavers pure and cleansing herbs wash off
> The clotted gore.   (1725–28)

But there is no need for further ransom or lustration: by blood Samson has been made clean.

The imagery of purgation relates Samson to Adam; the imagery of lustration relates him to Christ. To understand his catharsis is thus to understand the triadic pattern of *Paradise Lost, Paradise Regained,* and *Samson Agonistes.* This pattern was first observed by F. M. Krouse in his brilliant book on *Samson* and the Christian tradition.[22] I believe that the parallelism can be extended to the triple temptation in all three poems; however that may be, the essential outline is clear. In *Paradise Lost* we see man fallen; in *Paradise Regained,* we see man restored; in *Samson* we watch the agony of man between. The action of the drama repeats the pattern we have traced through history in the last two books of *Paradise Lost,* as Samson moves from the likeness of Adam to the likeness of Christ. Milton's tragedy is a mimesis of the redemptive process at work in the life of the individual and the race, an action not of men but of man. Krouse's argument has not won the acceptance I think it deserves, chiefly because of his too narrow insistence on Samson as an allegorical type of Christ. That Samson was so regarded, no reader of Krouse's book (or of seventeenth-century biblical commentary) can doubt. But in the Epistle to the Hebrews Samson is given a different and more general meaning. He is one of the great heroes of faith, those patriarchs and martyrs who, having finished the course, are become examples to all who follow them and who, compassed about with so great a cloud of witnesses, must run with patience the same race. Samson prefigures us: the poet, the reader, all who in darkness and bondage share the *agon* that leads from paradise lost to paradise regained.

The relation of Milton's Samson to Adam and to Christ is thus deeper and more universal than typology. Oddly enough Krouse neglects *De Doctrina,* the obvious and primary source for Milton's theology, where this relation is spelled out. There, human sin is presented and analyzed largely in terms of Adam's fall, while regeneration is our rebirth in Christ. The purpose of Christ's ministry is twofold: that the divine justice may be satisfied, and that we may be conformed to his likeness, *ad imaginem Christi* (XV, 332). The image of Christ to which we are conformed includes his humiliation as well as his exaltation; and this humiliation, this self-emptying or *exinanitio*, consists not only in suffering and death but in servitude and hardship and temptation (XV, 305). The long day's dying which Samson undergoes is thus a mortifying into life, by which "the old man being destroyed, the inward man is regenerated by God after his own image" (XV, 367). By his fall, Samson is conformed to the image of the first Adam; by his humiliation, self-emptying, and sacrificial death, he is transformed into the image of the second. As he stands, head bowed and arms outstretched between the pillars, Milton's readers, familiar with Samson as a type of Christ, would not fail to detect the *imago Christi*. But it is not surprising that Krouse could find little trace of typological reference in the play.[23] Such reference could only blur its larger meaning, the sense in which Samson's tragedy is that of all men: "For as in Adam all die, even so in Christ shall all be made alive" (I Corinthians xv, 22). In Milton's drama, this universal truth takes on the immediacy and power of "true experience," making Samson's catharsis an action in which all may share—audience or reader as well as the hero and the chorus—dismissing us, like them, with calm of mind, all passion spent.

University of Rochester

NOTES

1. *Defensio Secunda*, IV, i, 585. Wherever possible, I have included references in my text. Quotations from Milton's prose works are taken (as here) from the Yale edition; quotations from *De Doctrina* and the poetry are from the Columbia edition.

2. *The Reason of Church-Government*, I, 815.

3. David Pareus, *A Commentary Upon the Divine Revelation of the Apostle and Evangelist John*, trans. Elias Arnold (Amsterdam, 1644), p. 20.

4. I take the well of life to represent grace. Euphrasy < Gr. εὐφρασία, cheerfulness, is clearly contrasted to rue as pleasure to pain, or joy to grief. The contrast emphasizes the double effect of tragedy as Milton and Pareus understand it. But Ophelia reminds us that even rue can be an herb of grace. There may be a further pun on Gr. *εὐφραζία < εὐ (well) and φραζειν (to speak). The *OED* gives only one nineteenth-century instance of "euphrasy" for fine speaking, but the invented etymology was no more beyond Milton than it was beyond *Fraser's Maga-*

zine. Adam's vision would then be purged by the angel's eloquence, the good counsel that causes him such pleasure and pain. The theme of vision restored, so significant in relation to *Samson*, recurs (ironically) at XI, 598 and at XII, 271, 274.

5. Note that this is not delight in imitation. It would be possible to avoid this difficulty by reading "with" in the phrase "with a kind of delight" as "accompanied by" rather than "by means of." But "temper" implies mixture, and Milton has precedent (e.g., Minturno) for the idea that pity and fear are purged by pleasure. And we have seen how Pareus' belief that Revelation comforts as well as warns is paralleled in *PL* XI–XII. Both there and in *Samson*, pity and fear are in fact gradually reduced by and mixed with wonder and a "kind of delight." The ascription of this delight to imitation seems to reflect the authority of Aristotle rather than Milton's actual practice.

6. *"Pathos* and *Katharsis* in *Samson Agonistes," ELH,* XXXI (1964), 156–74. Though I agree with Mueller's point, I am not indebted to him for it. I am, however, most gratefully indebted for his connection of clothing and washing imagery with catharsis.

7. Why did not Milton explain in his epistle that Samson is being purged? One can only note the dry reserve of the epistle, its condensation of dramatic fact (Manoa and Dalila become simply "other persons"), and Milton's lofty willingness to be misunderstood (though division into act and scene *is* omitted, the play has five acts, and we cannot understand its structure unless we recognize them). Milton has said enough to obviate certain elementary objections—"thus much before-hand may be Epistl'd"—and no more. The rest he left to that fit audience though few whom he thought capable of judging his play.

8. As pointed out by T. S. K. Scott-Craig, "Concerning Milton's *Samson," RN,* V (1952), 45–53.

9. *Devotions Upon Emergent Occasions,* ed. John Sparrow (Cambridge, 1923), p. 125.

10. *The Pilgrim's Progress, The Second Part,* in *Grace Abounding and The Pilgrim's Progress,* ed. Roger Shattuck (London, 1966), p. 327.

11. *Annotations Upon All the Books of the Old and New Testament,* 3rd ed., 2 vols. (London, 1657), I, on Judges xiii, 4.

12. *A Commentary Upon the Whole Booke of Juges* [sic] (London, 1615), pp. 742, 766.

13. "*Samson Agonistes* and Milton in Old Age," in *John Milton: Poet and Humanist* (Cleveland, 1966), p. 285.

14. "De la Purgatione de la Tragedia," in *Oratione e Discorsi di Lorenzo Giacomini Tebalducci Malespini* (Florence, 1597), p. 36. The resemblance of Giacomini's interpretation to Milton's has been noted by Martin Mueller, "Sixteenth-Century Italian Criticism and Milton's Theory of Catharsis," *SEL,* VI (1966), 139–50.

15. Punishment "as it is an evil, I esteem to be of two sorts, or rather two degrees only, a reprobat conscience in this life, and hell in the other world. Whatever else men call punishment, or censure is not properly an evil, so it be not an illegall violence, but a saving med'cin ordaine'd of God both for the publik and privat good of man" (*Reason of Church-Government,* I, 835). Cf. the discussions of punishment in *De Doctrina,* XV, 209, 387–91.

16. *Nichomachean Ethics,* 1115 b.

17. Donne, *Devotions*, p. 121.

18. For the importance to Milton of the paradox of strength from weakness, see John Steadman, *Milton and the Renaissance Hero* (Oxford, 1967), pp. 36–37. For its application to Milton himself, see *Defensio Secunda* IV, i, 589–90, and for its relevance to Samson and the other heroes of faith who "out of weakness were made strong," see Heb. xi, 34.

19. "*Samson Agonistes* and Religious Drama," in *Frontiers of Drama*, 2nd ed. (London, 1946), p. 27.

20. The importance of the Epistle to the Hebrews to the interpretation of *Samson* can hardly be exaggerated. Everyone agrees that Milton bases his conception of Samson as a hero of faith on his mention in Heb. xi. No one, I think, has noticed that this occurs in the longest (though intermittent) passage of *agon* imagery in the New Testament—and the whole passage is relevant to *Samson*. The heroes of faith are *agonists*, and so are we, as no classically trained reader would fail to recognize: cf., e.g., Henry Hammond, *A Paraphrase, and Annotations, Upon All the Books of the New Testament . . .*, 2nd ed. (London, 1659), pp. 762–63. What Hebrews has to say about fear or terror in x, 31, about suffering as the chastening of a father and as exercise in xii, 5–11, about faith and the temptation to surrender to weariness and despair in xii, 12–13, about the likeness and difference between the Father of spirits and the fathers of our flesh in xii, 9–10— all this is directly relevant to *Samson*. And it is in Hebrews that we find Christ described as the great *agonist* whom we are to follow and imitate, and as the priest whose self-sacrificial offering makes that imitation an acceptable likeness. These are the terms in which the relation between Samson and Christ is suggested in Milton's play. For the meaning of that relation, see the end of this essay.

21. All these have Christological significance, but in Milton's tragedy this significance is hinted obliquely and ironically. The blood in which Samson is washed is that of Philistines, and the ransom that is offered for him is Manoa's gold. Justification is figured as being clothed in the righteousness of Christ (Rev. xix, 8 and *De Doctrina*, XVI, 29) and so Samson is washed and clad in fresh garments, but these are the "state Livery" of the Philistines. Yet even in this guise we recognize the likeness of one who also took on the form of a "public servant" —indeed, the most public of all (1615–16). Circumcision typifies the covenant of works, which cannot justify; but it also suggests repentance, the circumcision of the heart, by which we die and are reborn with Christ (*De Doctrina*, XVI, 167; XV, 361, 383 and Col. ii, 11–13). It is in such a context of veiled and partial symbolism that we should interpret the phoenix, which has one meaning for the chorus of Hebrews and another for the Christian reader.

22. *Milton's Samson and the Christian Tradition* (Princeton, 1949).

23. Ibid., pp. 120, 122.